OUT . . .

. . . OF . . .

. . . BOUNDS

Out of Bounds

SPORTS,

MEDIA, AND

THE POLITICS OF

IDENTITY

EDITED BY *Aaron Baker and Todd Boyd*

INDIANA
University Press

Bloomington & Indianapolis

THIS BOOK IS A PUBLICATION OF

INDIANA UNIVERSITY PRESS
601 NORTH MORTON STREET
BLOOMINGTON, IN 47404-3797 USA

HTTP://IUPRESS.INDIANA.EDU

Telephone orders 800-842-6796
Fax orders 812-855-7931
Orders by e-mail IUPORDER@INDIANA.EDU

THE PAPER USED IN THIS PUBLICATION MEETS THE MINIMUM REQUIREMENTS OF
AMERICAN NATIONAL STANDARD FOR INFORMATION SCIENCES PERMANENCE OF
PAPER FOR PRINTED LIBRARY MATERIALS, ANSI Z39.48-1984.

∞™

MANUFACTURED IN THE UNITED STATES OF AMERICA

LIBRARY OF CONGRESS CATALOGING-IN-PUBLICATION DATA

OUT OF BOUNDS : SPORTS, MEDIA, AND THE POLITICS OF
    IDENTITY / EDITED BY AARON BAKER AND TODD BOYD.
        P. CM.
    INCLUDES BIBLIOGRAPHICAL REFERENCES AND INDEX.
    ISBN 0-253-33228-1 (CL : ALK. PAPER). — ISBN 0-253-21095-X
    (PA : ALK. PAPER)
        I. MASS MEDIA AND SPORTS—UNITED STATES. 2. SPORTS—
    SOCIAL ASPECTS—UNITED STATES. I. BAKER, AARON.
    II. BOYD, TODD.
    GV742.088   1997
    070.4'49796—DC20   96-19729

    3 4 5 6 7 07 06 05 04 03 02

CONTENTS

ANATOMY OF A MURDER
O.J. and the Imperative of Sports in Cultural Studies

TODD BOYD

Believe it or not, we began working on this collection well before the infamous O.J. Simpson case ever came about. Yet an anthology on sports, media, and the politics of identity would not be complete if we did not address the significance that this case has had in America, and what it says about the relevance of sports in cultural studies.

On one hand, one could ask, what is there to say about the O.J. Simpson case that has not been said already? In many ways the case and the commentary on it represent the redundancy of media in our daily lives in the worst way. On the other hand, this is the type of situation about which we can probably never say enough. As far as *Out of Bounds* is concerned, this case justifies our aim in a way that no academic endorsement could ever claim to. The situation involving O.J. Simpson and the resulting discourse surrounding his trial for the double murder of his ex-wife, Nicole, and her friend Ronald Goldman has been tailor-made for cultural studies. The implications that result from this rather strange set of circumstances address issues of race, class, gender, and an overall politics of identity in multiple ways, while at the same time the case brings these concerns together in a fashion seldom seen before. Be it O.J.'s exaggerated quest for class mobility, the repeated bouts of spousal abuse, and the racism of the LAPD, or the divisiveness that has come about in defining one's cultural identity through the mediated presentation of the event, the study of popular culture in America will be forever enriched because of this landmark event.

Now that the O.J. case ranks as one of the major soap operas in the history of television, we can look at the levels of discourse being articulated in multiple directions. Much has been said about a poor Black man in America who used sports as a vehicle to elevate his class status, and ultimately attempted to make less significant his racial identity. For those of you who cannot remember, O.J. was once employed by ABC sports, yet his inability to grasp the fundamentals of mainstream English contributed to an early dismissal. He went to elocution classes to rid himself of the culturally distinct diction that goes with being formerly poor and always Black.

Yet in the process of all the evaluations that have taken or will take place both in the media and in conversation, we have to return to the source as to the production of meaning relative to contemporary American culture. Black men have always struggled, and continue to do so, in navigating the maze of mainstream America every day. Many of them end up in a courtroom, many end up in jail. So why are we all of a sudden engulfed in the suspense of this particular trial? It would be easy to describe this case as a footnote to a much larger issue—a sidebar, if you will. On the other hand, it becomes important to ask, what makes O.J.'s case different? The answers to this question define the cultural imperative alluded to in the title of this piece.

We should know that this case would never have made the news if a troubled San Francisco teenager had not discovered the track to social mobility known as football. Sports occupies a special place in our society. It is like a reserved space, knowingly off limits to most but vicariously participated in by many. When sports participants win, this is shared with many people who have nothing to do with the actual sport itself, but who use this success as a form of cultural identity. It can be equated with winning in our own lives. When these athletes lose, we often feel as though they have failed us, though we in no way have the same things at stake as they or their employers do. Even so, certain people still see O.J. as having failed America.

Sports and its presentation in the media has become a multi-million-dollar entity. The ideas that mediated sports produce are hammered home repeatedly. These moral lessons are cleverly integrated into our cultural psyche. In O.J.'s case, we have heard many times the story of how a young Juice was schooled by baseball superstar Willie Mays on the merits of using sports as a way out of the seemingly endless detours of the ghetto. For this we applaud him. The Juice took heed and went on to become, arguably, the best player at his position in the history of the game.

With this success came life, liberty, and the pursuit of happiness in America—the accumulation of capital, both economic and cultural. O.J. could now shed the old baggage of racial and class inferiority, in favor of money and recognition. No one ever asked him for his autograph in the ghetto; now when he went out in public, it was like being on *Cheers:* everybody knew his name. America readily accepts sports as one of the few viable options left for struggling ghetto youth looking for a legitimate way out. Yet, as *Hoop Dreams* points out so cleverly, making it to college, much less the pros, can be a daunting task indeed.

There was a time when unskilled, uneducated labor had an option of factory work or, at worst, the military. With these options now gone, the pressure to succeed through sports seems that much more of an imperative. And though the chances of winning the lottery are probably much higher, many pursue that dream of unlimited access to capital and fame that sports can provide. O.J.'s problem, and in many ways America's problem, is that this pursuit of happiness went overboard. The plush surroundings of the NFL and life as a recognizable star created a monster. While O.J. constantly received adulation and cultural significance, this only increased his desire for more. Eventually he overdosed on the spoils of capitalist excess, like so many professional athletes, and so many Americans, do on a regular basis.

O.J. tried as best as possible to blend in with the elite white world of Brentwood, his diction now intact. Eventually he tried to act as though the projects in San Francisco were as fictional as the characters he played in those horrible *Naked Gun* movies. Yet all one need do is listen to the infamous 911 tape to hear that the diction and everything else was possibly the best acting he had ever done. O.J. was a poor Black man who had learned that being poor and Black meant very little, yet he also learned that in Hollywood, one's real self was much less important that one's fictional self, so he opted for a public persona based on an erasure of race and racially distinct behavior. So saying that he sold out is an understatement, more appropriately, that O.J. bought into.

There is something quite criminal about a system that subsumes disadvantaged young men in their prime, exposes them to a world few real people will ever see, and then after a few years of life-threatening performance tells them that their bodies are no longer able to compete with a group of younger bodies who are going through the same thing they went through years before. O.J.'s lifestyle of the rich and famous, his own attempts at escaping the bondage of being poor and Black in America, may have ultimately cost him his freedom.

With the media having made sports such a fundamental part of American culture, their significance as reification for the most essential of American ideals is foregrounded. Sports, and the discourses that surround them, have become one of the master narratives of twentieth-century culture. We can always count on assessing the American character by using sports as our barometer. Up until now, sports has received limited attention in cultural studies. Yet when we consider the significance accorded the O.J., Nancy Kerrigan and Tonya Harding, and Mike Tyson cases, among others, we see that the amount of money and audience attention surrounding sports should make them an integral component of popular culture. This is not only necessary, but inevitable.

ACKNOWLEDGMENTS

I write these acknowledgments after watching the HBO documentary "Arthur Ashe: Citizen of the World." In addition to being reminded of the invaluable humanistic contribution Ashe made to society, I found that my belief in sports as an integral venue of American culture and identity was confirmed once again. The life of Arthur Ashe suggests the impetus behind this book in a most convincing fashion.

No project would ever be complete without a sincere expression of gratitude to those who assisted, directly or indirectly, in making the finished project a reality. I would begin by offering a special thanks to my wife, Michele, whose continued encouragement, advice, and support are invaluable. I would also like to thank Edward and Mozelle Boyd, Bonnie, Willis, Kellye, and Jason Mosley, Enone, Lloyd, Ericka, and Eric Collier. Thanks to Ken Shropshire and Kellan Winslow. Special thanks to the USC School of Cinema-Television, especially my colleagues in the Critical Studies Department. I would also like to thank Joan Catapano at Indiana University Press. Peace.

Todd Boyd

This collection has come about through collaboration. Vivian Sobchack and Henry Jenkins made helpful suggestions about contributors and direction. My colleagues in the Humanities Program at Arizona State University, especially Charles Dellheim and Michael Vanden Heuvel, gave advice and encouragement. Joan Catapano's belief in this project, and her useful criticism as it progressed, have been invaluable. Finally, I would like to give special thanks to Juliann Vitullo, who has helped in too many ways to describe.

Aaron Baker

INTRODUCTION

Sports and the Popular

AARON BAKER

Media representations of American professional sports are extremely "popular" in the sense that Stuart Hall uses the term to describe those cultural texts that are widely consumed by a large audience.[1] *USA Today* has created an unparalleled sports section, occupying more than 25 percent of the editorial space of each issue, to build the largest circulation of any daily newspaper in the United States.[2] The all-sports network ESPN, currently seen in 95 million households worldwide, was the most important asset in the recent Disney takeover of Capitol Cities/ABC. Executives from both ABC and Disney explained the value of sports programming as its "universal appeal" and ability to "offend no political position."[3] Yet the popularity of professional sports as represented by this lucrative symbiosis with the media does not depend exclusively on their appeal as commercial entertainment. Media representations of sports are also popular in a second sense described by Hall: they function "in a continuing tension (relationship, influence and antagonism) to the dominant culture."[4] The contributors to this collection employ both of these assumptions about popular culture in their analyses of how media sports texts present competing discourses about class, race, and gender—especially masculinity. These essays therefore challenge media mogul wisdom about the apolitical nature of sports by examining how they contribute to the contested process of defining social identities.

While in recent years scholars have produced a substantial amount of work on film and television using a cultural studies approach, relatively little of this scholarship has focused on the media representation of professional sports in North America. For example, at present no book-length critical study of sports films has been published, and most of the writing that has been done on the coverage of athletics by American television emphasizes the economic influence of the medium on the sports industry rather than the broader cultural meaning of their symbiosis. Some important work with a cultural studies methodology has been done in Great Britain, but much of it analyzes sports there. As Todd Boyd states in his preface to this volume, the vast amount of commentary about issues of class, gender, and race generated by the Mike Tyson, Nancy Kerrigan/Tonya Harding, and O.J. Simpson cases has highlighted the importance of sports to cultural studies, and this volume is a response to that need.

All the contributors to this collection of essays share a common view of culture as a site of ideological conflict between dominant and subaltern groups over the construction of social identities. In order to maintain hegemonic control, dominant interests attempt to represent subject positions that they favor as serving the interests of all people in the society, while, for their part, subordinate groups try to reappropriate the discourse that constitutes their identity so as to have a voice in their own definition.[5] To analyze the overdetermined and pluralistic nature of such cultural relations, these essays employ modes of analysis that draw on various critical disciplines and bodies of knowledge including African American studies, gender studies, Marxism, psychoanalysis, and reception theory.

Several of the contributors to this collection examine how professional sports use spectacle to neutralize our ability to respond critically. Since the inception of the sports industry in the United States at the end of the nineteenth century, and especially with the development of television after World War II, media coverage of professional athletics has contributed significantly to this spectacle. Not only has the pleasure of spectacle increased audience interest in professional sports, it has also played an important role in defining their ideological meaning. As Guy Debord points out, spectacle can function as "the existing order's uninterrupted discourse about itself, its laudatory monologue," providing an "instrument of unification" and celebrating the order of things "as something enormously positive, indisputable and inaccessible."[6]

Unlike conservative spectacle, more progressive texts have traditionally sought to employ a system of representation that foregrounds the negotiation between different ways of viewing the world rather than the assertion of that which is "true" or "natural." Roland Barthes referred to this representational difference when he stated that "left-wing myth is inessential."[7] Nonetheless, some media representations of sports employ spectacle to question hegemonic values, rather than just reaffirming them. For example, both Henry Jenkins, in his essay about WWF wrestling, and Todd Boyd, in his analysis of an image of black masculinity embodied by certain NBA stars, describe forms of spectacle that, although contradictory, are to a certain degree progressive in regard to class, masculinity, and race.

In recent years, Hollywood has demonstrated that it has learned from television the importance of spectacle in the representation of sports. Since its inception, the American movie industry has produced hundreds of fictional narratives about athletics, but after the Academy Award and box office success of *Rocky* (1976), sports films increased their emphasis on the rhetoric of visual spectacle, as evidenced by the popularity of the *Rocky* sequels, *Raging Bull* (1980), *The Natural* (1984), *Field of Dreams* (1987), *Bull Durham* (1988), *White Men Can't Jump* (1992), *A League of Their Own* (1992), and the *Major League* films (1989 and 1994). While most of these recent sports films employ spectacle to endorse conservative views on issues such as family, class, gender, race, and nationalism, a few, including *Raging Bull, Eight Men Out,* and *White Men Can't Jump,* also use it to question hypermasculinity, acknowledge the achievement of working-class athletes, or celebrate African American cultural values.

Whatever the politics of spectacle, its prominent role in the representation of professional athletics requires the broadening of traditional definitions of sports. While most of the activities that are the subject of this collection fit the definition of professional sports as rule-governed physical contests for which the competitors are paid to participate, WWF wrestling is more staged than competitive, and professional bodybuilding, such as that described in Chris Holmlund's essay, emphasizes static images of a certain physical ideal as much as narrative contests. Yet, how different are these activities from more traditional sports whose stars are as well-known for their performances in often spectacular ads for everything from athletic shoes to fast food as they are for their performances in competition?

While they note that television sports often try to construct "a uniquely masculine experience of spectatorship," Ava Rose and James Friedman show how the male spectator is also interpellated as distracted. This distraction in their view "both reflects the ideological contradictions of masculine identity, and destabilizes the theoretical feminization of consumer culture." In his essay, Dan Streible also revises the traditional association of sports spectatorship with conservative masculinity by describing how exhibitors of the popular film recording of the 1897 heavyweight championship fight between James Corbett and Robert Fitzsimmons attracted women viewers to offset threats of government censorship. Streible claims that this (albeit isolated) instance of female access to a previously taboo male domain "represented a sign of disruption of the gendered order of things." This opportunity for women to look at the near-nude male prizefighters indicates that, as recent work on film and masculinity has begun to demonstrate, we must revise "the notion that cinema has historically constructed a heuristic male audience with [only] female bodies as the objects of its gaze."[8]

Henry Jenkins's essay also describes a revised notion of athletic masculinity. He reads professional wrestling on television as combining traditionally masculine subject matter such as homosocial relations between men, an emphasis on the public sphere, and physical means of conflict resolution with a mode of presentation that includes aspects generally considered feminine such as a serial narrative structure, a focus on multiple characters and their relationships, and an appeal to viewer speculation and gossip. As a result, wrestling "merges sports with melodrama and therefore provides a space for the release of masculine emotion," normally unexpressed within the confines of male stoicism. Jenkins concludes that wrestling combines "anti-hegemonic and reactionary elements" and reveals certain "contradictions within the social construction of masculinity." This analysis becomes all the more important when one considers that the apparently contradictory elements which Jenkins describes in wrestling occur in most representations of men's sports on television.

With the help of feminism and Title IX, women's involvement in professional sports has increased somewhat in the last three decades. Media representations of women's professional sports still remain marginal at best, however, and most of these reinforce the priority of a traditional notion of beauty for the female athlete at the expense of attaining the self-assertion (both physical and financial) emphasized in male professional sports. As Chris Holmlund makes clear in her essay about women's bodybuilding, those female athletes who seek to assert the characteristics associated with male sports figures, in this case a certain level of muscularity and strength, are often represented as aberrant or freakish. While tennis star Martina Navratilova has received generally favorable representation in the media despite defining herself outside conventional notions of heterosexual femininity, the Tonya Harding/Nancy Kerrigan incident shows how media discourse about women athletes can still be used to privilege a traditional notion of middle-class femininity and represent as undeserving—or even conflate with criminality—any challenge to its dominance.[9]

The essays by Kent Ono, John Sloop, and Todd Boyd emphasize the issue of race. Ono examines the racist aspect of American nationalism as it has been expressed in media coverage of Japanese investment in the Seattle Mariners baseball team. He shows how protectionist discourses feminized Major League Baseball and the city of Seattle, and raised the fear of miscegenation with a masculinized Japanese Other. According to Ono, these discourses recalled not only racist characterizations of the Japanese during World War II that legitimated the use of the atomic bomb, but also arguments used often in American culture about the sexual threat of the racial Other, the danger of AIDS, and environmental contamination.

Although he makes clear that "I do not (indeed, cannot) presume to know the ultimate guilt or innocence of [Mike] Tyson and am attempting to neither exonerate nor condemn him," John Sloop argues in his essay that cultural discourses and mass-media representations of the prizefighter as black and working-class positioned him as guilty of rape even before he was convicted in 1992. Sloop combines the archaeological and genealogical methods of Michel Foucault to construct a synchronic "snapshot" of these discourses while at the same time showing how they fit within preexisting constructions of African American men, boxers, and Tyson himself. Sloop also shows how representations of rape victim Desiree Washington as having been raised in a predominantly white, upper-middle-class neighborhood, and as a sexually naive college student who taught Sunday school, helped to pre-construct Tyson's guilt by positioning her outside the stereotype of the promiscuous black female and therefore evoked fears of sexual miscegenation similar to those Ono describes. The racist representation of Tyson that played on stereotypes of the black male has been repeated in the media spectacle surrounding the O.J. Simpson case, most notably by the infamous *Newsweek* cover; both these cases illustrate how media spectacle can promote progressive interests (by the attention they have focused on the problem of violence against women) and also reaffirm conservative beliefs (here in regard to race).

Todd Boyd examines a similar ideological contradiction as it is represented by a historically informed image of empowered black masculinity in American popular culture in general and in NBA basketball and the star image of Charles Barkley in particular. His analysis focuses on the use of the term "nigga" to refer to the class dimension of this notion of black masculinity, and how it combines progressive tendencies with misogynist and hegemonic attitudes.

Like Chris Holmlund, Aaron Baker and Vivian Sobchack analyze how Hollywood films about sports represent some of the contradictions that challenge dominant notions of identity. Baker looks at how Depression-era boxing films represent what Henry Jenkins calls "the fundamental contradictions of the American populist tradition." Baker argues that Hollywood films about prizefighting use the sport as a dramatic metaphor for the rugged individualism that has been a central part of its mythology. Yet he also claims that those made during the Depression responded to the skepticism of that period by endorsing a populist ideology, which not only reinforced the value of self-reliance through the strength and determination of an often ethnic or black fighter, but also showed that his success depended upon group support and promoted traditional agrarian notions of the common good. Sobchack looks at how baseball films since 1942 have used the game to define a nostalgic discourse of national identity. She analyzes how even films of recent years, such as Ken Burns's documentary *Baseball* (1994), that address "the discontinuities and contradictions embedded in the national pastime" still resist the breakdown of "commonality" caused by multicultural and transnational challenges to American nationalism.

As the essays in this collection show, media representations of sports contribute to the contested process of identity construction in American culture. These analyses taken as a whole demonstrate that, although professional sports may often reproduce the conservative values of the corporate interests that own and represent them, there are also important examples of athletic texts that define identities outside the bounds established by dominant practice.

NOTES

1. Stuart Hall, "Notes on Deconstructing 'The Popular,'" in *People's History and Socialist Theory,* ed. Raphael Samuel (London: Routledge and Kegan Paul, 1981), p. 231.

2. *Working Press of the Nation* (New Providence, N.J.: National Register Publishing, 1993), p. 8-1.

3. "The Trophy in Eisner's Big Deal," *New York Times,* August 6, 1995, sec. 3, pp. 1, 11.

4. Hall, p. 235.

5. John Fiske describes the importance of this notion of hegemony in cultural studies in his essay "British Cultural Studies and Television," in *Channels of Discourse,* ed. Robert C. Allen (Chapel Hill: University of North Carolina Press, 1987), p. 255.

6. Guy Debord, *Society of the Spectacle* (Detroit: Black and Red, 1970), sections 3, 12, 24.

7. Roland Barthes, *Mythologies,* trans. Annette Lavers (New York: Hill and Wang, 1972), p. 147.

8. For example, see *Screening the Male: Exploring Masculinities in Hollywood Cinema,* ed. Steven Cohan and Ina Rae Hark (London: Routledge, 1993).

9. See *Women on Ice: Feminist Essays on the Tonya Harding/Nancy Kerrigan Spectacle,* ed. Cynthia Baughman (New York: Routledge, 1995).

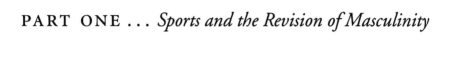

PART ONE ... *Sports and the Revision of Masculinity*

AVA ROSE AND JAMES FRIEDMAN

1 ... *Television Sports as Mas(s)culine Cult of Distraction*

> One chides the Berliners for being *addicted to distraction,* but this is a
> petit-bourgeois reproach. . . . The tension to which the working masses
> are subjected . . . [is] an essentially formal tension which fills their day
> fully without making it fulfilling. Such a lack demands to be compen-
> sated, but this need can only be articulated in terms of the same surface
> sphere which imposed the lack in the first place. The form of entertain-
> ment necessarily corresponds to that of enterprise.
>
> —Siegfried Kracauer[1]

The pursuit of distraction observed by Kracauer in the 1920s has perhaps
reached its hyperbolic expression in the consumption of sports on American
commercial television.[2] If early film audiences sought escapist entertainment
and superficial fulfillment in the picture palaces of Berlin, today's family of
consumers have access to diversion in their own homes. And perhaps the
strongest—certainly the most consistent—lure to the screen is televised
sports. Nowhere is there a more spectacular celebration of the surface sphere,
a more explicit correspondence between enterprise and entertainment, nor a
more pervasive reiteration of dominant values.

In using Kracauer's theory of distraction as a paradigm for our analysis of
television sports, we hope to suggest a relationship between masculine forms
of mass entertainment and some of those "tensions to which the working
masses are subjected." Our intention is to destabilize the theoretical feminization of mass consumption in general, and of distraction in particular. At the
same time, we hope to avoid the kinds of "petit bourgeois reproaches" which
have too often characterized critical theories of "mass" consumption. In other
words, we hope to articulate a relationship between distracted spectatorship
and ideology, while allowing for the diversity of actual "readings."

DISTRACTION

In 1926, Kracauer understood distraction as symptomatic of the tensions
and inadequacies associated with modernity. Rather than dismissing the

consumption of mass entertainment as a passive and reasonless addiction, Kracauer's essay appreciates distraction as a form of cultural consumption that makes sense as a response to the tensions and unfulfilled needs created by a reasonless society. Although Kracauer's "cult of distraction" is theoretically a non-gender-specific mass-cultural phenomenon, his description of mass spectatorship is intimately bound up with the image of the "little shop girls who go to the movies."[3] This association of the feminine with mass consumption is not unique to Kracauer: several contemporary critics have noted the implicit (and sometimes explicit) feminization of modernity and mass culture in critical theory.[4]

Surprisingly, contemporary theories of film and television spectatorship have in many ways reiterated this gender distinction, aligning female reception with distraction, while assuming the male gaze to be voyeuristic, linear, and contemplative.[5] In our view, formalist readings of certain "feminine" modes of programming and reception have contributed to the characterization of distracted spectatorship as *implicitly feminine*, by drawing the correspondence between the rhythms of women's work in the home, and the "flow" of daytime television.[6]

At the same time, feminist theories of spectatorship have reinforced the view that mass cultural consumption is—like the soap opera spectator herself—essentially passive, manipulated, and lacking. Moreover, this "distracted" consumption tends to be understood in relation—and opposition—to an insufficiently problematized "classical" model of masculine spectatorship. While this classical mode of spectatorship may in fact be offered to male viewers by some televisual texts some of the time, it is our contention that a contemplative and voyeuristic spectatorship is not typical of the dominant position offered the male viewer by American network television.

By looking at that quintessentially masculine genre, television sports, we will show how those texts which most explicitly address the male viewer (or, more precisely, address the viewer *as male*) interpellate the spectator simultaneously as "masculine" and as distracted. We will suggest—against more conventional readings of televised sports as linear, goal-oriented, and fetishistic—that sports programs are in fact open-ended, cyclical, and melodramatic, and that they are reflective (as well as constitutive) of a distracted experience of reception.

Despite commonly held assumptions that distraction is symptomatic of female spectators and daytime television, Rick Altman has pointed out that "an inseparable mixture of watching and non-watching" must be understood as a "general style of viewing behavior" for commercial television spectators.[7] Because television is generally consumed in the home—or in other environments which compete for the attention of its viewers—TV must constantly address, enlist, and hold onto a potentially distracted spectator. It therefore makes sense to understand distraction as an organizing principle of television sports, which are more often consumed intermittently than contemplatively.

After all, women are not the only TV spectators who are distracted by their viewing environments. Men are also interpellated by what Altman calls the "household flow," and programming addressed to the male viewer must also compete with the demands of work and family, the lapses in attention, the social interactions, and, yes, even the domestic duties which occupy men's supposed leisure time (mowing the lawn, working on the car, fixing leaky faucets, and so on). Thus, rather than providing an escape from the routines of everyday life, the mass consumption of television sports must be seen as an integral part of masculine work and play.

In order to attract and hold its viewers, television discourses interpellate spectators through direct address, a sense of immediacy and liveness, and the illusion that "those images seem to be made just for us."[8] TV sports programs, in particular, position the audience as part of a fluid and ongoing dialogue: inviting him to look, and look again; to interpret the image; to respond to the emotional content of the spectacle; and, in a literal sense, to participate in the metadiscourse of sports.

Thus, as television insinuates itself into the fabric of men's everyday lives, the discursive address of sports programming invites the viewer not only to watch sports on television, but to be part of its universe. The television provides its viewers with access to a continuously evolving world, a community to which the sports fan can belong simply by tuning in. While this mode of readership is remarkably similar to the "complex exchange between viewer and text" which Robert Allen has identified in soap opera reception, the symbolic and actual community constructed by sports spectatorship in America is as masculine as the playing of the games themselves.[9]

ENTERTAINMENT AND ENTERPRISE

There are many ways in which television sports constructs a uniquely masculine experience of spectatorship. On the one hand, TV sports is similar to soap opera in its distracted reception, its construction of a gendered viewing community, and many of its discursive strategies and textual effects. At the same time, the skills upon which it depends, and the values that it reifies, are distinctly masculine.

In "The Rhythms of Reception," Tania Modleski extends the theory of distraction to an analysis of daytime television reception, suggesting that the distracted and "maternal" gaze of the soap opera viewer corresponds to the rhythms and demands of women's work in the home. According to Modleski, television soap opera rationalizes and reifies the conditions of patriarchal femininity by positioning the (female) spectator as "a sort of ideal mother, a person who possesses greater wisdom than all her children, whose sympathy is large enough to encompass the conflicting claims of her family (she identifies with them all)."[10]

Thus, in their very structure, soaps habituate women to the "interruption, distraction, and spasmodic toil" which is characteristic of housework.[11] At the same time, by focusing the female spectator's gaze on others, encouraging her to read their needs, desires, and intentions from facial expressions and body language, the soap opera reflects and reinforces the cultural imperative which requires women to do the emotional work in their relationships.

By contrast, one might expect a masculine mode of spectatorship to avoid the emotional register, emphasizing instead the classical masculine pleasures in voyeurism and objectification, and constructing a more linear, goal-oriented structure of looking. In fact, this is precisely the way in which Margaret Morse interprets sports spectatorship. In her essay "Television Sports: Replay and Display," Morse argues that TV sports spectatorship involves a "gaze at maleness" which depends upon—while masking—a fetishistic pleasure in objectifying the male body.[12] While we would not deny the homoerotic pleasures in sports participation and spectatorship, we would like to suggest that the sports fan's visual pleasure is not based primarily on a classical model of masculine desire. The sports gaze depends not on distance, fragmentation, or objectification, but on identification, nearness, and participation. The male viewer's relationship to the image is in fact quite similar to that of the female soap viewer: he is alternately absorbed in multiple identifications and distracted. Rather than emphasizing a voyeuristic and objectifying gaze, television sports seems to invite the viewer to engage in a distracted, identificatory, and dialogic spectatorship which may be understood as a masculine counterpart to soap opera's "maternal gaze." The sports fan is like the "brother" on the sidelines: he shares the greater wisdom and perspective of the commentators, while identifying alternately with players, coaches, and fans.

The sports spectator is thus engaged in a process of reading others which stresses the intuitive over the analytical, and privileges the reactions of others over the action itself. This is less a scientific inquiry (as Morse suggests) than a psychological one. The hermeneutic process of reading and evaluating athletic performances certainly requires a degree of fetishization of the male body, which, as Morse argues, the "scientific" discourse of stats may serve to disavow. However, this analytical discourse is ultimately qualified by the *melodramatic*: the human angle, the personal drama, and the insistence on "mind over matter" which inform each assessment of the physical play of the game.

Further, this attention to subjective factors over objective actions should not be conceived as a deviation from masculine modes of attention. In fact, the skills which this hermeneutic process cultivates are as fundamental to male work as interruptibility and other-orientation are to women's domestic labor. What is ultimately at stake in our argument, then, is a reconceptualization of masculine modes of consumption and production: we are suggesting that the distracted, decentered, and other-oriented consumption of sports by television spectators reflects and reifies the patterns of perception and the skills required of the postindustrial male worker.

While classical masculine spectatorship corresponds to the goal-oriented and linear production of industry, and reflects the industrial worker's attention to a single task, men's work in our consumer society depends on different skills, and a different mode of attention. In fact, postindustrial labor may—like housework—actually require distraction. In the service sector, management, and sales-oriented occupations, men and women alike are expected to concentrate on several tasks at once, to be constantly interruptible, and to focus on the needs of others.

THE SPORTS COMMENTATOR: ONE OF THE GUYS

The discourse of the TV sports commentators provides a model of sports consumption which reinforces the mode of attention demanded by postindustrial work. As with most television programming, the soundtrack of any televised sports event is addressed simultaneously to the attentive spectator and the distracted fan. In TV sports, the commentators in particular mediate between the flow of sports programming and the distractions of the viewing situation. The direct address of the commentators is thus central to the discursive organization of the sports narrative, and to the placement of spectators in relation to the sports metatext, and to each other.

Because the dimensions of the sports narrative preclude the possibility of its mastery by any one subject, the collective discourse of the commentators provides coherence and a site for the production of meaning. Like soaps, TV sports programming must constantly supply background information so that the spectator can make sense of the action and engage in the process of interpretation and speculation which characterizes TV sports spectatorship.

This is precisely the role of the "color man," who reminds the viewer of statistics, past achievements, and world records, and places current events in historical perspective. The commentary of the color man functions like the gossip of soap operas, providing the fan with all the inside information that surrounds the events which are unfolding on the screen. Significantly, this insider discourse is frequently accompanied by close-ups of the players and coaches, replays of spectacular moments, and reaction shots—in other words, the melodrama of sports.

While the color man puts the game in its emotional and historical perspective, the play-by-play commentator narrates the action in the representation of sports, enabling the distracted viewer to keep up with the game, and calling him back to the screen for the highlights. His is the discourse of *liveness,* and it is the play-by-play commentator who lends a sense of immediacy and virtual reality to the representation of sports on TV.

In sports, both the analysis of the game and the synthesis of past and present always point toward the future. The teleological momentum of the game—and of each sport—is reinforced by the commentators' discourse of anticipation and speculation. However, this apparently linear trajectory does not lead to resolution or closure in the classical sense. Like daytime soaps, but unlike the majority of prime-time and weekend programming, television sports is serial: it is ongoing, continuous, and always to-be-continued.

As with any serial, the consumption of television sports cannot be defined by the viewing of a single program.[13] Each game is perceived in relation to the entire season, the history of each sport, and the yearly cycle of sports representation on television. In this way, the outcome of a game is never the end: there is always a next game, the next season, and the next star player—not to mention the next sport. The commentators are the discursive glue which binds these metatexts together, and facilitates their consumption by spectators whose access to the narratives of sports is always partial and interrupted.

Perhaps the most important discursive function of the sports commentators is to address the male spectator as "one of the guys," establishing a collective male identity through television sports. This is achieved through the form as well as the content of the commentators' discourse. In providing knowledge, gossip, and narrative information, the commentators give the viewer the tools he needs to perform a dominant reading of the sports text. These tools enable the sports fan to engage in a range of discourses and practices that connote "maleness" in our culture.

Together, the commentators model the ideal spectator. In their discursive exchange, they embody the utopic ideals of sports reception and participation. In fact, they present sports reception *as* participation, as a dialogue between at least three men: the play-by-play commentator, the color man, and the viewer at home. This dialogue—with its mixture of information, anecdote, and anticipation—engages the sports fan in the participatory reception characteristic of sports viewing: inviting him to call the plays, argue with the referees, and coach "his" players from the simulated sidelines.

The boundary of the television screen apparently dissolves, as the symbolic exchange of sports becomes actual, and the spectator is literally absorbed in the virtual reality of television sports.[14] This breakdown of boundaries is remarkably similar to Tania Modleski's description of daytime soap opera reception:

> Soap operas tend, more than any other form, to break down the distance required for the proper working of identification. But rather than seeing these cases as pathological instances of *over*-identification . . . I would argue that they point to a different *kind* of relationship between spectator and characters. . . . The viewer does not *become* the characters . . . , but rather relates to them as intimates, as extensions of her world.[15]

While Modleski is offering a positive alternative to theorizations of female "over-identification," the "different kind" of spectatorship which she describes is still understood as implicitly feminine: characteristic of daytime television, female viewers, and an essentially feminine (if not female) desire for nearness. At the same time, Modleski assumes that "the proper working of identification" requires distance, which is presumably an essential component of masculine (if not biologically male) spectatorial pleasure.

However, the male fan who participates in the dialogic activity of television sports reception is not the solitary, voyeuristic spectator of classical film theory. Alternately absorbed in multiple identifications and distracted, the TV sports spectator has much more in common with the daytime soap opera viewer. While in his fantasies the fan may become the hero of sports, the text does not interpellate him in this kind of classical identification. Instead—like the female soap fan—he relates to the characters of sports as intimates, as "extensions of his world." At the same time, he experiences each program not as a discrete text but as an open, continuous, and never-ending story, which penetrates—at the same time that it takes him away from—his own reality.

As he experiences that "partial loss of touch with the here and now" that Margaret Morse associates with distraction, the sports fan tests his own evaluative skills in the otherworld of sports.[16] In this world of entertainment which is the shadow of enterprise, the working man can question authority and vent frustration—at the same time that he engages in those very discourses which facilitate his own incorporation. In his leisure time, then, the sports fan is sharpening the skills he will need to succeed in the world of work: judgment, evaluation, speculation, teamwork, competitiveness. Meanwhile, TV sports offers what Morse calls that "attenuated fiction-effect" of distraction which, to paraphrase Kracauer, "fills our days fully without making them fulfilling."[17]

REIFICATION AND UTOPIA

In his writings of the 1920s, Kracauer draws the correspondence between the forms of mass entertainment and alienated labor in order to show how mass culture reflects and rationalizes the tensions created by a capitalist system. Recent theorists of popular culture have similarly pointed to the exposure of conflict and ideological contradictions in such forms as the musical, film noir, and especially melodrama.

In her essay "Notes on Sirk and Melodrama," Laura Mulvey argues that women's melodrama functions "as a safety valve for ideological contradictions centred on sex and the family."[18] We would like to suggest that television sports may similarly be read as the representation of moral and ideological conflicts around *masculine* identity and social roles. At the same time, sports programming on television is a vehicle for the utopic imaging—and reification—of corporate and patriarchal ideals of the masculine.

Like melodrama, sports narratives highlight personal struggle, social tension, and moral conflict. The extremes of emotion are exaggerated, and opposing forces are pitted against each other in absolute dualisms. Everything in sports representation reiterates this "moral Manichaeism": from the clashing of team helmets generated by the opening computer graphics on Monday Night Football, and the visual contrasts between the teams' colors and opposing movements, to the endless juxtapositions of close-ups highlighting the personal inner struggles of coaches and players from the two sides.[19] Even the referees are visually coded as the arbiters of this conflict: wearing the black and white stripes which symbolize their "objective" position as mediators between opposing forces.

On the one hand, television sports embraces the ideals of democracy: equal opportunity, fairness, and a balance between individual achievement and the collective good. However, as in American society at large, these ideals are frequently in conflict with the values of capitalism, generating a tension between workers and owners, ethics and efficacy, teamwork and Social Darwinism. The games themselves simultaneously encourage collective effort and reward competitiveness, and the rhetoric of sports paradoxically praises individual feats of heroism while demanding self-sacrifice.

The conflicting values of sports manifest themselves in a tension that is visible both on and off the playing field. The irreconcilable ideals of masculinity come to a head-on collision on these organized battlegrounds, where macho aggressivity is both required and punished. The star athlete must be tough, determined, and unstoppable—until the whistle blows; he must be monomaniacally focused on his goal, indifferent to opposition, and yet respectful of the rules of the game. Television sports coverage glorifies the supreme capitalist ethic of survival of the fittest; and yet, unruly athletes are condemned when they exercise their power outside the bounds of the game.

Sports in America embodies all the illusions of opportunity and upward mobility that our nation holds dear. At the same time, the economic and political realities of sports give the lie to the myths of democracy, equal opportunity, and integration. For example, many popular critics have argued that the image of the sports superstar functions as a kind of lure for disenfranchised youth: a magical fantasy of escape which is unrealistic for all but a handful of athletes. In this way, the utopic universe of sports may serve to distract its fans from the harsh realities of economic and racial inequality with a mythic fantasy of integration which ultimately reiterates conservative American values.

While this is structurally a question of class, it is manifestly an issue of race, for an overwhelming percentage of professional athletes in the United States are black. The extraordinary visibility of blacks in sports embodies the ideals of equal opportunity and integration which characterize official discourses about race in America. However, this visibility cuts both ways: on the one hand, the success of black athletes is real, and the prevalence of black sports stars on television provides spectators from all racial and ethnic groups with "positive images" of black men.[20] On the other hand, the images of upward mobility and personal achievement which these black stars present is contained within traditional discourses which champion individual excellence rather than collective empowerment.

Moreover, the realities of discrimination, exploitation, and unequal opportunity cannot be completely resolved by the utopic discourses of sports on TV. If blacks are overrepresented as athletes, they are still grossly underrepresented as coaches, managers, owners, officials, and even quarterbacks. This imbalance is consistent with the historical exploitation of blacks in certain entertainment industries (especially music), where people of color have been accepted as performers, while positions of management and power have been reserved for whites. Against this (actual) racial inequality, the high visibility of (a limited number of) blacks in these industries is invoked as (symbolic) proof that equal opportunity does in fact exist.

Thus, the utopic discourses of television sports seem to work in the way that Richard Dyer described in his discussion of the musical: by evoking a utopic sensibility that reflects and responds to real social needs and ideological contradictions.[21] In sports, tensions between black and white, the individual and the collective, the "in group" and the "other," the personal and the corporate, desire and the law, are played out—not only on the playing fields, but within the discourses of the representations themselves.

In this way, social tensions and ideological oppositions are displaced onto—and contained by—the dramatic conflicts between teams and between players.

The televisual representation of athletic competition both embodies and rationalizes a complex and value-laden oppositional structure. Sports on television embraces a range of dualisms, from the game-specific conflicts between teams, individual players, coaches, and owners, to the broader antagonisms between the fans, who identify themselves with a given side in the conflict.

This brings into play a discourse of civic and national pride, loyalty, and, of course, competition. The discourse engendered between fans of opposing teams is always one of rivalry: the stakes range from one's pride in a home team, or faith in a personal favorite, to the more "rational" powers of assessment with which one picks a winner. The excessive overidentification which is an integral part of sports spectatorship, and the blurring of boundaries—in which the sports fan's sense of self-worth is bound up with the performance of "his" team—work to draw the sports fan into the conflicts of sports. He is interpellated by a discourse of "us and them," which has implications for the cultivation of nationalism and ethnocentrism, as well as all those discourses which depend on binary thinking: racism, sexism, homophobia.

THE MAS(S)CULINE CULT OF DISTRACTION

While the "little shop girls" who go to the movies and the housewives who watch daytime television have been the subjects of critical theory's scrutiny of the "cult of distraction," a closer look at masculine forms of mass cultural consumption reveals that distraction is not a uniquely feminine mode of consumption or production. Distraction seems in fact to be equally—if somewhat differently—endemic to masculine and feminine forms of entertainment and enterprise in our postindustrial culture.

While there is still a significant disparity between men's and women's economic, political, and cultural power, the *skills* required of both men and women in the workplace—and in both the public and private spheres—appear to be growing increasingly similar. Along with the shift from an industrial to a service economy, and the heightened economic and social imperatives of conspicuous consumption, there seems to be a destabilization of the historical association of masculinity with active production, and femininity with passive consumption. As women move into (and out of) more active subject positions and social roles, and men are increasingly appealed to by advertising and the culture industry, the realities of production and consumption for both sexes no longer fit into neat categories of activity/passivity.

At the same time, both men and women may look increasingly to mass culture not only for distraction but for the exposure of contradictions, the utopic resolution of conflict, and the collective affirmation of identity that mass entertainment offers. TV sports may perform for male viewers a function similar to that effected by women's daytime television: exposing the ideological contradictions of masculine identity in a capitalist, racist, and patriarchal society. However, the dominant position offered the male viewer by TV sports appears to be more conservative of the status quo than that offered women by soaps.

In his early writings on distraction, Kracauer distinguished between a reasonless and rationalized distraction, which leads away from—or masks—truth, and a distraction which offers the possibility of redemption. He argued that distraction leads away from truth when it is "an end in itself," when contradictions are "forced back into a unity that no longer exists, [and when,] rather than acknowledging the state of disintegration which such shows ought to represent, they glue the pieces back together after the fact and present them as organic creations."[22] Thus, for Kracauer, distraction has a redemptive function only if it exposes itself—and therefore society—in its true disorder. When, on the other hand, mass culture seeks to resolve contradiction, to mask tensions and present a false order, it offers nothing more than diversion and reification.

While television sports does expose social tensions and ideological contradictions around race, class, and masculine identity, it does *not* "acknowledge disintegration," nor does it expose itself—or society—as disordered. On the contrary, the rhetoric of sports reiterates an ethic of integration and incorporation: insisting that individuals put aside differences, put the team first, and play by the rules. In this way, sports discourse seems ultimately to reify the dominant values of corporate America. This should not be surprising, since the average sports spectator (more often white, most often straight, and almost always male) has an investment in the corporate Social Darwinism of sports. He has a lot to lose by exposing the contradictions of mainstream ideology, and even if the system has not served him well, he feels entitled to the American Dream that sports promises him.

While many of the women who watch soaps may also cling to dominant values, the exposure of ideological tension which is an inevitable part of melodrama is in fact more likely to affirm than to threaten the female spectator's sense of entitlement. On the other hand, those mass-cultural forms which reiterate hegemonic structures may be more likely to affirm masculine privilege. It is ironic, then, that female spectators have been associated with the passive and uncritical consumption of mass culture. The promises offered by these reified forms are certainly *no less* appealing to the male spectator. Indeed, as Andreas Huyssen points out,

> The claim that the threats (or, for that matter, the benefits) of mass culture are somehow "feminine" has finally lost its persuasive power. If anything,

a kind of reverse statement would make more sense: certain forms of mass culture, with their obsession with gendered violence, are more of a threat to women than to men. After all, it has always been men rather than women who have had real control over the productions of mass culture.[23]

The masculine universe constructed by television sports seems to work to reinforce this patriarchal power structure. Distracted and decentered, exposed to social tensions and systemic inadequacies, the sports spectator is nevertheless firmly anchored in the discourses of production and consumption which define him as threatening, rather than threatened.

While any text can be read against the grain, the distraction which the sports text offers the mainstream viewer both embodies and utopically resolves the contradictions of masculinity in our culture. However, a spectator who does not fully identify with this position may engage in a very different reading, and may not, in fact, see the text as resolving all contradictions. As Steve Neale has argued, "'address' is not simply synonymous with textual address . . . [for while] the latter can be analyzed and has an effectivity," the *ideological effect* of a text must be understood in relation to the conjuncture of all those discourses and practices which inform its production and consumption.[24] Thus, while the discourses of film and television construct preferred positions for the spectator, each viewer is always simultaneously interpellated by a number of discourses (cultural, institutional, personal) which define him as a subject and have an impact on his reading of any text.

Stuart Hall has articulated this nonequivalence of textual address and actual readings as a "lack of fit" between the codes which inform the encoding and decoding of a given text.[25] Referring only to news (or informational) programming, Hall suggests three broad categories for decoding, in which the dominant position is either taken up, opposed, or "negotiated." While this may be a bit schematic even for explicitly ideological television texts such as the news, we suggest that the taking up of a preferred reading position is even more complex in relation to ostensibly nonideological (entertainment) programming such as television sports.

For example, the very pleasures involved in sports spectatorship may involve some degree of taking up the dominant position offered by sports texts: identifying with normative masculine points of view, celebrating the utopic fantasies of integration and incorporation, and engaging in a discursive practice which rationalizes ideological contradictions and disintegration with artificial oppositional structures. However, it would be simplistic to assume that any spectator who derives pleasure from TV sports spectatorship is unproblematically taking up the hegemonic values of television sports.

Nor would we want to suggest that pleasure is somehow antithetical to critical reception.

Indeed, the formal lack of resolution in television sports, as well as its discursive insistence on dialogic spectatorship, may in fact encourage a degree of reading against the grain. If the TV sports fan is indeed continually moving in and out of multiple identifications, constantly negotiating the interpenetration of text and reality, and actively engaged in re-reading the image and second-guessing the narrative, he may in fact be more disposed to perceive a lack of fit between representation and (his view of) reality. After all, no matter how much the utopic discourse of sports works to resolve tensions, there are always conflicts in the universe of sports which cannot be neatly contained by the rules and representations of the game.

A study of the actual responses of television sports audiences might explore the extent to which viewers perceive sports as exposing and/or resolving ideological contradictions. "Ethnographic" studies of television viewers such as David Morley's *The "Nationwide" Audience,* and the work on American soap opera reception by Ellen Seiter et al. ("Don't Treat Us Like We're So Stupid and Naive") have demonstrated the limitations of extrapolating theories of the "mass spectator" solely from textual analyses.[26] The study of soap audiences in particular illustrates the dangers in assuming a congruence between the *ideal feminine spectator* constructed by soap operas, and the *actual readings* performed by female viewers.

These readings suggest, for example, that Tania Modleski may have exaggerated the extent to which soap viewers identify with "all their children." Similarly, to insist that the visual pleasures in television sports spectatorship consist predominantly in classical objective omnipotence, objectification, and closure would be to confuse the *textual possibilities* of voyeurism, fetishism, and "objectivity" with the *actualities* of sports reception. While our analysis of the discursive address of television sports suggests that the sports fan is in fact offered multiple points of identification, encouraged to relate to the "characters" of sports as "extensions of his world," and invited to transgress the classical boundaries between subject and text, we hesitate to draw absolute conclusions about sports reception from an analysis of the programming alone.

It is time to subject masculine mass-cultural consumption to the same kinds of critical analysis with which feminists have scrutinized soap operas. We believe that a closer look at the texts which are addressed to males—as well as at the "masculine cult of distraction" which characterizes the consumption of these texts—would expose some of the tensions and contradictions inherent in patriarchal masculinity. By problematizing the mass production of masculinity, we believe that such a project would help to destabilize the theoretical alignment of femininity with passive, distracted, and "uncritical" consumption.

NOTES

1. Siegfried Kracauer, "The Cult of Distraction" (1926), reprinted in *New German Critique* 40 (Winter 1987).
2. Because our understanding of television sports as a "masculine cult of distraction" is derived from our analysis of American commercial broadcasting and cultural practices, we will refer specifically to American television and its reception in making our argument. Our intention is not to suggest that this masculine cult of distraction should be viewed as a national cultural phenomenon, but rather to respect the textual and historical particularities of our objects (and subjects) of study. In fact, our theoretical argument would suggest that the operations which we have identified in American sports programming and reception can be extended to the texts and practices of TV sports in other postindustrial cultures.
3. Siegfried Kracauer, "Die Kleinen Ladenmadchen gehen ins Kino" (1927), in *Das Ornament der Masse* (Frankfurt: Suhrkamp, 1977), pp. 279–94.
4. See, for example, Andreas Huyssen, "Mass Culture as Woman: Modernism's Other," in Tania Modleski, ed., *Studies in Entertainment* (Bloomington: Indiana University Press, 1986); Tania Modleski, "Femininity as Mas(s)querade: A Feminist Approach to Mass Culture," in Colin McCabe, ed., *High Theory, Low Culture* (Manchester: University of Manchester Press, 1986); Patrice Petro, "Modernity and Mass Culture in Weimar: Contours of a Discourse on Sexuality in Early Theories of Perception and Representation," *New German Critique* 40 (Winter 1987).
5. See, for example, Laura Mulvey, "Visual Pleasure and Narrative Cinema," *Screen* 16, no. 3 (Autumn 1975); and Mary Ann Doane, *The Desire to Desire* (Bloomington: Indiana University Press, 1987).
6. See especially Tania Modleski, "The Rhythms of Reception," and Sandy Flitterman-Lewis, "The *Real* Soaps: TV Commercials," in E. Ann Kaplan, ed., *Regarding Television* (Los Angeles: AFI, 1983).
7. Rick Altman, "Television Sound," in Modleski, ed., *Studies in Entertainment,* p. 42.
8. Altman, p. 50. For a discussion of the function of "liveness" in attracting and holding viewers, see Jane Feuer, "The Concept of Live Television: Ontology as Ideology," in Kaplan, ed., *Regarding Television.*
9. Robert C. Allen, "On Reading Soaps: A Semiotic Primer," in Kaplan, ed., *Regarding Television,* p. 100.
10. Modleski, p. 92. Modleski's use of the phrase "all her children" is a play on the name of a very popular daytime soap opera, "All My Children" (ABC).
11. Modleski, p. 71.
12. Margaret Morse, "Television Sports: Replay and Display," in Kaplan, ed., *Regarding Television.*
13. As Raymond Williams first pointed out, no television program can be understood as a discrete text: each show is embedded in the "flow" of television (commercials, station breaks, other programs, other channels, etc.). See Raymond Williams, *Television: Technology and Cultural Form* (New York: Shocken, 1974). However, the narrative closure of many prime-time programs (TV movies, documentaries, dramatic series, sitcoms, etc.) does mark these texts as "discrete" in a way that serial programs never are.
14. Margaret Morse, "An Ontology of Everyday Distraction: The Freeway, the Mall, and Television," in Patricia Mellencamp, ed., *The Logics of Television* (Bloomington: Indiana University Press, 1990).
15. Modleski, pp. 68–69.
16. Morse, "An Ontology of Everyday Distraction," p. 193.

17. Ibid.

18. Mulvey, "Notes on Sirk and Melodrama," *Movie* 25 (Winter 1977-78).

19. Peter Brooks, *The Melodramatic Imagination: Balzac, Henry James, Melodrama, and the Mode of Excess* (New Haven and London: Yale University Press, 1976).

20. For a discussion of the problematic of "positive images," see Robert Stam and Louise Spence, "Colonialism, Racism and Representation: An Introduction," *Screen* 24, no. 2 (January-February 1983). Examples of "positive/negative" image analyses of blacks in Hollywood are Donald Bogle, *Toms, Coons, Mulattoes, Mammies and Bucks* (New York: Bantam, 1974), and Thomas Cripps, *Slow Fade to Black* (New York: Oxford University Press, 1977). For theoretical discussions of racial stereotyping, see Homi Bhabha, "The Other Question: The Stereotype and Colonial Discourse," *Screen* 24 (November-December 1983), and Steve Neale, "The Same Old Story: Stereotypes and Differences," *Screen Education* 32/33 (Autumn-Winter 1979-80).

21. Richard Dyer, "Entertainment and Utopia," *Movie* 24 (Spring 1977). Reprinted in Rick Altman, ed., *Genre: The Musical* (London: RKP, 1981).

22. Kracauer, pp. 94-95.

23. Andreas Huyssen, "Mass Culture as Woman: Modernism's Other," in Tania Modleski, ed., *Studies in Entertainment* (Bloomington: Indiana University Press, 1986).

24. Steve Neale, "Propaganda," *Screen* 18, no. 3 (Autumn 1977): 34.

25. Stuart Hall, "Encoding/Decoding," in *Culture, Media, Language* (London: Hutchinson, 1980), p. 131.

26. See David Morley, *The "Nationwide" Audience: Structure and Decoding*, BFI Television Monographs 11 (London: British Film Institute, 1980); and Ellen Seiter, Hans Borcher, Gabriele Kreutzner, and Eva-Maria Warth, "'Don't Treat Us Like We're So Stupid and Naive': Towards an Ethnography of Soap Opera Viewers," in Ellen Seiter et al., eds., *Remote Control: Television, Audiences and Cultural Power* (London and New York: Routledge, 1989).

2 . . . *Female Spectators and the Corbett-Fitzsimmons Fight Film*

Throughout the nineteenth century, the spectator sport of prizefighting grew in popularity, though its audience remained almost entirely male. Newspapers and sporting tabloids helped boxing gain a wider following, even as actual prizefights—illegal in many locales—were held in distant or secretive settings to avoid police interference. Motion picture coverage significantly changed the sport and its dubious social status. The first genuine prizefight recorded was the Corbett-Fitzsimmons title bout of 1897. The feature-length film garnered six-figure profits as it became a cinematic sensation during its theatrical roadshowing. As Charles Musser, Miriam Hansen, and other film scholars have noted, an unintended consequence of the film's widespread exhibition was the appearance of a female constituency for the prizefight pictures. The event of women watching the *Corbett-Fitzsimmons Fight* was socially problematic in the gendered public sphere of the time. While the phenomenon was short-lived, it raised important questions about the nature and function of motion pictures as a mediating force and social institution.[1]

On St. Patrick's Day, 1897, in the wake of three years' anticipation, delay, and hype, boxers Jim Corbett and Bob Fitzsimmons fought for the heavyweight championship in Carson City, Nevada. Underdog Fitz dethroned the popular Gentleman Jim with a much-discussed "solar plexus punch" in the fourteenth round. Under the direction of cinematographer Enoch Rector and the promotion of Texas gambler Dan A. Stuart, motion pictures of the entire event were successfully taken and prominently exhibited across the United States and abroad by their Veriscope Company.

The eleven thousand feet of film taken and projected by Rector's "veriscope" became one of the earliest individual productions to sustain public commentary on the cinema. From the time of its proposed creation in 1894 until its release two months after the actual fight, the public and the press discussed the filmed reproduction. Its lengthy run and re-run—a new film exhibition experience—invited further commentary on the quality of cinematic reproduction, results of the contest, the social effects of the film,

Ringside, Carson City, Nevada, St. Patrick's Day, 1897. A photograph of the heavy-weight title fight between James J. Corbett (*right*) and Robert Fitzsimmons shows Gentleman Jim's revealing boxing trunks. Courtesy of the Todd-McLean Collection, University of Texas at Austin.

and the nature of its audience. Yet in writings on the history of cinema, the *Corbett-Fitzsimmons Fight* remains but a well-worn footnote, characterized as an atypically long actuality that presaged the boom in feature-length films.[2]

For several reasons, the *Corbett-Fitzsimmons Fight* offers a rich case study for an investigation of early cinema. First, the film was in one sense not an aberration at all, but rather an expected installment in the series of boxing pictures which were already considered *de rigueur* for film producers. Second, even though its running time and manner of exhibition departed from previous motion picture practice, the *Corbett-Fitzsimmons Fight* must have been for many viewers their first memorable contact with cinematic presentations. Finally, the film's unique qualities were not grounds for dismissal by its contemporaries; rather, the novel Veriscope pictures received a great deal of attention precisely because they were more auspicious. As such, the nineteenth-century archival sources which are usually mute on the subject of cinema are rife with details about the *Corbett-Fitzsimmons Fight.*

After briefly recounting the film's production and exhibition history, I analyze the reception of Veriscope's *Corbett-Fitzsimmons Fight,* focusing on public debates about censorship and the attempts to offset that censure by highlighting the film's female patronage. The fact that women in large numbers turned out to view scenes of a prizefight surprised many observers in 1897. For contemporary media studies, the phenomenon of the film's female reception is also the most salient and provocative aspect of this historical episode. The simultaneous unease and pleasure that various parties expressed upon discovering that women were attending the *Corbett-Fitz-simmons* picture demonstrates that the Veriscope exhibitions represented a significant disruption of the gendered order of things in "sporting and theatrical" circles. A consideration of the fight film's female reception points to important historical shifts in the gendered nature of audiences for sports, cinema, and other forms of public entertainment. While prizefighting remained a male-oriented affair, cinema proved a mediating institution that provided women access, however limited, to previously forbidden arenas. This cinematic look into a taboo world also had a strong sexual dynamic, as women gazed at the nearly nude physiques of athletes, especially matinee idol Corbett. As such, the case of the female audience for the *Corbett-Fitzsimmons Fight* encourages further revision of the notion that cinema has historically constructed a heuristic male audience with female bodies as the object of its gaze.

THE BUILDUP

Audience interest in a film of the Corbett-Fitzsimmons competition was piqued by long-running newspaper coverage of promoters' attempts to conduct a match without interference from the authorities. Gossip and press stories abounded about the problems of staging the event and of filming it. In fact, the potential for motion picture exploitation of the fight played a large role in determining when, where, and how the bout would take place.

In 1894, during the first months of Thomas Edison's public presentation of his company's kinetoscope technology, brothers Gray and Otway Latham contracted with Edison to form their Kinetoscope Exhibition Company for the purpose of filming and exhibiting boxing pictures. Enoch Rector, an engineer, and silent partner Samuel Tilden, Jr., son of a prominent politician, joined the venture. Following the successful recording of a modest sparring scene, the *Leonard-Cushing Fight,* in June 1894, the Lathams paid heavyweight champion Corbett to stage a boxing exhibition before the Edison cameras. In September, on the second anniversary of his taking the title from the legendary John L. Sullivan, Corbett posed for six choreographed and abbreviated rounds with an unknown pugilist, Peter Courtney. Owing to the champion's considerable celebrity, *Corbett and Courtney before the Kinetograph* became one of the most popular and profitable kinetoscope subjects.

The Lathams began negotiating for a higher-profile fight film. The optimal scenario was an on-location recording of a championship tilt between Corbett and the top-ranked contender, Bob Fitzsimmons. The pair had been publicly feuding and created a grudge match atmosphere that led to the signing of articles of agreement in October. Hoping to capture the event on film, the Lathams pushed W. K. L. Dickson and the other Edison engineers to expand the capacity of their camera—at least to the limits of the three-minute rounds of legitimate prizefights. By November the improvements in the technology had progressed sufficiently for Gray Latham to attempt to intervene in the contracted plans to hold the Corbett-Fitzsimmons fight in Jacksonville, Florida. The theatrical and sporting journal the *New York Clipper* published Latham's "startling proposition."

> [Since the fight will likely not be allowed in Florida] we propose to make you an offer, which will certainly demand consideration. This offer would have been made at the time the several clubs were bidding for the championship contest, but for the fact that we were not then in a position to enter the competition . . . because the experiments at three minute subjects with the kinetograph had not proved entirely successful. Now, however, we shall not only be able to take each three minute round of the fight, but also the action of the seconds, etc., during the one minute rest between rounds.
> . . .
> Our offer is a plain one. The fight must be held in the morning, and, in case the date selected should prove a cloudy day, we will ask for a postponement until a clear day comes round. . . . We want the fight before November 1, 1895, and will give $50,000 for it. . . . We are enabled to offer this amount of money without depending upon the gate receipts, because, while a good many tickets will be sold, that is an entirely after consideration with us.[3]

The fight failed to come off as first planned, but the groundwork had been laid for an unprecedented and highly lucrative enterprise—staging the heavyweight championship contest for the primary benefit of movie cameras, rather than live spectators, and milking profits from the much bigger audience that could be reached via repeated exhibitions of the fight recording. It would be two and a half years before the *Corbett-Fitzsimmons Fight* materialized, and the Lathams would not be involved. During this interim, the American press daily chronicled the activities surrounding the two boxers, their attempts to fight, and their promoters' efforts to capture them on film.

Dan A. Stuart, a prominent entrepreneur and "sporting man" based in Dallas, Texas, formed a syndicate to promote the Corbett-Fitzsimmons fight. His organization eventually engineered the boxing event that others had been unable to realize—and successfully managed its film coverage as well.

However, Stuart first had to overcome considerable opposition to his prizefight. When he announced plans to hold the bout at the 1895 Texas State Fair, his long-time political enemy Charles A. Culberson, now the governor, called a special session of the state legislature "to denounce prizefighting . . . and prohibit the same." An attempt to move the fight to Arkansas met with more direct intervention. The governor there had both Corbett and Fitzsimmons placed under arrest.[4] To make matters worse for Stuart and for the Kinetoscope Exhibition Company, which was banking heavily on a second Corbett film, the champion went into semi-retirement. In a dig at Fitzsimmons, Corbett unofficially resigned his title to the lesser-rated heavyweight Peter Maher. Although Corbett retained the popularity of a champion and prospects for a Corbett-Fitzsimmons scrap remained the subject of discussion, attention now focused on a Maher title defense.

The Maher-Fitzsimmons fight of February 21, 1896, proved to be one of boxing's most storied events. The participation of "moving picture men" contributed to the conspicuous affair. Although cinematography of the fight ultimately failed, the publicity surrounding the battle only spurred anticipation of the Corbett-Fitzsimmons showdown.[5]

Well before the actual contest, the quest for a heavyweight championship was again thrust into the national spotlight. As state after state legislated against prizefighting, Capitol Hill also took steps to ensure that the Fitzsimmons-Maher fight in particular would not take place on federal land, passing a law against prizefighting in the Territories.[6] Despite these rebuffs, Stuart sought to recoup part of his investment in the Corbett fight by handling the Fitzsimmons-Maher affair. He grandiosely proposed that the championship be part of a "fistic carnival" near El Paso and promised motion picture coverage. Stuart secured an agreement with the Kinetoscope Exhibition Company. Although the Lathams had departed to form their own motion picture venture, Rector had maintained the Edison company's favor and possessed four cameras that would enable him to do ringside photography.[7]

Under the watch of Texas Rangers, western lawmen Bat Masterson and Judge Roy Bean supervised production of the illegal prizefight on a sandbar in the dry Rio Grande. Two hundred fight fans traveled by rail with Stuart and Rector to the site outside of Langtry, Texas. Workers quickly constructed an elevated boxing platform and a ringside "frame compartment" for the movie cameras. Fitzsimmons knocked out his rival halfway through the first round. Overcast skies and a light rain apparently ruined Rector's efforts to film the colorful scene. Reporters wrote that "the kinetoscope man, came to [Fitzsimmons] with a proposition to fight Maher six rounds in front of his machine, which would not work to-day because of the dark weather." But the boxer refused to spar for the cameras without the same $5,000 that his nemesis Corbett had gotten for the same work.[8]

Although Fitzsimmons chose not to imitate Corbett's success in kinetoscope films, in the months after his victory over Maher the presence of cinema expanded so dramatically that all members of the prizefight establishment welcomed the opportunity to appear on film. Throughout 1896–97, big-screen projections of moving pictures replaced single-viewer peep shows. When the *Corbett-Fitzsimmons Fight* hit the market in the spring of 1897, it joined a host of other offerings presented by competing "screen machines." The proliferation of such novelties—some hits, others barely functional— became the subject of topical satire. The very week that Rector filmed the Corbett-Fitzsimmons bout, Weber & Fields' Broadway Music Hall presented a sketch entitled "The Lobsterscope," billed as "a burlesque of all animated picture machines (patent protected!)." The turn featured performers before a black curtain illuminated by a flickering strobe light and included "a burlesque of the Corbett-Fitzsimmons prize fight."[9]

Even before the bout, moving picture shows helped publicize the battle between the two boxers. Many exhibitors revived the dozens of available boxing subjects for their topical appeal, joining in the nationwide interest in the event. In particular, the *Corbett-Courtney Fight* remained a popular title. "The Great Corbett Fight" became an important attraction for many of the earliest film operations, including William T. Rock's Vitascope Hall in New Orleans (July-August 1896), Thomas Tally's Los Angeles film parlor (December 1896), and Siegmund Lubin's first cineograph projections in Philadelphia (March 1897). Patrons were invited to "get pointers [for the Nevada bout] by seeing Corbett fight."[10]

This burgeoning market in motion pictures also entailed a new level of commercial competition among film companies. Of the Edison licensees that originally vied for fight subjects in 1894, only the Rector-Tilden partnership remained when Corbett finally signed to meet Fitzsimmons. However, the duo no longer operated under the aegis of the Kinetoscope Exhibition Company or with the aid of specially built Edison cameras. After the failure of the modified Edison kinetographs at the Fitzsimmons-Maher fight, Rector experimented with his own camera-projector system. Improving on the Edison "prizefight machine," Rector built a smaller, lighter, hand-cranked model that employed a wide, large-format film stock and required less light. His "veriscope" tested well and covered the width of a boxing ring better than other cameras.[11]

PRODUCING THE CARSON CITY FIGHT FILM

With the increasing commercial possibilities of cinema and the technological success of the veriscope, Dan Stuart's contract for a heavyweight championship and Rector-Tilden's exclusive film deal with Corbett both took on greater potential value. Although anti-prizefight protests had multiplied, the sport continued to grow. Newspapers increasingly devoted attention to sports in general and boxing in particular.[12] Stuart negotiated a legal venue for his much-hyped contest in Nevada, which agreed to re-legalize the sport in hopes of gaining publicity and capital.[13] A huge arena was built in Carson City for the March 17 battle.

As with the Langtry fight, the construction featured ringside housing for film equipment. Despite his earlier failure, Stuart again engaged the photographic services of Rector. On the day of the fight, when photographic conditions were deemed acceptable, the center-of-the-ring preliminaries commenced and were directed toward the camera: the introduction of John L. Sullivan, his manager Billy Madden, and referee George Siler; the entrance, posing, and disrobing of the boxers.

Once the bell sounded, the Veriscope equipment captured all of the action.[14] Eleven thousand feet of film, running nearly two hours, were exposed without interruption. Some of the footage had photographic flaws, but all of the action was visible in the finished documentary record that Rector released. The climax of the film, Fitzsimmons's solar plexus punch that crippled his opponent, even seemed to show a camera-conscious Corbett. As the *San Francisco Examiner* suggested: "The field of the camera, which took the final kinetographs [sic] did not include the space near the ropes into which Corbett crawled. . . . The pictures show him painfully crawling out of the camera's field, and at the end his head, arms, and shoulders are out of the picture."[15] Although commentators often erroneously referred to the apparatus used in Carson City as a "kinetoscope," the Veriscope Company planned to present full-length, projected exhibitions to theater audiences across the country. For the first time, scenes of an actual professional fight would be shown to "mixed" audiences of men and women, fans of boxing and curious onlookers. But two months of controversy and commentary over the fight pictures preceded their exhibition.

ANTICIPATION OF THE FIGHT PICTURES: CENSORSHIP AND "NEGATIVE" PUBLICITY

With eleven reels of Veriscope film in the can, the "production" of the *Corbett-Fitzsimmons Fight* had only just begun in a sense. Threats of censorship, rumors about the quality of the photography, and exploitative cinematic imitations of the fight helped generate public discourse about the film on an almost daily basis. Deftly channeled by Stuart, the publicity led to a highly visible and successful roadshowing of the *Corbett-Fitzsimmons Fight* that lasted through the turn of the century.

Attempts to censor the fight pictures arose immediately. In February 1897, the U.S. Congress, which one year earlier had enacted preemptive legislation against the heavyweight title fight, initiated a campaign against all forms of media publicity for the event. A failed bill aimed "to forbid the transmission by mail or interstate commerce of any picture or description of any prize fight."[16] Religious and civic reform groups supported the legislation as part of their larger Purity Crusade against vices of all sorts. The 300,000-strong Women's Christian Temperance Union (WCTU) spearheaded the campaign, arguing that the bill would "protect our boys from brutality."[17] As Gregory A. Waller points out, those opposed to the exhibition of the *Corbett-Fitzsimmons Fight* were among the first to question the "insidious influence of this new mechanical means of 'life-like' reproduction." Others warned against the power of the "hypnotic exhibition," implying an apprehension of the medium's perceived potency.[18] Two days after the Corbett-Fitzsimmons bout, a new Congress introduced legislation to specifically "prohibit the reproduction in the District of Columbia and the Territories, by kinetoscope or kindred devices, of such pugilistic encounters and fights as are forbidden" by existing law.[19] Opponents of prizefighting lobbied for passage. In April, for example, a collection of prominent public men issued a memorial "Against Prizefight Pictures." With signatories including a U.S. Supreme Court justice, three governors, and many religious leaders, the petition condemned the "brutal encounter" between Corbett and Fitzsimmons, as well as the press's exploitation of "the disgraceful event." Though many other constituencies expressed similar condemnation, the measure never came to a vote.[20]

Congressional inaction against the *Corbett-Fitzsimmons Fight* did not indicate a lack of interest or political will with regard to the matter, but rather a realization that individual states could act more swiftly than the new administration in Washington. Less than a week after the fight, the *New York Tribune* commented on a trend toward such legislative intervention: "If a prizefight is a brutal and degrading performance, properly forbidden by law the pictorial reproduction of it by kinetoscope can scarcely be edifying or elevating and may properly also be forbidden by law. Some States, it is pleasant to observe, are enacting special laws against such exhibitions."[21] The *New York Times* also sided with "the moralists" in condemning the films: "It is not very creditable to our civilization perhaps that an achievement of what is now called the 'veriscope' that has attracted and will attract the wildest attention should be the representation of the prizefight."[22]

In the end, few authorities acted upon the initial furor of proposals and apocalyptic rhetoric. One of the chief reasons that the unprecedented censorship campaign against movies stalled was that the Veriscope Company conducted an effective publicity counteroffensive. Stuart first allowed the activists and legislators to cool. Then he co-opted a female constituency for his film. This gave the appearance of balancing the attacks by women's reform groups such as the WCTU that had seemingly threatened his venture in the first place.

Stuart selectively released to the press false, misleading, and conflicting facts about the condition of the photographic negatives. While legislators debated a ban on fight films, the Veriscope Company suggested that such statutes would be laughable because its precious negatives had not been exposed properly. The Hearst news syndicate, which had heavily promoted the Corbett-Fitzsimmons fight, helped Stuart by chronicling the fortunes of the pictures on an almost daily basis. On April 4, its Sunday papers ran a front-page telegraphic headline: "Kinetoscope Scheme Is a Failure—Negatives of Great Fight Show Many Defects—Big Venture That Promised Great Returns Will Be Profitless—Efforts to Restore the Films to Usefulness May Prove Futile—Projector of the Enterprise Has Given Up All Hope of Success." The report cited "E. J. Rector" and developers at the Edison labs in New Jersey as confirming that the film contained "every defect known to photography."

> Rector is not losing any sleep over what various legislative bodies may do to "knock out" his pictorial prizefight enterprize *[sic]*, so he says. . . . He is laughing in his sleeve at the misguided legislators. He thinks it is a great joke that so much space in the statute books should be used to prohibit something that is impossible of accomplishment.[23]

As threats of censorship steadily fell away, a series of increasingly favorable evaluations gradually replaced these stories of ruined negatives. By May it was clear that in fact the complete fight had been captured cleanly on film. The Veriscope Company offered screenings to the press in New York. Hearst and other newspapers carried both written descriptions and prominent page-one illustrations based on the Veriscope scenes.

By any measure, the strategy to publicize the Veriscope pictures was successful. The press releases managed by Stuart, along with the fighters' agents, William A. Brady and Martin Julian, consistently avoided direct combat with the moralist forces. By the eve of the Veriscope premiere, the new heavyweight champion was hobnobbing with the distinguished gentlemen of the U.S. Senate, who had tabled the bill against fight films only a week before.[24]

VERISCOPE EXHIBITION: ACADEMIES, OPERA HOUSES, AND FAIRGROUNDS

The first complete public Veriscope exhibition of the *Corbett-Fitzsimmons Fight* occurred on a Saturday evening, May 22, 1897, at the Academy of Music in New York City. Within a few weeks, a number of Veriscope projectors with prints of the film were traversing the United States and nations abroad. Traveling Veriscope units reproduced the entire bout for audiences paying up to one dollar for admission. Stuart's primary targets were prestige venues such as the Academy of Music, opera houses, and high-class vaudeville halls. The mass popularity of the pictures soon led to their exhibition in various other amusement places as well—fairgrounds, storefronts, and parks—where they reached a broader audience than those who could afford to see the initial roadshow presentations. By creating an international distribution plan, sustaining publicity in the press, and elevating admission prices, Stuart's enterprise garnered the first fortune in motion picture history: an estimated gross of $750,000, and well over $100,000 in net profits for his company.[25]

More to the point, by exhibiting the *Corbett-Fitzsimmons Fight* under these conditions, Stuart brought prizefighting to a broad new audience. Even as the sport was being excoriated and outlawed by one element of the ruling class, Veriscope was receiving the tacit imprimatur of another. Rather than cater to and recruit the traditional fight fan—perceived to be a rowdy, less desirable class of patron—Veriscope recruited more genteel audiences. Setting itself up in the trappings of high-class theaters and opera houses, Veriscope specifically invited "ladies" to attend its shows. When some did, it claimed them as proof of its legitimacy.

The first screenings of the *Corbett-Fitzsimmons Fight* were press shows that Stuart organized in advance of the Veriscope's public premiere. Other motion picture entrepreneurs had offered publicity displays for newspaper reporters. But these had been to show off the capabilities of technology. Stuart and his agents used the previews to color perceptions and plant stories about what the films revealed. Initially, screenside lecturers, such as Corbett's manager William A. Brady, told reporters how to watch for particular controversial moments in the fight. As news of the *Corbett-Fitzsimmons* film circulated, however, the "angle" about women attending the screenings began to be increasingly hyped by the film's promoters and reporters.

With the aid of the press, Veriscope began its far-flung and lengthy tour. It had unprecedented success, playing for several years in a variety of venues. An examination of Veriscope exhibition practices demonstrates how it crossed into arenas of high, middle, and low social status. Employing protean exhibition and promotional strategies, the *Corbett-Fitzsimmons Fight* reached from the sublime to the pedestrian, playing academies of music and opera houses, fairgrounds and circuses.

Stuart sought to capture the high ground first. As early as April 24, his first trade advertisement informed theatrical proprietors that "this picture will be given throughout this country in theatres as a dramatic representation."[26] In a bold and unusual marketing of motion pictures, Stuart distributed the entire *Corbett-Fitzsimmons Fight* as a hundred-minute feature that would constitute a complete theatrical attraction. The film's extra-wide 60mm format also made it incompatible with other projectors on the market and thus heightened the exclusivity of Veriscope's presentations.

The Veriscope's initial and most lucrative runs were in the large, prominent theaters of major urban centers. The gala circumstances of the film's premiere at New York's Academy of Music were not unlike many of the screenings which followed it. As its name suggested, the academy typically hosted refined cultural events (though it had also hosted live "boxing entertainments").[27] The rowdy connotation of "prizefight" was therefore toned down for its presentation of "the Veriscope Pictures of the Corbett-Fitzsimmons Sparring Contest." With reserved seats priced from one dollar to twenty-five cents, middle- and upper-class patrons predominated. The *New York Tribune* reported that the 2,100-seat theater was "full of people," "as if a big melodrama full of icebergs and noble sentiments had been announced." Theatrical papers also took note of the "enormous crowd" at the Veriscope shows, including a "'goodly sprinkling of ladies,' who appeared as much interested in the exhibition as those made of stronger stuff."[28]

One noteworthy aspect of this mode of exhibition facilitated attendance by ladies and genteel audiences in general: the use of an on-stage narrator. He described key moments in the match, identified ringside celebrities, and detailed the veriscope's technological achievements. The live narrator's presence connected the fight film exhibition to the tradition of the illustrated lecture. As Musser has shown, the screen practice of narrated stereopticon programs was a precedent for the full-length program which fight pictures and passion-play films adopted. Specializing in the travelogue genre (which in its own way the Nevada fight film resembled), touring lecturers began incorporating motion pictures into their lantern-slide shows in 1897–98.[29] An explanatory boxing lecture, therefore, helped diffuse the unsavory blood-and-guts aspect of the exhibition by suggesting the more genteel style of presentation used in illustrated lectures on the bourgeois lyceum circuit.

Dozens of other cities hosted the Veriscope in the same way and with the same results as the Academy of Music. In each case the prestige and box office of the film remained high. Admission prices continued to be set at up to one dollar, with matinee and evening "performances." While competing motion picture displays could be found in vaudeville halls, Veriscope units consistently filled legitimate theaters, academies of music, and grand opera houses in these urban areas.

Such lavish treatment, however, could be sustained only in areas with large populations. People residing in smaller towns and rural areas saw the Veriscope show in more modest circumstances. As local histories of early film exhibition increase in number, one of the emerging constants across these studies has been the late-nineteenth-century institution of the opera house in small American towns. Distinct from the "grand opera house" of the metropolis, the provincial opera house served as the center for all major commercial entertainment. The local opera house of the 1890s was where small-town America often saw its first motion picture demonstrations, including the *Corbett-Fitzsimmons Fight*.

One detailed account of the veriscope's appearance in such a provincial opera house is Gregory A. Waller's profile of pre-nickelodeon film exhibition in Lexington, Kentucky. The Lexington Opera House, a 1,250-seat structure, introduced motion picture technology to Lexington in December 1896 (with a between-act display by the *cinématographe*). Other inventions—the Vita-scope, Phantoscope, Magniscope—passed through town the following year. By the time of the Corbett-Fitzsimmons controversy, Lexington citizens were familiar enough with motion pictures that the Second Presbyterian Church could ask the board of aldermen to pass "an ordinance prohibiting the exhibition in our city of any picture, however made, or representation of such fights." As was the case in many other cities, however, no censorship action was taken. Instead the *Corbett-Fitzsimmons Fight* received a favorable reception when it played the local opera house that fall.

With only small populations from which to draw audiences, opera-house exhibitions were scheduled for short runs, Lexington's occurring from September 30 to October 2. However, ticket prices remained as high as they had been for the New York premiere, with reserved box seats still one dollar. Evening and matinee show times were also maintained, with "larger and more enthusiastic" crowds reported at night. Afternoon presentations were less well attended, but conspicuously were "largely made up of ladies." As Waller notes, the fight film exhibitor had to take special pains to construct the event as "perfectly proper" for more genteel audiences. Lexington's opera-house manager, therefore, reported that "thousands of ladies and gentlemen" were taking great interest in the veriscope.[30]

If proprietors of opera houses and urban theaters were careful to control the circumstances of Veriscope shows so as to attract a more bourgeois clientele (and segregate them from the raucous fight fans in the cheap seats), a third line of exhibition offered freer access to the *Corbett-Fitzsimmons Fight*. The carnivalesque settings of fairgrounds, amusement parks, and circuses were frequently used as more casual spaces for Veriscope displays. Here the film shed its trappings of exclusivity, allowing crowds of mixed gender, class, ethnicity, and age to see and comment on the reproduction together. In some areas this may have been the predominant form of Veriscope exhibition. The Rhode Island WCTU, for example, protested the "debasing influence . . . exerted by the side shows of many of our fair grounds," taking particular note of "the vitascopic exhibition of prize fights" that fair associations had sponsored in 1897.[31] In other instances, such as the summer movie shows at New Orleans's Athletic Park in June 1898, the *Corbett-Fitzsimmons Fight* appeared in open-air exhibitions only after it had completed its high-priced run in the city.[32]

During its run, the recording of the great prizefight remained a durable and lucrative show business property. As the history of its multifaceted exhibition demonstrates, Veriscope promoters took advantage of its unique level of publicity to reach an unusually great number and diversity of places and audiences.

THE QUESTION OF RECEPTION: FEMALE SPECTATORS AT THE VERISCOPE

Amid all of the fight film publicity and debate, the variety in exhibition formats, and the mixed reception of the film in different milieux, one constant and historically surprising motif recurs in documentation about the Veriscope: women in unexpected numbers patronized the *Corbett-Fitzsimmons Fight*. Several film historians have recently noted this phenomenon and have argued its importance for revising the historiography of early film reception. Miriam Hansen has described it as not less than an "exemplary moment of crisis" in the history of film spectatorship.[33] After reviewing the available evidence concerning female attendance and reception of the Veriscope, I conclude by considering some of the possible implications of this historical incident for rethinking theories of the history of film audiences, particularly ones which conceptualize films as articulations of a patriarchal system that position spectators as masculine subjects.[34]

Again it was Musser who brought the attention of the field to the fact that the *Corbett-Fitzsimmons Fight* attracted a substantial female clientele. Citing newspaper reports, he notes that "although men of sporting blood were the veriscope's intended audience," there arose quite a different response. Not only were members of the upper crust and the nonsporting public turning out for the newsworthy fight films, but many women were as well. "In Boston, women were reported to form 'a considerable portion of the audience,' and according to at least one source, women constituted fully 60 percent of Chicago's patronage. In many other cities and towns, a similar pattern emerged. To male reporters, it was a puzzle."[35]

Other local reviews support Musser's findings. That summer, the *San Francisco Examiner* mentioned that "women as well as men watch the changing pictures of the veriscope with eagerness." A Dallas report pointed out in the fall that "hundreds of ladies have witnessed these exhibitions," while the following spring, the New Orleans press was still noting that women attended evening shows, as well as the "special matinees . . . given especially for the convenience of ladies and children."[36]

While it is certain that many women did see Veriscope presentations, there is reason to question the degree to which their turnout was accurately reported. The accounts of public response to the *Corbett-Fitzsimmons Fight* often appear to have been colored by or derived from prepared publicity material distributed by the film's promoters. Stories about the film's appeal to women were an element of this publicity which the Veriscope Company planted in the press. Several facts support this premise. First, many of the Veriscope write-ups have a great degree of sameness about them, down to particular descriptive words and detailed facts about the film (repeated mention is made, for example, that it was "one and a half miles" long, that it consisted of "189,000 exposures," etc.).

Second, we know that both Stuart and Brady exploited newspaper connections to keep stories about their boxers and the Veriscope almost constantly in print. Among the methods employed were wiring press releases directly to news offices, spreading rumors or exaggerated stories purely for the sake of gossip columns, and running ghostwritten pieces signed by their boxers. Brady himself claimed to emulate Joseph H. Tooker, the theatrical showman who stirred up publicity, pro and con, by fabricating outlandish letters, sermons, fan mail, and news items.[37]

Third, even if the company did not literally distribute written materials ("press kits" of the sort that became routine during the feature-film era),[38] it provided advance screenings, "Press Nights," in which Veriscope views were run for the benefit of local newspapers. The lecturer and/or operator who traveled with the films had motive, means, and opportunity to supply reporters with the appropriate angle on how the fight reproduction would be received by the public.

Fourth, the Hearst press syndicate, which dominated coverage of the Corbett-Fitzsimmons affair, poured a great deal of its money and resources into promoting the fight: buying exclusive interview rights, sending celebrity reporters and artists to Carson City, chartering express trains, etc. Although they had no share in film profits, Hearst papers and other yellow journals had a vested interest in milking the story of the Great Fight. The idea that genteel ladies were flocking to peek at this sensational heavyweight slugfest contains all of the elements of classic yellow journalism. Like so many fabricated stories of the era, it had allusions to crime, sexual transgression, exotic locale, social taboo, sporting life, and popular science—all with the veneer of a "true story."[39]

Without documentation from the Veriscope offices, it is impossible to substantiate how much of this story was orchestrated hype and how much was fair reporting of a genuine phenomenon. Isolating one particular case of a local Veriscope exhibition, however, strengthens the case for the former. Looking at Lexington, Kentucky's, history of film exhibition, Gregory A. Waller offers a skeptical view of the claims about female patronage. He notes that the local opera-house proprietor, Charles Scott, who booked the *Corbett-Fitzsimmons Fight*, also provided both Lexington papers with a "promotional article a week before the fight films were to be shown," in which he claimed that "one of the most remarkable features of the veriscope pictures of the contest is the great interest shown in the exhibition by women." Waller concludes: "True or false, this 'fact' established a precedent, and Scott provided a 'perfectly proper' opportunity for taking in the fight films by scheduling matinee showing 'especially for ladies.'"[40]

Waller's case study also provides evidence as to why the Veriscope interests would have benefited from publicity about the film's finding a female audience. As was true in other areas, the Lexington press's principal discussion of motion pictures prior to the Veriscope arrival at the local opera house had been during the national debate on fight film censorship in March 1897. Since that campaign was led by the WCTU (who ranked it second only to suffrage on their annual agenda),[41] press accounts represented the film as a "stag" entertainment venture meeting feminine grassroots opposition. Stuart's management proved capable of defeating censorship measures threatened by all-male legislatures (stories abounded about congressmen's own desires to see the big fight); co-opting female resistance to his enterprise would help assuage the remaining moralist antipathy.

To implement such a strategy for channeling the film's reception, Veriscope representatives sought out high-class exhibition venues and, rather than protect women and children from exposure, encouraged "ladies" to come see this "illustration" of the boxing contest. The result for women was a socially problematic conjunction of two cultural practices: attending the theater and becoming a spectator of the male domain of prizefighting. In order to have any insight into the horizons of reception possible for American women in 1897, one must reconstruct the historical context of female spectatorship with regard to both theater and boxing.

The latter is easier to measure, since by all accounts the nineteenth-century ringside was an almost entirely male purview. While other organized sports encouraged female patronage (e.g., baseball, with its "Ladies' Days" as early as the 1860s),[42] boxing remained "stag" well into the next century. Whether at organized athletic club contests, mining-camp mills, or clandestine bouts, women remained excluded from the violent and rowdy social setting of prizefights. Period photographs and drawings corroborate this. Although some women may have gotten secondhand knowledge by reading about boxing in the emerging sports pages of the day, such material was intended for male readers. But by the 1890s, mass-circulation dailies also solicited female readers by featuring women reporters. When Hearst papers titillated readers by sending their star female writer, "Annie Laurie," to cover a prizefight, she told her audience: "Men have a world into which women cannot enter."[43]

Female spectatorship at fights was thus consistently represented as an act of transgression. Annie Laurie could watch, it was said, only "from behind a curtained booth." The figure of the lone, disguised woman at ringside became a recurring one in tabloid stories of the 1890s; some were intended to be comical, others sensationalistic. In the Corbett-Fitzsimmons era, such anecdotes peppered the pages of the widely read boxing bible, the *Police Gazette*. Colorful items such as "How a Female Sport Saw a Fight," in which a cigarette-smoking blonde sat near ringside dressed as a man, drew upon boxing lore which dated back to at least the days of John L. Sullivan (when his girlfriend, Ann Livingston, reportedly attended the Sullivan-Charlie Mitchell fight "dressed as a boy").[44] The *Gazette* also frequently presented readers with illustrated stories about female pugilists. These accounts were read as comic inversions, emphasizing the distance between boxing and prevailing perceptions of femininity and masculinity. By suggesting that the "manly art" was being usurped in "these days of women's rights" ("these degenerate days"), they also revealed a male perception of female threat. As sports historian Steven A. Riess has shown, American men of this period saw amateur boxing as a method of countering a perceived "feminization" of social life.[45]

The lone woman at ringside took on a particular identity when Rose Julian Fitzsimmons, the boxer's wife, became noted for her insistence on sitting in her husband's corner. Like Annie Laurie, she initially watched bouts from hidden peephole vantage points; but at Carson City the former vaudeville acrobat broke with social decorum by making herself highly visible in the first row. Her "boisterous and Amazonian action" was widely reported and sermonized against. Those who did not find her cheering deplorable spoke of it as comical.[46]

As a public figure, the wife of the champion was perhaps granted some license with her appearance, but other women at the Nevada fight were not. One sports writer remarked: "The most curious members of the spectators were a few women who had braved public opinion for the new sensation. They were mostly of the per-oxide blonde order and some of them were not particularly difficult to classify."[47] This thinly veiled reference to prostitutes bolsters the applicability of Hansen's argument that to consider the historical role of women as participants in any public activity, we must remember that the "public sphere was gendered from the start," that it began as "an arena of civic action for the 'public man,'" at a time when the idea of a "public woman" was synonymous with prostitution.[48]

Yet the spectacle of pugilism was not completely closed to women in 1897. As Timothy J. Gilfoyle shows in his history of prostitution, "public women" of the urban "underground" certainly had contact with the male sporting life.[49] But "respectable" ladies had limited exposure as well. Through various types of theatrical performance—sparring exhibitions, physical culture shows, living pictures, illustrated lectures, and melodramas starring prizefighters— women had access to a controlled form of the sport, its celebrities, and their displayed bodies. Jim Corbett's status as a matinee idol was well known, and both he and Fitzsimmons attracted female followings during the theatrical tours which followed their title match.[50] Through this medium of theatrical re-presentation, the Veriscope invited women to experience what was then their closest contact with an authentic prizefight.

Even this legitimated and regulated public space of the theater was not an unproblematic one for American women of the Gilded Age to enter. As Robert C. Allen demonstrates in his history of burlesque, the nineteenth century was a period of "cultural reorientation" for the American theater. By the 1890s the association between prostitution and female theater attendance was still less than a generation old. Prior to the Civil War, commercial theaters and concert saloons catered to a public that was mostly male and working-class. Few women attended the raucous shows. Unescorted women who did were often known (or reputed) to be prostitutes. Such activity was tacitly condoned by theater managers who allowed the use of a separate entrance that led to a notorious "third tier" or upper gallery where prostitutes rendez-voused with male clients.

Allen charts the reconstruction of American theatrical institutions as a steady process of gentrification, in which working-class audiences and forms were "excorporated" into separate spheres (burlesque, minstrelsy, et al.) by managers who increasingly sought the patronage of an ascending middle class. Theatrical entrepreneurs began to recruit women and their families. Their attendance not only increased profits but also served as a marker of social acceptability, "sanctifying" and "feminizing" theatergoing for the American bourgeoisie. Following the earlier leads of cagey showmen such as P. T. Barnum and Moses Kimball (who gave women access to stage shows via their "museums"), New York theaters in 1865 began scheduling Saturday afternoon matinees for women. Intended to coincide with the urban woman's afternoon shopping excursions, the strategy proved successful. Accommoda-tions were made in both the theatrical space and performances. Proprietors transformed the male-dominated "pit" (main floor) into the "parquette," allowing women a choice of seating beyond the conspicuous loge. Finally, as Allen and many other theater historians point out, the valorization and recruitment of a female audience was consolidated by the efforts of variety promoter Tony Pastor in the 1880s, and the institutionalization of "clean," "polite" vaudeville by B. F. Keith and other theater owners of the 1890s. As Keith himself wrote in 1898, both "the house and the entertainment [should] directly appeal to the support of ladies and children. . . . My playhouse must be as 'homelike' an amusement resort as it was possible to make it."[51] Vaudeville became, Allen says, the "first form of commercial theatrical enter-tainment to draw unescorted, middle-class women in significant numbers."[52] At the time of the *Corbett-Fitzsimmons Fight,* therefore, many women had only just begun to find the environs of the theater to be a receptive, legiti-mated social space.

THE MATINEE GIRL

The majority of those women who ventured into the opera houses of America to see the Veriscope pictures were recruited and accommodated by the "ladies' matinee" trappings of their exhibition. From the *Boston Herald* to the *Lex-ington Herald,* publicity announced the fight films not as a transgression, but as the "proper" thing for ladies to see.[53] But how did they react to the flickering black-and-white images of Fitzsimmons knocking out Corbett?

What did their attendance mean to them and to others? Preliminary answers to these questions have been made by Musser and Hansen, suggesting that the *Corbett-Fitzsimmons Fight* was a brief, utopian moment in the history of female spectatorship in which socially restricted middle-class women were temporarily free to indulge in the pleasure of "perusing" "well-trained male bodies in semi-nudity."[54] Such interpretations are not invalid, but surviving reviews by a pair of female reporters—New York's "Matinee Girl" and San Francisco's Alice Rix—suggest a more complicated reception.

Writing from the point of view of the female theater patron, a columnist for the *New York Dramatic Mirror* wrote a brief notice of the *Corbett-Fitzsimmons Fight's* debut in Manhattan. Under the *nom de plume* "the Matinee Girl," the presumably female reporter told readers of the theatrical trade paper:

> I saw the prize fight at the Academy. . . . Of course I mean the Veriscope. I saw lots of girls I knew there, but I didn't pretend to notice they were there. I felt as much ashamed of it as they were!
>
> It is a pity Corbett doesn't win. He is a great favorite with us, but he's been knocked out of our hearts by his recent defeat.
>
> Mr. Brady will have to give away some very expensive souvenirs if he ever expects to have his star regain his popularity with the Saturday afternoon audiences. Fitzsimmons isn't pretty—but oh, my![55]

From the perspective of one in the theatrical world, the propriety of the ladies' matinee functioned precisely as the promoters wished. Treated to "souvenirs," the "Saturday afternoon audiences" flocked to the theater even in the somewhat embarrassing circumstances of a prizefight exhibition. Since the writer was clearly an "insider" (she knows William Brady as Corbett's manager) reporting to other trade members, her account may be read as yet another item driven more by publicity than by reportage. But she does represent the motives and reactions of her constituency in a way consistent with Hansen's interpretation. The female spectator of fight pictures is lured by the sight of a "pretty" athlete. Hansen compares the display of boxers to the selling of Rudolph Valentino's bare torso to female fans of the 1920s. She describes the Veriscope phenomenon, however, as an "accident" in which women were allowed a pleasurable glimpse at the athletes' bodies. Whether their pleasure involved looking at physiques for sexual desire or a general attraction to the individual man remains uncertain. As the Matinee Girl notes, it was their "great favorite" Gentleman Jim whom they specifically came to see. Other pugs would not have evoked the same response.

Another aspect of the event which anyone seeing either the *Corbett-Fitzsimmons* or *Corbett-Courtney* films cannot fail to spy is the Gentleman's prominently displayed gluteus. The bare-cheeked trunks he sports in the filmed bouts were not ones often found on other fighters. One can only assume that his daring choice of costume calculatedly played on his awareness of his "ladies' man" image. Although journalistic accounts successfully repressed any mention of his state of undress, it is difficult to imagine that those who saw the sight would have paid no notice. If word of mouth had not gotten around after Corbett's kinetoscope appearance, the well-circulated motion pictures of him disrobing (literally) in Carson City must have provoked comment, however *sotto voce.* With this in mind, the matinee girls' feeling "much ashamed" and pretending not to see each other suggest not just a social embarrassment at partaking in the male act of ringside spectatorship, but also a blushing at the explicit physical display—what Hansen calls the "forbidden sight"[56]—of Corbett as they had never before seen him.

The degree to which watching moving pictures of Corbett and Fitzsimmons was an erotic experience for women, akin to the Valentino cult, is impossible to measure conclusively. The Matinee Girl's claim to Corbett as a "great favorite . . . knocked out of our hearts" is as close as public commentary came to speaking in terms of female desire. Even assuming an attraction to the boxer's body on the part of (heterosexual) women, the potential eroticism of the moment was tempered by the violence of the bout, the knockout of the star, and the spotty quality of the reproduction, as well as the unprecedented publicness of such an experience for women of the day.

ALICE RIX AT THE VERISCOPE

These complicating factors—which question the premise that women flocked to the Veriscope to see the bodies of boxers on display—are raised in a lengthy feature story written by a newspaperwoman attending the San Francisco debut of the *Corbett-Fitzsimmons Fight.* "Alice Rix at the Veriscope," an exposé on the film's exhibition at the Orpheum vaudeville palace in July 1897, appeared in the Sunday magazine supplement to Hearst's *Examiner.*[57] This fascinating document is worth examining for several layers of evidence not found in other sources. Authored by a woman, primarily for women readers, on the subject of female audiences, it offers a specific and illustrated description of an exhibition and a live audience's responses.

In order to gauge the value of this account as a representation of the film's reception, one must consider the circumstances of its production. Who was Alice Rix, and why was she "at the Veriscope"? The name was not a pseudonym but belonged to a San Francisco society woman whose surname was known as one of the prominent families who had settled the Bay Area after the 1849 gold rush.[58] Her byline appeared weekly as part of the *Examiner's* colorful Sunday supplement. The Sunday edition had been a recent part of William Hearst's strategy to increase mass circulation in general and female readership in particular.[59] The "Sunday Magazine," as its masthead proclaimed, covered "art, music, drama, fashion, society, sport, fiction and news." Among the more prominent "women's features" were floridly written, dramatic stories by female reporters. As in the sporting world, women in journalism were conspicuous by their very presence. Hearst editors exploited their conspicuousness by giving them prominent bylines and assigning them to sensational stories. Often, as historian Barbara Belford points out, they were placed in taboo or "dangerous situations to titillate readers." "Sob sister" journalists (as they were later dubbed) —writers such as Rix and her better-known pseudonymous counterparts Nellie Bly, Dorothy Dix, and Annie Laurie—sought out the "secret" story which "only a woman could extract."[60] In 1897, therefore, Rix's Veriscope report was just one in a series of Sunday exposés in which she revealed to readers the inside scoop on such local subjects as the "Girl Slaves of Chinatown," the "Women Tramps of Oakland," "Sausalito Pool Halls," exploited migrant workers, and the interior of San Quentin prison.

Interestingly, her essay begins by insinuating that the circulating story about women clamoring to see the prizefight pictures was a fabricated male fantasy misreported by newspapers such as her own:

> Well?
>
> Where is she?
>
> Where is woman at the prize fight?
>
> Where is that fierce, primitive savage thing, that harpy, that bird of prey, that worse-than-man who was expected to sit six rows deep before the Veriscope at the Olympia and gloat over the bloody sport of the ring? Where is the brute?
>
> I do not see her on Monday night. But, then, as somebody reminds me, Monday is Press night.
>
> It is on Tuesday then that I may expect her?
>
> Yes, certainly. She will be there on Tuesday.
>
> Various simple ostriches [i.e., women] of my acquaintance assure me there will be a crush of women at the Olympia every night and a bigger crush still at the matinees. That is woman's first opportunity, you know, to see a prize fight with the blessing of the world upon her head and she would rather lose the head than miss it. Why? Look at her in New York where the Veriscope was running at the Academy of Music. I saw her at the Veriscope in New York, of course, sitting fierce-eyed and dry-mouthed before the screen with her thumbs down? No? I read about her, then? And saw the pictures in the papers?
>
> I see [cheap, sporting men] at the entrance to the Olympia. They are waiting there, as one of them remarks, to watch the women pour in.
>
> . . . A short line forms before the box office. There is not a woman in it.

Eventually, Rix reports, only sixty women—out of about a thousand people—made their way into the theater. She notes with some detail the social typology of the crowd, arranged by custom in the various sections of seats. The gallery, as usual, was occupied by the more boisterous working-class element, while the more middle-class "sporting men incline[d] to the boxes." The dress circle, where one might expect to find the "proper" ladies reputed to be in attendance, was noted as empty. Instead, women at the Olympia sat in the main parquette section and were "dressed down." Rix describes them as either demure, quiet wives and mothers with their families, or well-bred society girls escorted by young sports.

Among these scattered women viewers, reportedly few were there in earnest to see the boxers; nor were they particularly captivated by the pictures. Despite elements of presentation designed to enhance the exhibition—a musical overture by a mandolin orchestra and pianist, along with the standard screenside announcer—most of the audience failed to respond with much enthusiasm. Men familiar with prizefighting found the silent, monochromatic reproduction lacking.

> But the women said nothing. During the next intermission they yawned and moved about restlessly in their chairs. . . .
> The Veriscope is a bloodless battle, fought on canvas by the wraiths and shades of men. . . .
> The San Francisco woman sat calmly before the Veriscope.
> So did the San Francisco man.

One might have expected 'Frisco audiences, as they saw their hometown hero dethroned, to be more subdued that those elsewhere. But, at least from Rix's perspective, it was not just the content of the film but the medium of cinema itself to which she and her fellow viewers failed to warm. Rather than marveling at their magical qualities, she found moving pictures "awful."

> I am reminded suddenly of a long-forgotten childish terror of the Magic Lantern show. The drawing-room in darkness, the ghastly white plain stretching away into the unknown world of shadows. It was all very well to call it a linen sheet, to say it was stretched between innocent familiar folding doors, it nevertheless divided the known and safe from the mysterious beyond where awful shadows lived and moved with a frightful rapidity and made no sounds at all.
> And they were always awful, no matter how grotesquely amusing the shape they took, and they followed me to the nursery in after hours and sat on my heart and soul the black night through. And sometimes even

"The Interested and the Disinterested": This drawing of women watching the *Corbett-Fitzsimmons Fight* accompanied an essay, "Alice Rix at the Veriscope," in the Sunday magazine section of Hearst's *San Francisco Examiner*, July 18, 1897. Rix's rare firsthand account of a woman watching a prizefight film confirms that there was a female audience for the Corbett-Fitzsimmons pictures, but she suggests that talk about the phenomenon was exaggerated.

morning light could not drive them quite away, and now forsooth, it seems they have withstood the years.

I would not go to see the Veriscope often. It is, as one of the girls in front of me said, "A little too leary for me."

Although this evocative description reinforces the historical discursive connection between cinema and dreams, it is a far cry from the stereotype which soon developed of the enchanted, movie-mad female spectator.

Further contradictions and complexities concerning the figure of the female movie viewer accompany Rix's essay in the form of an illustration by

Mary Harrison (or Davidson). With the caption "The Interested and the Disinterested," the drawing depicts two opposite reactions by women at the Veriscope. The "interested" party, a smiling woman, leans forward in her box seat, enjoying her view of the shadow Corbett. Behind her stands the "disinterested" companion, looking away, her back to the screen.

The two figures parallel two modes of female reception. The first is suggested by the New York Matinee Girl, an unmarried theater habitué and adoring Corbett fan. The second is that of Alice Rix, the society matron and arbiter of taste who denied that anything untoward was occurring with those few San Francisco women who ventured to see the Veriscope pictures. Looking over the shoulder of the seated (apparently younger) woman, we follow her line of sight to the movie screen, where the silhouette of Corbett's famous figure is the object of her gaze. Although the directness of her looking is attenuated by a veil and a hand fan which partially guard her expression, she obviously takes not only interest but pleasure in the experience. She delights in the transgression of looking as well as the image itself. Her counterpart not only seems disinterested but even wears a look of slight dismay at the other's keen interest. However one reads their expressions, it is certain that the artist's rendering of female spectators at the Veriscope suggests a more intriguing dynamic of reception than Rix's essay of disinterest.

This illustration holds even greater significance for an interpretative assessment of female spectatorship during this period, given its notable similarity to the genre of Paris Opera paintings and prints in circulation a few years earlier. Film historian Antonia Lant points out that Mary Cassatt, Auguste Renoir, and other artists produced a series of works—including *At the Opera* (1880) and *La Loge* (1880)—representing women (and some men) in the "activity of looking out of and into an elevated opera box." As Lant points out, these depictions make clear that for the nineteenth-century woman/spectator, in this public space the very activity of looking and of being allowed to "overtly scrutinize her surroundings" was more important than what was being looked at.[61] So it was for Veriscope audiences. However, the sketch of the San Francisco loge also differs from those in Paris in one important aspect. Presented with a moving-picture image, the women in the *Examiner* illustration do react to the specific spectacle being presented. While one looks away from the image with a chaperone's sense of social impropriety, the other leans forward to secure a more concerted view. This latter gesture suggests two things: (1) that cinema, with its darkened setting, encouraged viewers to attend less to the activity within the theater and more to the presentation itself, and (2) that some female patrons, in this particular case, found something especially intriguing in the reproductions of Corbett and Fitzsimmons.

As Lant's reflections on theories of female spectatorship put it, representations such as these hint at the nuances of "the social and psychic conditions of the nineteenth-century female's public life." Knowledge of such conditions is crucial to understanding the type of possibilities that existed for the reception of prizefight films or any other sort of public presentation. Yet with such limited source materials it is difficult to venture beyond those outlines and determine what women or men actually thought when viewing fight reproductions.

In fact, the lack of documentation may be even more problematic in evaluating the specific subtleties of the modes of male spectatorship and reception. If the boxers' dress and display had erotic connotations for some women, one must assume that there also were sexual dynamics involved in the spectatorship of the larger male audience. Whether hetero- or homosexual, the audience was one of men watching men. Thomas Waugh's 1991 essay "Strength and Stealth: Watching (and Wanting) Turn of the Century Strongmen" suggests some historical understanding of this phenomenon. He takes the 1894 kinetoscope of Strongman Eugen Sandow's muscle-flexing and speculates how it, and other artifacts such as the *Corbett-Courtney* pictures, may have "accommodated the homoerotic gaze."

To what degree was there a gay male audience for prizefight films such as *Corbett-Fitzsimmons?* As Waugh shows in historical detail, "many emerging cultural forms" at the time—academic nude photography, sports photographs, *Police Gazette* illustrations, physical culture magazines and postcards, as well as some early films—made the male athlete a spectatorial object. A century later, he argues, these appear to represent "the first stirrings of the homoerotic construction of the male body." Just as we know that the constituency for prizefighting was men, Waugh points out that for these related practices "the institution of looking at the male body was overwhelmingly male." But it is difficult to reliably say much more. Much as discourse about female desire was repressed in the discussion of women attending fight films, Waugh concludes that the same was true of men writing about physical culture: "Specific documentation of the homoerotic articulation and appropriation of the strongman image is as scanty as a fig leaf." At most we can "presume that the homosocial [i.e., all-male] infrastructure" and "sexual atmosphere" of the physical culture movement "legitimized the pleasure of looking at male beauty" and "sheltered an important (if superficially invisible) gay constituency."[62]

Although there are similarities, there are also key differences between the aesthetics of physical culture that Waugh describes and turn-of-the-century prizefighting. The sleek, clean, Grecian-sculptured, statuesque poses of Sandow differ markedly from that of the stereotypical plug-ugly prizefighter.

Corbett aside, the boxer of the period was represented by his disfiguring ring scars—broken noses, cauliflower ears—and his ability to maul, seldom for his beauty. Physical culture was a still-life display of idealized bodies; prizefighting was blood sport, a spectacle of men damaging one another's bodies. If it was a standard of male beauty that might have attracted gay men, as well as heterosexual women, to Sandow and Corbett, the dynamics and aesthetics of prizefighting largely worked against that. Gilfoyle's *City of Eros* has even documented how the sporting press in particular was virulently homophobic in its presentation of boxing as a symbol of "manliness." The world of boxing was more likely to comport to the traditional, patriarchal culture of stereotypical masculinity than it was to a gay subculture. Homosexual or bisexual men may well have been motivated to watch the sport for the same reason heterosexuals did, but erotic attractions were tempered.[63]

Although I have discussed how and why claims about a veritable craze by women to see the *Corbett-Fitzsimmons Fight* are exaggerated, there can be no doubt that a female audience of some size saw the films. As both Hansen and Musser argue, women's contact with this widely circulated set of prizefight pictures can be seen as an important historical moment, one which gave women access to the segregated male domain of prizefighting and to the sight of boxers in action. But that access was always limited, mediated, and socially controlled. The moment was indeed momentary as well. The sport itself remained primarily male, more so than any other. Subsequent fight films, even those showing Jim Corbett, never again attracted female patrons in significant numbers. The few trade reports of women at the boxing films which later appeared treated the event as a mere oddity.[64] Though an invited "ladies" audience helped legitimize the Veriscope enterprise, throughout the ensuing Progressive Era fight film promoters often had to pledge to bar women (and children) from the more closely regulated nickelodeons.

The case of the *Corbett-Fitzsimmons Fight* remains in many ways an atypical example of early cinema. Its format, fame, controversy, longevity, and profitability stood out from the increasing traffic in motion pictures in 1897. Despite its enormous financial success, it did not offer a paradigm for cinema form or practice. And the limited number of big fight films which followed did not draw the same sort of audience.

Yet the *Corbett-Fitzsimmons Fight*'s nonpareil status still suggests some rethinking of film historiography. In general, the great degree of social commentary and public discourse that surrounded a film of so little aesthetic or formal interest testifies to the need to pay more attention to the social conditions of exhibition and reception when evaluating a film's place in the history of cinema.

More particularly, and more important, the question of this boxing film's reception by women calls into question the larger conceptions we have about the historical development of cinematic form and cinema audiences. The strong argument that has been made for classical Hollywood cinema has often been applied to early film as well: that cinema was constructed for a heuristic male viewer, with women as the object of the gaze. Given the voyeuristic, peepshow aesthetic of so many early cinema subjects—dancing girls, disrobing acts, etc.—this conception holds. But with both the male boxer (especially the exhibitionistic Corbett) as film subject and the female viewer as audience member, we should re-evaluate the actual dynamic that was in play during the early years of moving-picture presentation. While there can be no doubt that these boxing events were intended foremost as male entertainment, the evidence suggests that women also sought pleasure from them on occasion. Not only did some female audiences make Corbett's physique the object of their gaze, but they may well have enjoyed other, more overtly "stag" displays as well. Contemporaneous representations of young women peering into mutoscope peep shows (looking at striptease scenes and the like) may support the evidence of the Veriscope's female audience. Images such as John Sloan's lithograph "Fun 1¢" (1905), or any of several photographs taken at turn-of-the-century Coney Island depicting similar scenes, bolster the notion of a female audience for male-oriented entertainment.

Even though the female clientele that may have taken an unintended pleasure in seeing the Veriscope pictures did so only during a brief moment in the early history of cinema, the fact remains that it was a significant rupture in the expected course of events. The fact that the film and its audience's reactions invited such simultaneous pleasure and outrage makes the *Corbett-Fitzsimmons Fight* an intriguing and problematic artifact from America's early cinema.

NOTES

1. Charles Musser, *The Emergence of Cinema: The American Screen to 1907* (New York: Scribner's, 1990), pp. 194–200; Miriam Hansen, "The Spectatrix: Individual Responses," *Camera Obscura* 20–21 (1989–90): 179. A fuller version of the history of the *Corbett-Fitzsimmons Fight* film appears in Daniel Gene Streible, "A History of the Prizefight Film, 1894–1915," Ph.D. dissertation, University of Texas at Austin, 1994 (and a forthcoming book by Smithsonian Institution Press).

2. Paul Rotha's passing comment on the film typifies the general treatment of the subject: "exceptionally dull as this enormous length of film must have been, its novelty was probably astounding." *The Film Till Now* (London: Spring Books, 1967), pp. 69–70.

3. "The Championship Match," *New York Clipper*, November 4, 1894, p. 562.

4. Leo N. Miletich, *Dan Stuart's Fistic Carnival* (College Station, Tex.: Texas A&M University Press, 1994); William Brady, *The Fighting Man* (Indianapolis: Bobbs-Merrill,

1916), p. 130; James J. Corbett, *The Roar of the Crowd* (Garden City, N.Y.: Garden City Publishing Co., 1926), p. 247; "The XXIV Legislature Meets," *Austin Daily Statesman,* October 3, 1895, p. 5.

See also *House Journal* of the Texas Legislature, October 1, 1895, p. 4; "Having Hot Times Down at Austin," *Dallas Times Herald,* October 2, 1895, p. 2; James William Madden, *Charles Allen Culberson: His Life, Character, and Public Service as County Attorney, Attorney General, Governor of Texas and U.S. Senator* (Austin: Gammel's Book Store, 1929); Elmer M. Million, "History of the Texas Prize Fight Statute," *Texas Law Review* (1938), pp. 152–59; "Gov. Culberson and Dan Stuart," *Dallas Times Herald,* October 8, 1895, p. 2; "That Grand Jury Down at Austin," *Dallas Times Herald,* October 9, 1895, p. 2; J. C. M., "Hot Springs Is the 'Hot' Town," *Dallas Times Herald,* October 10, 1895, p. 2; William A. Brady, *Showman* (New York: E. P. Dutton, 1937), pp. 165–70.

Details about Daniel Albert Stuart (1846–1909) before the Corbett-Fitzsimmons affair are sketchy. He was a successful merchant and trader who became influential in sporting and theatrical enterprises. Robert L. Wagner, "Governor vs. Gambler," *Texas Parade,* November 1963, pp. 22–24; *Memorial and Biographical History of Dallas County, Texas* (Chicago: The Lewis Publishing Company, 1892), p. 547; Frank X. Tolbert, "Stuart Proposed Fight in Balloon," *Dallas Morning News,* September 19, 1962, in *Tolbert's Texas Scrapbook* (Barker Texas History Center, University of Texas at Austin), vol. IX, p. 67a; and [Dan Stuart buys Turner Hall building for $10,000 and rents it to Thompson's Variety Theatre people], *Dallas News,* October 12, 1886, p. 8.

5. Jimmy Banks, "Roy Bean—Boxing Promoter," *Texas Parade,* September 1950, pp. 24–25; Damon Benningfield, "The Boxing Championship That Wasn't: Maher vs. Fitz-simmons on a Rio Grande Sandbar," *American West* 23, no. 1 (1986): 63–65; Dick King, "The Fight That Almost Kayoed Boxing," *Frontier Times,* Summer 1959, pp. 26–27, 56–57; Denis McLoughlin, *Wild & Woolly: An Encyclopedia of the Old West* (Garden City, N.Y.: Doubleday, 1975), p. 39; David Weiss, "Beer and Boxing," in John Durant, ed., *Yesterday in Sports: Memorable Glimpses of the Past as Selected from the Pages of "Sports Illustrated"* (New York: A. S. Barnes, 1956), pp. 48–49; and Grace Miller White, "When Judge Roy Bean Pulled a Prize Fight," *Frontier Times,* August 1941, pp. 477–80.

6. Report No. 256, accompanying H. R. 5566, 54th Congress, 1st Session, February 5, 1896 (Washington, D.C.: Government Printing Office, 1896); *Congressional Record,* February 5, 1896, p. 1344.

7. White, p. 478; Tolbert, p. 67a.

8. "The Big Mill Pulled Off," *Galveston Daily News,* February 22, 1896, pp. 1–2; "The World's Championship: Bob Fitzsimmons Easily Defeats Maher for the Title Which Corbett Declined to Defend," *Clipper,* February 29, 1896, p. 829; "The Day Was Too Dark for the Kinetoscope," *Austin Daily Statesman,* February 22, 1896, p. 1; Terry Ramsaye, *A Million and One Nights,* 1926 (rpt., New York: Simon and Schuster, 1986), pp. 281–84; William Naughton, *Kings of the Queensberry Realm* (1902), p. 219; Fred Dartnell, *"Seconds Out!" Chats about Boxers, Their Trainers, and Patrons* (New York: Bretano's Publishers, 1924), pp. 133–34.

9. Armond Fields and L. Marc Fields, *From the Bowery to Broadway: Lew Fields and the Roots of American Popular Theater* (New York: Oxford University Press, 1993), p. 131 (generously provided by Annie Bright); *New York Clipper,* April 3, 1897, p. 81. Lobster implies "a victim of deception," "one easily duped." Harold Wentworth et al., eds., *Dictionary of American Slang* (New York: Thomas Y. Crowell, 1975), p. 322. C. Francis Jenkins, *Animated Pictures* (Washington, D.C.: H. L. McQueen, 1898), p. 24, lists 110 "'scope' and 'graph' machines which have already appeared."

10. Sylvester Quinn Breard, "A History of the Motion Pictures in New Orleans, 1896–1908," M.A. thesis, Louisiana State University, 1951; Dan Streible, "A History of the Boxing Film, 1894–1915: Social Control and Social Reform in the Progressive Era," *Film History* 3, no. 3 (1989): 237 (broadside of Tally's and "The Great Corbett Fight" provided by Richard Koszarski); Musser, p. 169.

11. Ramsaye, pp. 284–87; Musser, p. 195. Kemp R. Niver, "From Film to Paper to Film," in *Wonderful Inventions* (Washington, D.C.: Library of Congress, 1985), p. 203.

12. John Rickard Betts, "Sports Journalism in Nineteenth-Century America," *American Quarterly,* Spring 1953, p. 56; Betts, *America's Sporting Heritage, 1850–1950* (Reading, Mass.: Addison-Wesley, 1974), pp. 61–64, 160–69; Elliott J. Gorn, *The Manly Art: Bare-Knuckle Prize Fighting in America* (Ithaca: Cornell University Press, 1986), pp. 41–42, 121–22; Melvin Adelman, *A Sporting Time: New York City and the Rise of Modern Athletics, 1820–1870* (Urbana: University of Illinois Press, 1989), pp. 230, 237–38.

13. "[Referee George] Siler Gives His Views," *San Francisco Examiner,* March 18, 1897, p. 10. Boxing historian Barratt O'Hara wrote, "Nothing short of a genius is Stuart. . . . Straight to Nevada he hurried, and lobbied a bill through the legislature." In *From Figg to Johnson: A Complete History of the Heavyweight Championship* (Chicago: Blossom Book Bourse, 1909), p. 171.

14. According to "The Fistic Kinetoscope Exhibits" (*Clipper,* April 10, 1897, p. 96), "the machine got to work five minutes before the fight began and the scenes start with the arrival of the fighters at the ringside, in their bathrobes. The whole fourteen rounds are on the films, and the pictures go on for ten minutes after the last round, showing the crowd jumping into the ring."

15. "Kinetoscope Views Are Good in Spots," *Examiner,* April 18, 1897, p. 26.

16. Report No. 3046 [to accompany H. R. 10369], "Transmission by Mail or Interstate Commerce of Picture or Any Description of Prize Fight," 54th Congress, 2d Session, February 26, 1897, n.p. See also *Congressional Record,* XXIX, p. 2392.

17. All quotations from *Congressional Record,* pp. 2587–89.

18. Gregory A. Waller, "Situating Motion Pictures in the Prenickelodeon Period: Lexington, Kentucky, 1897–1906," *Velvet Light Trap* 25 (1990): 12–28; "A Knock-Out for Kinetoscopic Reproductions of the Corbett-Fitzsimmons Fight Planned by Women," *Lexington Herald,* March 24, 1897, p. 1 (from a photocopy graciously provided by Waller); [Pennsylvania legislature's bill to prevent hypnotic exhibition], *Clipper,* May 8, 1897, p. 171.

19. "To Stop Pugilism by Kinetoscope," *New York Tribune,* March 25, 1897.

20. "Against Prizefight Pictures," *New York Tribune,* April 16, 1897. Of the forty-two signers, the article named "Justice [Stephen Johnson] Field of the U.S. Supreme Court; Governors Oferrall of Virginia, Cooke of Connecticut, and Grout of Vermont; Bishops Whitaker, Coleman, and Cheney; Revs. John Hall, Teunis S. Hamlin, Theodore L. Cuyler, Henry M. Field, and H. L. Wayland; Robert Treat Paine; [Prohibitionist leader] Neal Dow and others. . . ." See also *Congressional Record,* May 12, 1897, p. 1046.

21. *New York Tribune,* March 22, 1897, p. 6; "Anti-Kinetoscope Fight Bills," *New York Tribune,* March 20, 1897, p. 1; "To Prohibit Prize-Fight Pictures," *Examiner,* March 21, 1897, p. 9; "Opposed to Prize-Fight Pictures," *Clipper,* March 26, 1897, p. 3; "The Ring," *Clipper,* March 27, 1897, p. 63; "Against Fight Pictures," *Clipper,* April 3, 1897, p. 80, and May 8, p. 171; "No Kinetoscope for Canada," April 16, 1897, *Examiner,* p. 8; "To Bar Fight Pictures," *Examiner,* June 5, 1897, p. 3.

22. *New York Times,* May 26, 1897, cited by Garth Jowett, *Film: The Democratic Art* (Boston: Little, Brown, 1976), pp. 109–10.

23. *Examiner,* April 4, 1897, p. 1. See also "Another Fight Anticipated," *Examiner,* April 5, 1897, p. 3. A cartoon by Jimmy Swinnerton played upon the rumor of defective negatives of the *Corbett-Fitzsimmons* film: "When They Heard That the Kinetoscope Pictures Were a Failure," *Examiner,* April 8, 1897, p. 8.

24. "Fitz Hobnobs with Greatness," *Examiner,* May 19, 1897, p. 3.

25. Sources for the $750,000 figure include Brady, *Fighting Man,* pp. 131–48. Musser, p. 200, cites the lower, net profit amount.

26. *Clipper,* April 24, 1897, p. 134.

27. Musser, p. 193.

28. "The Veriscope Exhibited," *New York Dramatic Mirror,* May 29, 1897, p. 13; "The Championship Fight Reproduced," *Clipper,* May 29, 1897, p. 214; "The Veriscope Shows the Fight," *New York Tribune,* May 23, 1897, p. 8.

29. Musser, chapter 7, "Full-Length Programs: Fights, Passion Plays, and Travel," especially pp. 221-23; Charles Musser with Carol Nelson, *High-Class Moving Pictures: Lyman H. Howe and the Forgotten Era of Traveling Exhibition* (Princeton, N.J.: Princeton University Press, 1990).

30. Waller, "Situating Motion Pictures in the Prenickelodeon Period," pp. 12-28; and "Introducing the 'Marvelous Invention' to the Provinces: Film Exhibition in Lexington, Kentucky, 1896-1897," *Film History* 3, no. 3 (1989): 223-34. Also "A Knock-out," *Lexington Herald,* March 24, 1897, p. 1; Veriscope ad, *Lexington Herald,* September 27, 1897, p. 6; "Great," *Lexington Leader,* October 1, 1897, p. 3 (provided by Waller).

31. *Twenty-third Annual Meeting of the Women's Christian Temperance Union of Rhode Island Held in Olneyville, October 13 and 14, 1897* (Providence: Providence Press, 1897), p. 11.

32. Breard, pp. 48ff.

33. Miriam Hansen, "Individual Responses," *Camera Obscura* 20-21 (1989-90): 179. Hansen's other writings on the *Corbett-Fitzsimmons Fight* are "Reinventing the Nickelodeon: Notes on Kluge and Early Cinema," *October* 46 (Fall 1988): 178-98; "Adventures of Goldilocks: Spectatorship, Consumerism and Public Life," *Camera Obscura* 22 (1990): 51-72; and *Babel and Babylon: Spectatorship in American Silent Film* (Cambridge, Mass.: Harvard University Press, 1991).

34. For overviews of historical and theoretical scholarship concerning female film audiences, see Jackie Stacey, "Textual Obsessions: Methodology, History and Researching Female Spectatorship," *Screen* 34, no. 3 (Autumn 1993): 260-74; Janet Staiger, *Interpreting Films: Studies in the Historical Reception of American Cinema* (Princeton: Princeton University Press, 1992); "Spectatrix Issue," *Camera Obscura* 20-21 (1989-90).

35. Musser, p. 200.

36. "The Shadows of the Corbett and Fitzsimmons Fight," *Examiner,* July 18, 1897, p. 25; "Corbett and Fitzsimmons—The Carson Fight Pictures Reproduced to Large Audiences," *Dallas Morning News,* October 25, 1897, p. 4; *New Orleans Picayune,* March 28, 1898, p. 12, March 30, p. 10; and *New Orleans Democrat,* March 30, 1898, p. 3, both cited in Breard, pp. 43-47.

37. Tooker promoted *The Black Crook,* an 1866 Broadway spectacle featuring chorus girls in flesh-colored tights, by inventing a "public indignation build-up." Brady, *Showman,* pp. 131-33.

38. Mark Stuart Miller, "Promoting Movies in the Late 1930s: Press Books at Warner Bros.," Ph.D. dissertation, University of Texas at Austin, 1993.

39. On "yellow journalism" see Sidney Kobre, *The Yellow Press and Gilded Age Journalism* (Tallahassee: Florida State University Press, 1964), and *Development of American Journalism* (Dubuque, Iowa: William C. Brown, 1969); Frank Luther Mott, *American Journalism* (New York: Macmillan, 1962); Edwin and Michael Emery, *The Press and America,* 4th ed. (Englewood Cliffs, N.J.: Prentice-Hall, 1978).

40. Waller, "Situating Motion Pictures in the Prenickelodeon Period," pp. 17-18; citations from *Lexington Herald,* September 26 and 27, 1897, p. 6, and *Lexington Leader,* September 20, 1897, p. 3.

41. *Twenty-third Annual Meeting of the WCTU,* p. 11.

42. Barbara A. Schreier, "Sporting Wear," in Claudia Brush Kidwell and Valerie Steele, eds., *Men and Women: Dressing the Part* (Washington, D.C.: Smithsonian Institution Press, 1989), p. 103.

43. Barbara Belford, *Brilliant Byline: A Biographical Anthology of Notable Newspaperwomen in America* (New York: Columbia University Press, 1986), p. 140. No date is given for the *Examiner* story written by Laurie [Winifred Black Bonfils]; "it was said she was the first woman to report a prize fight."

44. Nat Fleischer and Sam Andre, *A Pictorial History of Boxing* (New York: Citadel Press, 1959), pp. 62–63; *Police Gazette,* February 18, 1899, p. 10; "Sporty Young Woman at the Bouts," *Police Gazette,* May 26, 1900, p. 8; Brady, *Showman,* p. 77, alludes to a woman who smuggled herself into the Corbett-Sullivan fight (1892).

45. "Peep behind the Scenes—Two Women Fight with Gloves in Approved Pugilistic Style," *Police Gazette,* November 17, 1894, p. 3; *Police Gazette,* January 19, 1895, p. 5. Steven A. Riess, "Sport and the Redefinition of American Middle-class Masculinity," *International Journal of the History of Sport* 8, no. 1 (1991): 16–22, pointed out by Aaron Baker. Sports historians Jan Todd and Terry Todd point out that the *Gazette* promoted women boxers for a time, but abandoned them in the 1890s "in favor of women bag punchers" (letter to the author).

46. Sen. John J. Ingalls, "The Blow a Fluke," *San Francisco Examiner,* April 4, 1897, p. 1; Sammons, *Beyond the Ring,* pp. 54–55; Lardner, p. 104.

47. T. T. Williams, "One Punch Was Worth a Fortune," *Examiner,* March 18, 1897, p. 7.

48. Hansen, *Babel and Babylon,* p. 10.

49. Timothy J. Gilfoyle, *City of Eros: New York City, Prostitution, and the Commercialization of Sex, 1790–1920* (New York: W. W. Norton, 1992).

50. "Corbett and Fitzsimmons," *Examiner,* April 1, 1897, p.8.

51. B. F. Keith, "The Vogue of Vaudeville," *National Magazine* 9 (November 1898): 146–53, reprinted in Charles W. Stein, ed., *American Vaudeville as Seen by Its Contemporaries* (New York: Da Capo Press, 1984), p. 17.

52. Robert C. Allen, *Horrible Prettiness: Burlesque and American Culture* (Chapel Hill: University of North Carolina Press, 1991), p. 186; Hansen, "Adventures of Goldilocks," p. 52.

53. Waller cites the Lexington press advance publicity as telling "those thousands of ladies and gentlemen who, in a quiet way, take a keen interest in sporting matters" that Veriscope shows were "perfectly proper"; "Situating Motion Pictures in the Prenickelodeon Period," p. 17. Musser, pp. 200, 512, cites the *Boston Herald* as describing them as "quite the proper thing" for ladies.

54. Hansen, "Reinventing the Nickelodeon," p. 190; Musser, p. 200.

55. "The Matinee Girl," *New York Dramatic Mirror,* June 12, 1897, p. 14.

56. Hansen, "Adventures of Goldilocks," p. 52.

57. Alice Rix, "Alice Rix at the Veriscope," *Examiner,* July 18, 1897, p. 22.

58. *The Bay of San Francisco, the Metropolis of the Pacific Coast and Its Suburb Cities: A History,* vol. II (Chicago: Lewis Publishing Co., 1892), p. 313; Peggy Samuels and Harold Samuels, *Illustrated Biographical Encyclopedia of Artists of the American West* (Garden City, N.Y.: Doubleday, 1976), p. 402; John William Leonard, ed., *Women's Who's Who of America: A Biographical Dictionary of Contemporary Women of the United States and Canada, 1914–1915* (New York: American Commonwealth Co., 1914), p. 691; G. S. Rix, *Genealogy of the Rix Family* (1906).

59. Kobre, *Development of American Journalism,* pp. 357, 391–92; Emery and Emery, p. 245; Ishbel Ross, "Ladies of the Press," in Marion Marzolf, *Up from the Footnote: A History of Women's Journalism* (New York: Hastings House, 1977), p. 33.

60. Belford, pp. 2–5; Phyllis Leslie Abrahamson, *"Sob Sister" Journalism* (New York: Greenwood Press, 1990).

61. Antonia Lant, "Individual Responses," *Camera Obscura* 20–21 (1989–90): 217–19. In later correspondence with the author (August 12, 1994), Lant also points out that the "veiled profile" of the second Veriscope viewer resembles images painted by Manet, Cassatt, or Morisot.

62. Thomas Waugh, "Strength and Stealth: Watching (and Wanting) Turn of the Century Strongmen," *Canadian Journal of Film Studies/Review canadienne d'études cinématographiques* 2, no. 1 (1991): 1–20 (brought to my attention by Janet Staiger).

63. Gilfoyle, pp. 135–36. Gerald Early writes that boxing's spectacle of "male bodies often locked in embrace" represents only a "latent homosexuality" denied by most of its audience and practicers. In its violence, prizefighting arguably "becomes virulently antihomosexual theater." "James Baldwin's Neglected Essay: Prizefighting, the White Intellectual, and the Racial Symbols of American Culture," in *Tuxedo Junction: Essays on American Culture* (New York: Ecco Press, 1989), p. 189; Early, *The Culture of Bruising: Essays on Prizefighting, Literature, and Modern American Culture* (Hopewell, N.J.: Ecco Press, 1994).

64. "Women and Prizefights," *Moving Picture World,* July 13, 1907, p. 374.

3 ... "Never Trust a Snake": WWF Wrestling as Masculine Melodrama

> See, your problem is that you're looking at this as a *wrestling* battle—two guys getting into the ring together to see who's the better athlete. But it goes so much deeper than that. Yes, wrestling's involved. Yes, we're going to pound each other's flesh, slam each other's bodies and hurt each other really bad. But there's more at stake than just wrestling, my man. There's a morality play. Randy Savage thinks he represents the light of righteousness. But, you know, it takes an awful lot of light to illuminate a dark kingdom.
>
> —Jake "the Snake" Roberts[1]

> There are people who think that wrestling is an ignoble sport. Wrestling is not a sport, it is a spectacle, and it is no more ignoble to attend a wrestled performance of Suffering than a performance of the sorrows of Arnolphe or Andromaque.
>
> —Roland Barthes[2]

Like World Wrestling Federation superstar Jake "the Snake" Roberts, Roland Barthes saw wrestling as a "morality play," a curious hybrid of sports and theater. For Barthes, wrestling was at once a "spectacle of excess," evoking the pleasure of grandiloquent gestures and violent contact, and a lower form of tragedy, where issues of morality, ethics, and politics were staged. Wrestling enthusiasts have no interest in seeing a fair fight but rather hope for a satisfying restaging of the ageless struggle between the "perfect bastard" and the suffering hero.[3] What wrestling offers its spectators, Barthes tells us, is a story of treachery and revenge, "the intolerable spectacle of powerlessness" and the exhilaration of the hero's victorious return from near-collapse. Wrestling, like conventional melodrama, externalizes emotion, mapping it onto the combatants' bodies and transforming their physical competition into a search for a moral order. Restraint or subtlety has little place in such a world. Everything that matters must be displayed, publicly, unambiguously, and unmercilessly.

Barthes's account focuses entirely upon the one-on-one match as an isolated event within which each gesture must be instantly legible apart from any larger context of expectations and associations: "One must always understand everything on the spot."[4] Barthes could not have predicted how this focus upon the discrete event or the isolated gesture would be transformed through the narrative mechanisms of television. On television, where wrestling comes with a cast of continuing characters, no single match is self-enclosed; rather, personal conflicts unfold across a number of fights, interviews, and enacted encounters. Television wrestling offers its viewers complexly plotted, ongoing narratives of professional ambition, personal suffering, friendship and alliance, betrayal and reversal of fortune. Matches still offer their share of acrobatic spectacle, snake handling, fire eating, and colorful costumes. They are, as such, immediately accessible to the casual viewer, yet they reward the informed spectator for whom each body slam and double-arm suplex bears specific narrative consequences. A demand for closure is satisfied at the level of individual events, but those matches are always contained within a larger narrative trajectory which is itself fluid and open.

The WWF broadcast provides us with multiple sources of identification, multiple protagonists locked in their own moral struggles against the forces of evil. The proliferation of champion titles—the WWF World Champion belt, the Million Dollar belt, the Tag Team champion belt, the Intercontinental champion belt—allows for multiple lines of narrative development, each centering around its own cluster of affiliations and antagonisms. The resolution of one title competition at a major event does little to stabilize the program universe, since there are always more belts to be won and lost, and in any case, each match can always be followed by a rematch which reopens old issues. Outcomes may be inconclusive because of count-outs or disqualifications, requiring future rematches. Accidents may result in surprising shifts in moral and paradigmatic alignment. Good guys betray their comrades and form uneasy alliances with the forces of evil; rule-breakers undergo redemption after suffering crushing defeats.

The economic rationale for this constant "buildup" and deferral of narrative interests is obvious. The World Wrestling Federation (WWF) knows how to use its five weekly television series and its glossy monthly magazine to ensure subscription to its four annual pay-per-view events and occasional pay-per-view specials.[5] Enigmas are raised during the free broadcasts which will be resolved only for a paying audience. Much of the weekly broadcast consists of interviews with the wrestlers about their forthcoming bouts, staged scenes providing background on their antagonisms, and in-the-ring encounters between WWF stars and sparring partners which provide a backdrop for speculations about forthcoming plot developments. Read cynically, the broadcast consists purely of commercial exploitation. Yet this promotion also has important aesthetic consequences, heightening the melodramatic dimensions of the staged fights and transforming televised wrestling into a form of serial fiction for men.

Recent scholarship has focused on serial fiction as a particularly feminine form.[6] Television wrestling runs counter to such a sharply drawn distinction: its characteristic subject matter (the homosocial relations between men, the professional sphere rather than the domestic sphere, the focus on physical means to resolve conflicts) draws on generic traditions which critics have identified as characteristically masculine; its mode of presentation (its seriality, its focus on multiple characters and their relationship, its refusal of closure, its appeal to viewer speculation and gossip) suggests genres often labeled feminine. These contradictions may reflect wrestling's uneasy status as masculine melodrama. Critics often restrict their discussion of melodrama to the domestic melodrama, a form particularly associated with feminine interests and targeted at female audiences.[7] Such a definition ignores the influence of melodrama on a broader range of genres, including some, such as the western or the social-problem drama, which focus on a masculine sphere of public action. Our inability to talk meaningfully about masculine melodrama stems from contemporary cultural taboos against masculine emotion. Men within our culture tend to avoid self-examination and to hide from sentiment, expressing disdain for the melodramatic. After all, we are told, "real men don't cry." Yet masculine avoidance of the public display of emotion does not mean that men lack feelings or that they do not need some outlet for expressing them. Patriarchy consequently constructs alternative means of releasing and managing masculine emotion while preserving the myth of the stoic male. A first step toward reconsidering the place of male affective experience may be to account for the persistence of melodramatic conventions within those forms of entertainment that "real men" do embrace—horror films, westerns, country songs, tabloid newspapers, television wrestling, and the like. By looking more closely at these forms of sanctioned emotional release for men, we may be able to locate some of the central contradictions within our contemporary constructions of masculinity.

This chapter will thus consider WWF wrestling as a melodramatic form addressed to a working-class male audience. In focusing on this particular audience here, I do not mean to suggest that this is the only audience interested in such programming. The WWF's multifocused narrative creates space for multiple audience segments—children, young and older women, gays, etc.—who take their own pleasures in its narrative. Nor does my focus on the melodramatic imply that televised wrestling is not readable in terms of other generic traditions, such as the carnivalesque dimension John Fiske locates.[8] My subtitle, "WWF Wrestling as Masculine Melodrama," signals my focus on one of a number of possible readings of the program. As Peter J. Rabinowitz has suggested, "Reading is always 'reading as,'" and our decision about a generic frame shapes subsequent aspects of our interpretations.[9] This essay, thus, reads wrestling *as* masculine melodrama, placing particular emphasis upon its relationship to a masculine audience and a melodramatic tradition. Such a focus invites an inquiry into the complex interplay of affect, masculinity, and class, issues which surface in both the formal and the thematic features of televised wrestling, in its characteristic narrative structure(s), its audience address, its treatment of male bonding, and its appeal to populist imagery.

PLAYING WITH OUR FEELINGS

Norbert Elias and Eric Dunning's pathbreaking study *The Quest for Excitement: Sport and Leisure in the Civilizing Process* invites us to reconsider the affective dimensions of athletic competition. According to their account, modern civilization demands restraint on instinctive and affective experience, a process of repression and sublimation which they call the "civilizing process." Elias has spent much of his intellectual life tracing the gradual process by which Western civilization has intensified its demands for bodily and emotional control, rejecting the emotional volatility and bodily abandon that characterized Europe during the Middle Ages:

> Social survival and success in these [contemporary] societies depend . . . on a reliable armour, not too strong and not too weak, of individual self-restraint. In such societies, there is only a comparatively limited scope for the show of strong feelings, of strong antipathies towards and dislike of other people, let alone of hot anger, wild hatred or the urge to hit someone over the head.[10]

Such feelings do not disappear, but they are contained by social expectations:

> To see grown-up men and women shaken by tears and abandon themselves to their bitter sorrow in public . . . or beat each other savagely under the impact of their violent excitement [experiences more common during the Middle Ages] has ceased to be regarded as normal. It is usually a matter of embarrassment for the onlooker and often a matter of shame or regret for those who have allowed themselves to be carried away by their excitement.[11]

What is at stake here is not the intensity of feeling but our discomfort about its spectacular display. Emotion may be strongly felt, but it must be rendered invisible, private, personal; emotion must not be allowed to have a decisive impact upon social interactions. Emotional openness is read as a sign of vulnerability, while emotional restraint is the marker of social integration. Leaders are to master emotions rather than to be mastered by them. Yet, as Elias writes, "We do not stop feeling. We only prevent or delay our acting in accordance with it."[12] Elias traces the process by which this emotional control has moved from being outwardly imposed by rules of conduct to an internalized and largely unconscious aspect of our personalities. The totality of this restraint exacts its own social costs, creating psychic tensions which somehow must be redirected and released within socially approved limitations.

Sports, he argues, constitute one of many institutions which society creates for the production and expression of affective excitement.[13] Sports must somehow reconcile two contradictory functions—"the pleasurable de-controlling of human feelings, the full evocation of an enjoyable excitement on the one hand and on the other the maintenance of a set of checks to keep the pleasantly de-controlled emotions under control."[14] These two functions are never fully resolved, resulting in occasional hooliganism as excitement outstrips social control. Yet the conventionality of sports and the removal of the real-world consequences of physical combat (in short, sport's status as adult play) facilitate a controlled and sanctioned release from ordinary affective restraints. The ability to resolve conflicts through a prespecified moment of arbitrary closure delimits the spectator's emotional experience. Perhaps most important, sports offer a shared emotional experience, one which reasserts the desirability of belonging to a community.

Elias and Dunning are sensitive to the class implications of this argument: the "civilizing process" began at the center of "court society" with the aristocracy and spread outward to merchants wishing access to the realms of social and economic power and to the servants who must become unintrusive participants in their masters' lives. Elias and Dunning argue that these class distinctions still surface in the very different forms of emotional display tolerated at the legitimate theater (which provides an emotional outlet for bourgeois spectators) and the sports arena (which provides a space for working-class excitement): the theater audience is to "be moved without moving," to restrain emotional display until the conclusion, when it may be indicated through their applause; while for the sports audience, "motion and emotion are intimately linked," and emotional display is immediate and uncensored.[15] These same distinctions separate upper-class sports (tennis, polo, golf) which allow minimal emotional expression from lower-class sports (boxing, wrestling, soccer) which demand more overt affective display. Of course, such spectacles also allow the possibility for upper- or middle-class patrons to "slum it," to adopt working-class attitudes and sensibilities while engaging with the earthy spectacle of the wrestling match. They can play at being working-class (with working-class norms experienced as a remasculinization of yuppie minds and bodies), can imagine themselves as down to earth, with the people, safe in the knowledge that they can go back to the office the next morning without too much embarrassment at what is a ritualized release of repressed emotions.

Oddly absent from their account is any acknowledgment of the gender-specificity of the rules governing emotional display. Social conventions have traditionally restricted the public expression of sorrow or affection by men and of anger or laughter by women. Men stereotypically learn to translate their softer feelings into physical aggressiveness, while women convert their rage into the shedding of tears. Such a culture provides gender-specific spaces for emotional release which are consistent with dominant constructions of masculinity and femininity—melodrama (and its various manifestations in soap opera or romance) for women, sports for men. Elias and Dunning's emphasis upon the affective dimensions of sports allows us to more accurately (albeit schematically) map the similarities and differences between sports and melodrama. Melodrama links female affect to domesticity, sentimentality, and vulnerability, while sports links male affect to physical prowess, competition, and mastery. Melodrama explores the concerns of the private sphere, sports those of the public. Melodrama announces its fictional status, while sports claims for itself the status of reality. Melodrama allows for the shedding of tears, while sports solicits shouts, cheers, and boos. Crying, a characteristically feminine form of emotional display, embodies internalized emotion; tears are quiet and passive. Shouting, the preferred outlet for male affect, embodies externalized emotion; it is aggressive and noisy. Women cry from a position of emotional (and often social) vulnerability; men shout from a position of physical and social strength (however illusory).

WWF wrestling, as a form which bridges the gap between sport and melodrama, allows for the spectacle of male physical prowess (a display which is greeted by shouts and boos) but also for the exploration of the emotional and moral life of its combatants. WWF wrestling focuses on both the public and the private, links nonfictional forms with fictional content, and embeds the competitive dimensions of sports within a larger narrative framework which emphasizes the personal consequences of that competition. The "sports entertainment" of WWF wrestling adopts the narrative and thematic structures implicit within traditional sports and heightens them to ensure the maximum emotional impact. At the same time, WWF wrestling adopts the personal, social, and moral conflicts that characterized nineteenth-century theatrical melodrama and enacts them in terms of physical combat between male athletes. In doing so, it foregrounds aspects of masculine mythology which have a particular significance for its predominantly working-class male audience—the experience of vulnerability, the possibilities of male trust and intimacy, and the populist myth of the national community.

REMAKING SPORTS

Elias and Dunning offer a vivid description of the dramaturgy of the ideal soccer match: "a prolonged battle on the football field between teams which are well matched in skill and strength. . . . a game which sways to and fro, in which the teams are so evenly matched that first one, then the other scores." The emotional consequences of the close and heated action are viscerally felt by the spectators. Each subsequent play intensifies their response, "until the tension reaches a point where it can just be borne and contained without getting out of hand." A decisive climax rewards this active engagement with "the happiness of triumph and jubilation."[16] The writers emphasize many traits which football shares with melodrama—the clear opposition between characters, the sharp alignment of audience identification, abrupt shifts in fortune, and an emotionally satisfying resolution. Yet there is an important difference. While melodrama guarantees emotional release through its conformity to tried and true generic structures, actual athletic competition, unlike staged wrestling, is unrehearsed and unscripted. Matches such as the ones Elias and Dunning describe are relatively rare, since so much is left to chance. Where the actual competition lacks narrative interest, that gap must be filled by sports commentary which evokes and intensifies the audience's investment. However, as Barthes notes, wrestling is not a sport but rather a form of popular theater, and as such, the events are staged to ensure maximum emotional impact, structured around a consistent reversal of fortunes and a satisfying climax. There is something at stake in every match—something more than who possesses the title belts.

As a consequence, wrestling heightens the emotional experience offered by traditional sports and directs it toward a specific vision of the social and moral order. Peter Brooks argues that melodrama provides a postsacred society with a means of mapping its basic moral and ethical beliefs, of making the world morally legible.[17] Similarly, wrestling, Barthes argues, takes as its central problematic the restoration of moral order, the creation of a just society from a world where the powerful rule. Within the World Wrestling Federation, this battle for a higher justice is staged through the contest for the title belts. Like traditional melodrama, wrestling operates within a dualistic universe: each participant is either a good guy or a villain, a "fan favorite" or a "rule-breaker." Good guys rarely fight good guys, bad guys rarely fight bad guys. Championship is sometimes unjustly granted to rule-breakers but ultimately belongs to the virtuous. WWF wrestling offers its viewers a story of justice perverted and restored, innocence misrecognized and recognized, strength used and abused.

MIGHT MAKES RIGHT

Within traditional sports, competition is impersonal, the product of pre-scribed rules which assign competitors on the basis of their standings or on some prespecified form of rotation. Rivalries do, of course, arise within this system and are the stuff of the daily sports page, but many games do not carry this added affective significance. Within the WWF, however, all com-petition depends upon intense rivalry. Each fight requires the creation of a social and moral opposition and often stems from a personal grievance. Irwin R. Schyster (IRS) falsely accuses the Big Boss Man's mother of tax evasion and threatens to throw her in jail. Sid Justice betrays Hulk Hogan's friend-ship, turning his back on his tag team partner in the middle of a major match and allowing him to be beaten to a pulp by his opponents, Ric Flair and the Undertaker. Fisticuffs break out between Bret Hart and his brother, "Rocket," during a special "Family Feud" match which awakens long-simmering sibling rivalries. Such offenses require retribution within a world which sees trial by combat as the preferred means of resolving all disputes. Someone has to "pay" for these outrages, and the exacting of payment will occur in the squared ring.

The core myth of WWF wrestling is a fascistic one: ultimately, might makes right; moral authority is linked directly to the possession of physical strength, while evil operates through stealth or craftiness (mental rather than physical sources of power). The appeal of such a myth to a working-class audience should be obvious. In the realm of their everyday experience, strength often gets subordinated into alienated labor. Powerful bodies become the means of their economic exploitation rather than a resource for bettering their lot. In WWF wrestling, physical strength reemerges as a tool for per-sonal empowerment, a means of striking back against personal and moral injustices. Valerie Walkerdine argues that the *Rocky* films, which display a similar appeal, offer "fantasies of omnipotence, heroism and salvation . . . a counterpoint to the experience of oppression and powerlessness."[18] Images of fighting, Walkerdine argues, embody "a class-specific and gendered use of the body," which ennobles the physical skills possessed by the working-class spectator: "Physical violence is presented as the only way open to those whose lot is manual and not intellectual labor. . . . The fantasy of the fighter is the fantasy of a working-class male omnipotence over the forces of humiliating oppression which mutilate and break the body in manual labor."[19]

A central concern within wrestling, then, is how physical strength can ensure triumph over one's abusers, how one can rise from defeat and regain dignity through hand-to-hand combat. Bad guys cheat to win. They manipulate the system and step outside the rules. They use deception, misdirection, subterfuge, and trickery. Rarely do they win fairly. They smuggle weapons into the ring to attack their opponents while their managers distract the referees. They unwrap the turnbuckle pads and slam their foes' heads into metal posts. They adopt choke holds to suffocate them or zap them with cattle prods. Million Dollar Man purposefully focuses his force upon Roddy Piper's wounded knee, doing everything he can to injure him permanently. Such atrocities require rematches to ensure justice; the underdog heroes return next month and, through sheer determination and willpower, battle their antagonists into submission.

Such plots allow for the serialization of the WWF narrative, forestalling its resolution, intensifying its emotional impact. Yet at the same time, the individual match must be made narratively satisfying on its own terms, and so, in practice, such injustices do not stand. Even though the match is over and its official outcome determined, the hero shoves the referee aside and, with renewed energy, bests his opponent in a fair (if nonbinding) fight. Whatever the outcome, most fights end with the protagonist standing proudly in the center of the ring, while his badly beaten antagonist retreats shamefully to his dressing room. Justice triumphs both in the long run and in the short run. For the casual viewer, it is the immediate presentation of triumphant innocence that matters, that satisfactorily resolves the drama. Yet for the WWF fan, what matters is the ultimate pursuit of justice as it unfolds through the complexly intertwined stories of the many different wrestlers.

BODY DOUBLES

Melodramatic wrestling allows working-class men to confront their own feelings of vulnerability, their own frustrations at a world which promises them patriarchal authority but which is experienced through relations of economic subordination. Gender identities are most rigidly policed in working-class male culture, since unable to act *as* men, they are forced to act *like* men, with a failure to assume the proper role the source of added humiliation. WWF wrestling offers a utopian alternative to this situation, allowing a movement from victimization toward mastery. Such a scenario requires both the creation and the constant rearticulation of moral distinctions. Morality is defined, first and foremost, through personal antagonisms. As Christine Gledhill has written of traditional melodrama, "Innocence and villainy con-

struct each other: while the villain is necessary to the production and revelation of innocence, innocence defines the boundaries of the forbidden which
the villain breaks."[20] In the most aesthetically pleasing and emotionally grip-
ping matches, these personal antagonisms reflect much deeper mythological
oppositions—the struggles between rich and poor, white and black, urban
and rural, America and the world. Each character stands for something, draws
symbolic meaning by borrowing stereotypes already in broader circulation.
An important role played by color commentary is to inscribe and reinscribe
the basic mythic oppositions at play within a given match. Here, the moral
dualism of masculine melodrama finds its voice through the exchanges between two announcers, one (Mean Jean Okerlund) articulating the protagonist's virtues, the other (Bobby "the Brain" Heenan) justifying the
rule-breaker's transgressions.

Wrestlers are often cast as doppelgängers, similar yet morally opposite
figures. Consider, for example, how *WWF Magazine* characterizes a contest
between the evil Mountie and the heroic Big Boss Man: "In conflict are Big
Boss Man's and the Mountie's personal philosophies: the enforcement of the
law vs. taking the law into one's own hands, the nightstick vs. the cattle prod,
weakening a foe with the spike slam vs. disabling him with the nerve-crushing
carotid control technique."[21] The Canadian Mountie stands on one page,
dressed in his bright red uniform, clutching his cattle prod and snarling. The
former Georgia prison guard, Big Boss Man, stands on the other, dressed in
his pale blue uniform, clutching an open pair of handcuffs, with a look of
quiet earnestness. At this moment the two opponents seem to be made for
each other, as if no other possible contest could bear so much meaning,
though the Big Boss Man and the Mountie will pair off against other challengers in the next major event.

The most successful wrestlers are those who provoke immediate emotional
commitments (either positive or negative) and are open to constant rearticulation, who can be fit into a number of different conflicts and retain
semiotic value. Hulk Hogan may stand as the defender of freedom in his
feud with Sgt. Slaughter, as innocence betrayed by an ambitious friend in his
contest against Sid Justice, and as an aging athlete confronting and overcoming the threat of death in his battle with the Undertaker. Big Boss Man may
defend the interests of the economically depressed against the Repo Man,
make the streets safe from the Nasty Boys, and assert honest law enforcement
in the face of the Mountie's bad example.

The introduction of new characters requires their careful integration into
the WWF's moral universe before their first match can be fought. We need
to know where they will stand in relation to the other protagonists and
antagonists. The arrival of Tatanka on the WWF roster was preceded by a

"Close as Brothers": The Rockers celebrate their reunion moments before Shawn Michaels kicked his partner through the Barbershop window.

series of segments showing the Native American hero visiting the tribal elders, undergoing rites of initiation, explaining the meaning of his haircut, makeup, costume, and war shout. His ridicule by the fashion-minded Rick "the Model" Martel introduced his first antagonism and ensured the viewer's recognition of his essential goodness.

Much of the weekly broadcasts centers on the manufacturing of these moral distinctions and the creation of these basic antagonisms. A classic example might be the breakup of the Rockers. A series of accidents and minor disagreements sparked a public showdown on Brutus "the Barber" Beefcake's Barber Shop, a special program segment. Shawn Michaels appeared at the interview, dressed in black leather and wearing sunglasses (already adopting iconography signaling his shift toward the dark side). After a pretense of reconciliation and a series of clips reviewing their past together, Michaels shoved his partner, Marty Jannetty, through the barber-shop window, amid Brutus's impotent protests.[22] The decision to feature the two team members as independent combatants required the creation of moral difference, while the disintegration of their partnership fit perfectly within the program's familiar doppelgänger structure. *WWF Magazine* portrayed the events in terms of the biblical story of Cain and Abel, as the rivalry of two "brothers":

> [The Rockers] were as close as brothers. They did everything together, in and out of the ring. But Michaels grew jealous of Jannetty and became impatient to succeed. While Jannetty was content to bide his time, work to steadily improve with the knowledge that championships don't come easily in the WWF, Michaels decided he wanted it all now—and all for himself.[23]

If an earlier profile had questioned whether the two had "separate identities," this reporter has no trouble making moral distinctions between the patient Jannetty and the impatient Michaels, the self-sacrificing Jannetty and the self-centered Michaels. Subsequent broadcasts would link Michaels professionally and romantically with Sensational Sherri, a woman whose seductive charms have been the downfall of many WWF champs. As a manager, Sherri is noted for her habit of smuggling foreign objects to ringside in her purse and interfering in the matches to ensure her man's victory. Sherri, who had previously been romantically involved with Million Dollar Man Ted Dibiase, announced that she would use her "Teddy Bear's" money to back Michael's solo career, linking his betrayal of his partner to her own greedy and adulterous impulses. All of these plot twists differentiate Jannetty and Michaels, aligning spectator identification with the morally superior partner. Michaels's paramount moral failing is his all-consuming ambition, his desire to dominate rather than work alongside his long-time partner.

The Rockers' story points to the contradictory status of personal advancement within the WWF narrative: these stories hinge upon fantasies of upward mobility, yet ambition is just as often regarded in negative terms, as ultimately corrupting. Such a view of ambition reflects the experience of people who have worked hard all of their lives without much advancement and therefore remain profoundly suspicious of those on top. Wrestling speaks to those who recognize that upward mobility often has little to do with personal merit and a lot to do with a willingness to stomp on those who get in your way. Virtue, in the WWF moral universe, is often defined by a willingness to temper ambition through personal loyalties, through affiliation with others, while vice comes from putting self-interest ahead of everything else. This distrust of self-gain was vividly illustrated during a bout between Rowdy Roddy Piper and Bret "the Hitman" Hart at the 1992 Wrestlemania. This competition uncharacteristically centered on two good guys. As a result, most viewers suspected that one fighter would ultimately

"Struggling with Temptation": Good guy Rowdy Roddy Piper struggles with the urge to club his opponent with the bell.

be driven to base conduct by personal desire for the Intercontinental Championship belt. Such speculations were encouraged by ambiguous signs from the combatants during "buildup" interviews and exploited during the match through a number of gestures which indicate moral indecision: Rowdy stood ready to club Hart with an illegal foreign object; the camera cut repeatedly to close-ups of his face as he struggled with his conscience before casting the object aside and continuing a fair fight. In the end, however, the two long-time friends embraced each other as Piper congratulated Hart on a more or less fairly won fight. The program situated this bout as a sharp contrast to the feud between Hulk Hogan and Sid Justice, the major attraction at this pay-per-view event. Their budding friendship had been totally destroyed by Justice's overriding desire to dominate the WWF: "I'm gonna crack the head of somebody big in the WWF. . . . No longer is this Farmboy from Arkansas gonna take a back seat to anybody."[24] Rowdy and Hart value their friendship over their ambition; Justice lets nothing stand in the way of his quest for power.

PERFECT BASTARDS

WWF wrestlers are not rounded characters; the spectacle has little room for the novelistic, and here the form may push the melodramatic imagination to its logical extremes. WWF wrestlers experience no internal conflicts which might blur their moral distinctiveness. Rather, they often display the "undividedness" that Robert Heilman sees as a defining aspect of nineteenth-century melodramatic characters:

> [The melodramatic character displays] oneness of feeling as competitor, crusader, aggressor; as defender, counterattacker, fighter for survival; he may be assertive or compelled, questing or resistant, obsessed or desperate; he may triumph or lose, be victor or victim, exert pressure or be pressed. Always he is undivided, unperplexed by alternatives, untorn by divergent impulses; all of his strength or weakness faces in one direction.[25]

The WWF athletes sketch their moral failings in broad profile: The Mountie pounds on his chest and roars, "I am the Mountie," convinced that no one can contest his superiority, yet as soon as the match gets rough, he slides under the ropes and tries to hide behind his scrawny manager. The Million Dollar Man shoves hundred-dollar bills into the mouths of his defeated opponents, while Sherri paints her face with gilded dollar signs to mark her possession by the highest bidder. Ravishing Rick Rude wears pictures of his opponents on his arse, relishing in his own vulgarity. Virtue similarly displays itself without fear of misrecognition. Hacksaw Jim Duggan clutches an American flag in one hand and a two-by-four in the other.

The need for a constant recombination of a fixed number of characters requires occasional shifts in moral allegiances (as occurred with the breakup of the Rockers). Characters may undergo redemption or seduction, but these shifts typically occur quickly and without much ambiguity. There is rarely any lingering doubt or moral fence-straddling. Such characters are good one week and evil the next. Jake "the Snake" Roberts, a long-time hero—albeit one who enjoys his distance from the other protagonists—uncharacteristically offered to help the Ultimate Warrior prepare for his fight against the Undertaker. Their grim preparations unfolded over several weeks, with Jake forcing the Warrior to undergo progressively more twisted rituals—locking him into a coffin, burying him alive—until finally Jake shoved him into a room full of venomous snakes. Bitten by Jake's cobra, Lucifer, the Ultimate Warrior staggered toward his friend, who simply brushed him aside. As the camera pulled back to show the Undertaker standing side by side with Jake, the turncoat laughed, "Never trust a snake." From that moment forward, Jake was portrayed as totally evil, Barthes's perfect bastard. Jake attacks

Macho man Randy Savage's bride, Elizabeth, on their wedding day and terrorizes the couple every chance he gets.

The program provides no motivation for such outrages, though commentary both in the broadcasts and in the pages of the wrestling magazines constantly invites such speculation: "What makes Jake hate Savage and his bride so fiercely? Why does he get his jollies—as he admits—from tormenting her?" What Peter Brooks said about the villains of traditional melodrama holds equally well here: "Evil in the world of melodrama does not need justification; it exists, simply. . . . And the less it is adequately motivated, the more this evil appears simply volitional, the product of pure will."[26] Jake is evil because he is a snake; it's in his character and nothing can change him, even though in this case, less than a year ago, Jake was as essentially good as he is now totally demented. We know Jake is evil and without redemption, because he tells us so, over and over:

> I'm not really sure I have any soul at all. . . . Once I get involved in something—no matter how demented, no matter how treacherous, no matter how far off the mark it is from normal standards—I never back down. I just keep on going, deeper and deeper into the blackness, far past the point where any sensible person would venture. You see, a person with a conscience—a person with a soul—would be frightened by the sordid world I frequent. But Jake the Snake isn't scared at all. To tell you the truth, I can't get enough of it.[27]

Jake recognizes and acknowledges his villainy; he names it publicly and unrepentantly.

Peter Brooks sees such a process of "self-nomination" as an essential feature of the melodramatic imagination: "Nothing is spared because nothing is left unsaid; the characters stand on stage and utter the unspeakable, give voice to their deepest feelings, dramatize through their heightened and polarized words and gestures the whole lesson of their relationship."[28] The soliloquy, that stock device of the traditional melodrama, is alive and well in WWF wrestling. Wrestlers look directly into the audience and shove their fists toward the camera; they proclaim their personal credos and describe their sufferings. Tag team partners repeat their dedication to each other and their plans to dominate their challengers. Villains profess their evil intentions and vow to perform various forms of mayhem upon their opponents. Their rhetoric is excessively metaphoric, transforming every fight into a life-and-death struggle. Much as nineteenth-century theatrical melodrama used denotative music to define the characters' moral stances, the wrestlers' entry into the arena is preceded by theme songs which encapsulate their personalities. Hulk's song describes him as "a real American hero" who "fights for the rights of every man." The Million Dollar Man's jingle proclaims his compelling interest in "money, money, money," while Jake's song repeats "trust me, trust me, trust me."

This public declaration ensures the constant moral legibility of the WWF narrative and thereby maximizes the audience's own emotional response. Spectators come to the arena or turn on the program to express intense emotion—to cheer the hero, to boo and jeer the villain—without moral ambiguity or emotional complexity. (Wrestling fans sometimes choose to root for the villains, taking pleasure in their self-conscious inversion of the WWF's moral universe, yet even this perverse pleasure requires moral legibility.) Operating within a world of absolutes, WWF wrestlers wear their hearts on their sleeves (or, in Ravishing Rick Rude's case, on the seat of their pants) and project their emotions from every inch of their bodies. Much as in classic melodrama, external actions reveal internal states; moral disagreements demand physical expressions. As Brooks writes, "Emotions are given a full acting-out, a full representation before our eyes. . . . Nothing is *under*stated, all is *over*stated."[29] The Million Dollar Man cowers, covering his face and retreating, crawling on hands and knees backward across the ring. Sherri shouts at the top of her ample lungs and pounds the floor with her high-heel shoe. Rowdy Roddy Piper gets his dander up and charges into the ring. With a burst of furious energy, he swings madly at his opponents, forcing them to scatter right and left. Roddy spits in the Million Dollar Man's eyes, flings his sweaty shirt in his face, or grabs Sherri, rips off her dress, throws her over his knee, and spanks her. Such characters embody the shameful spectacle of emotional display, acting as focal points for the audience's own expression of otherwise repressed affect.

INVINCIBLE VICTIMS

Fans eagerly anticipate these excessive gestures as the most appropriate means of conveying the characters' moral attitudes. Through a process of simplification, the wrestler's body has been reduced to a series of iconic surfaces and stock attitudes. We know not only how the performer is apt to respond to a given situation but what bodily means will be adopted to express that response. Wrestlers perform less with their eyes and hands than with their arms and legs and with their deep, resounding voices. Earthquake's bass rumble and Roddy's fiery outbursts, Ric Flair's vicious laughter and Macho Man's red-faced indignation are "too much" for the small screen, yet they articulate feelings that are too intense to be contained.

This process of simplification and exaggeration transforms the wrestlers into cartoonish figures who may slam each other's heads into iron steps, throw each other onto wooden floors, smash each other with steel chairs, land with their full weight on the other's prone stomach, and emerge without a scratch, ready to fight again. Moral conflict will continue unabated; no defeat can be final within a world where the characters are omnipotent. If traditional melodrama foregrounded long-suffering women's endurance of whatever injustices the world might throw against them, WWF wrestling centers around male victims who ultimately refuse to accept any more abuse and fight back against the aggressors.

Such a scenario allows men to acknowledge their own vulnerability, safe in the knowledge that their masculine potency will ultimately be restored and that they will be strong enough to overcome the forces which subordinate them. Hulk Hogan has perfected the image of the martyred hero who some-how captures victory from the closing jaws of defeat. Badly beaten in a fight, Hulk lies in a crumpled heap. The referee lifts his limp arms up, once, twice, ready to call the fight, when the crowd begins to clap and stomp. The mighty hero rises slowly, painfully to his feet, rejuvenated by the crowd's response. Blood streams through his blond hair and drips across his face, but he whips it aside with a broad swing of his mighty arms. Hulk turns to face his now-terrified assailant.

"SEEING IS BELIEVING"

Such broad theatricality cuts against wrestling's tradition of pseudorealism; the programs' formats mimic the structures and visual style of nonfiction television, of sports coverage, news broadcasts, and talk shows. The fiction is, of course, that all of this fighting is authentic, spontaneous, unscripted. The WWF narrative preserves that illusion at all costs. There is no stepping outside the fiction, no acknowledgment of the production process or the act of authorship. When the performers are featured in *WWF Magazine,* they are profiled in character. Story segments are told in the form of late-breaking news reports or framed as interviews. The commentators are taken by surprise, interrupted by seemingly unplanned occurrences. During one broadcast, Jake the Snake captured Macho Man, dragging him into the ring. Jake tied him to the ropes and menaced him with a cobra which sprang and bit him on the forearm. The camera was jostled from side to side by people racing to Macho's assistance and panned abruptly trying to follow his hysterical wife as she ran in horror to ringside. A reaction shot shows a child in the audience reduced to tears by this brutal spectacle. Yet, at the same time, the camera refused to show us an image "too shocking" for broadcast. Macho Man's arm and the snake's gaping mouth were cen-sored, blocked by white bars, not unlike the blue dot that covered the

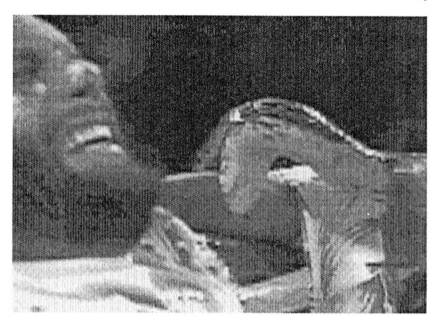

"Never Trust a Snake!": Jake "the Snake" Roberts's deadly cobra bites into "Macho Man" Randy Savage's arm.

witness's face at the William Kennedy Smith rape trial that same week. (A few weeks later, the "uncensored" footage was at last shown, during a prime-time broadcast, so that viewers could see "what really happened.") The plot lines are thus told through public moments where a camera could plausibly be present, though such moments allow us insight into the characters' private motivations.

As Ric Flair often asserted during his brief stay in the WWF, "Pictures don't lie; seeing is believing," and yet it is precisely seeing and not believing that is a central pleasure in watching television wrestling. What audiences see is completely "unbelievable," as ring commentators frequently proclaim—unbelievable because these human bodies are unnaturally proportioned and monstrously large, because these figures who leap through the air seem to defy all natural laws, and, most important, because these characters participate within the corny and timeworn plots of the nineteenth-century melodrama. The pleasure comes in seeing what cannot be believed, yet is constantly asserted to us as undeniably true. Fans elbow each other in the ribs, "Look how fake," taking great pride in their ability to see through a deception that was never intended to convince.

Such campy self-acknowledgment may be part of what makes male spectators' affective engagement with this melodramatic form safe and acceptable within a traditionally masculine culture which otherwise backs away from overt emotional display. Whenever the emotions become too intense, there is always a way of pulling back, laughing at what might otherwise provoke tears. WWF wrestling, at another level, provokes authentic pain and rage, particularly when it embraces populist myths of economic exploitation and class solidarity, feeds a hunger for homosocial bonding, or speaks to utopian fantasies of empowerment. The gap between the campy and the earnest reception of wrestling may reflect the double role which Elias and Dunning ascribe to traditional sports: the need to allow for the de-controlling of powerful affects while at the same time regulating their expression and ensuring their ultimate containment. The melodramatic aspects are what trigger emotional release, while the campy aspects contain it within safe bounds. The plots of wrestling cut close to the bone, inciting racial and class antagonisms that rarely surface this overtly elsewhere in popular culture, while comic exaggeration ensures that such images can never fully be taken seriously.

ROMANCE IN THE RING

WWF's plots center on the classic materials of melodrama: "false accusation. . . . innocence beleaguered, virtue triumphant, eternal fidelity, mysterious identity, lovers reconciled, fraudulence revealed, threats survived, enemies foiled."[30] The ongoing romance of Macho and Elizabeth bears all of the classic traces of the sentimental novel. The virginal Miss Elizabeth, who almost always dresses in lacy white, stands as the embodiment of womanly virtues. WWF fans were fascinated by her struggle to civilize her impassioned and often uncontrollable Macho Man, withstanding constant bouts of un-reasoning jealousy, tempering his dirty tactics. As a profile of Miss Elizabeth explained, "She embodies the spirit of a grass-roots American wife. She cares for her man. She provides him with comfort in the midst of chaos. She provides him with a sense of unity when his world seems to be disintegrating. Elizabeth calmly handles these difficult situations with grace and tact."[31] WWF fans watched the course of their romance for years, as Macho rejected her, taking up with the sensuous and anything-but-virtuous Sherri, but he was reunited with Elizabeth following a devastating defeat in a career-ending match against the Ultimate Warrior. They followed her efforts to rebuild her Macho Man's self-confidence, his fumbling attempts to propose to her, and their spectacular pay-per-view wedding. They watched as the beloved coupled were attacked during their wedding party by Jake and the Undertaker, as Macho begged the WWF management to reinstate him so that he could avenge himself and his wife against this outrage, and as he finally returned to the ring and defeated the heartless Snake during a specially scheduled event. No sooner was this conflict resolved than Ric Flair produced incriminating photographs which he claimed show that Elizabeth was his former lover. In a locker-room interview, Ric and Mr. Perfect smirkingly revealed the photographs as evidence that Elizabeth is "damaged goods," while the fumbling announcer struggled to protect Elizabeth's previously unquestioned virtue. Once again, this domestic crisis motivated a forthcoming bout, creating narrative interest as the all but inarticulate Macho defended his wife with his muscles.

The Macho Man-Elizabeth romance is unusual in its heavy focus on domestic relations, though not unique: Sherri's romantic entanglements with the Million Dollar Man and Shawn Michaels offer a similar (albeit morally opposite) narrative, while the complex family drama of the Hart family (whose patriarch, Stew, was a long-time wrestler and whose four sons have all enjoyed WWF careers) has motivated images of both fraternal solidarity and sibling rivalry. More often, however, the masculine melodrama of WWF wrestling centers on the relationships between men, occupying a homosocial space which has little room for female intrusions. There are, after all, only two women in the WWF universe—the domestic angel, Elizabeth, and the scheming whore, Sherri. A more typical story involved Virgil, the black bodyguard of the Million Dollar Man, who, after years of being subjected to his boss's humiliating whims, decided to strike back, to challenge his one-time master to a fight for possession of his "Million Dollar Belt." Virgil was befriended by the feisty Scotsman Rowdy Roddy Piper, who taught him to stand tall and broad. The two men fought side by side to ensure the black man's dignity. The antagonism between Virgil and the Million Dollar Man provoked class warfare, while the friendship between Virgil and Roddy marked the uneasy courtship between men.

Here and elsewhere, WWF wrestling operates along the gap that separates our cultural ideal of male autonomy and the reality of alienation, themes that emerge most vividly within tag team competition. The fighter, that omnipotent muscle machine, steps alone, with complete confidence, into the ring, ready to do battle with his opponent. As the fight progresses, he is beaten down, unable to manage without assistance. Struggling to the ropes, he must admit that he needs another man. His partner reaches out to him while he crawls along the floor, inching toward that embrace. The image of the two hands, barely touching, and the two men, working together to overcome their problems, seems rich with what Eve Sedgwick calls "male homosocial desire."[32] That such a fantasy is played out involving men whose physical appearance exaggerates all of the secondary masculine characteristics frees male spectators from social taboos which prohibit the open exploration of male intimacy. In their own brutish language, the men express what it is like to need (and desire?) another man. Consider, for example, how *WWF Magazine* characterizes the growing friendship between Jake the Snake and Andre the Giant:

> At a glance, Andre gives the impression of granite—unshakable, immutable and omnipotent. Inside, there is a different Andre. His massive size and power belie the fact that his spirit is as fragile as anyone's. And that spirit was more bruised than was his body. Like Andre, Jake projects a sense of detachment from the world of the average guy. Like Andre, Jake has an inner self that is more vulnerable than his outer shell.[33]

The story describes their first tentative overtures, their attempts to overcome old animosities, and their growing dependency on each other for physical and emotional support. As Jake explains:

> Andre was afraid of serpents. I was afraid of people—not of confronting people, but of getting close to them. We began to talk. Slow talk. Nothing talk. Getting to know one another. The talk got deeper. . . . I never asked for help from anybody. I never will. But Andre decided to help me; I won't turn him down. I guess we help one another. You might call it a meeting of the minds.[34]

Jake's language carefully, hesitantly negotiates between male ideals of individual autonomy ("I never asked for help") and an end to the isolation and loneliness such independence creates. Will Jake find this ideal friendship with a man who was once his bitter enemy, or does he simply lay himself open to new injuries? These images of powerful men whose hulking bodies mask hidden pains speak to longings which the entire structure of patriarchy desperately denies.

Such a narrative explores the links that bind and the barriers that separate men. Yet, at the same time, its recurring images of betrayed friendship and violated trust rationalize the refusal to let down barriers. Texas Tornado describes his relationship to his former tag team partner: "I know the Warrior as well as any man in the World Wrestling Federation. . . . Of course, in wrestling, you never get too close with anybody because one day you might be facing him on the other side of the ring. Still, Warrior and I have traveled and trained together. We've shared things."[35] Wrestling operates within a carefully policed zone, a squared ring, that allows for the representation of intense homosocial desire but also erects strong barriers against too much risk and intimacy. The wrestlers "share things," but they are not allowed to get "too close."

Consider what happened when the Beverley Brothers met the Bushwhackers at a live WWF event at the Boston Gardens. The two brothers, clad in lavender tights, hugged each other before the match, and their down-under opponents, in their big boots and work clothes, turned upon them in a flash, "queer baiting" and then "gay bashing" the Beverley Brothers. I sat there with fear and loathing as I heard thousands of men, women, and children shouting, "Faggot, faggot, faggot." I was perplexed at how such a representation could push so far and spark such an intense response. The chanting continued for five, ten minutes, as the Bushwhackers stomped their feet and waved their khaki caps with glee, determined to drive their "effeminate" opponents from the ring. The Beverley Brothers protested, pouted, and finally submitted, unable to stand firm against their tormentors. What may have necessitated this homophobic spectacle was the need of both performers and spectators to control potential readings of the Bushwhackers' own physically intimate relationship. The Bushwhackers, Butch and Luke, are constantly defined as polymorphously perverse and indiscriminately oral, licking the faces of innocent spectators or engaging in mutual face-wetting as a symbolic gesture of their mutual commitment. By defining the Beverley "Sisters" as "faggots," as outside of acceptable masculinity, the Bushwhackers created a space where homosocial desire could be more freely expressed without danger of its calling into question their gender identity or sexual preference. This moment seems emblematic of the way wrestling more generally operates—creating a realm of male action which is primarily an excuse for the display of masculine emotion (and even for homoerotic contact) while ensuring that nothing which occurs there can raise any questions about the participant's "manhood."[36]

POPULIST PLEASURES

One key way that wrestling contains this homoerotic potential is through the displacement of issues of homosocial bonding onto a broader political and economic terrain. If, as feminism has historically claimed, the personal is the political, traditional masculinity has often acknowledged its personal vulnerabilities only through evoking more abstract political categories. Populist politics, no less than sports, has been a space of male emotional expression, where personal pains and sufferings can be openly acknowledged only through allegorical rhetoric and passionate oratory. Melodramatic wrestling's focus on the professional rather than the personal sphere facilitates this shift from the friendship ties between individual males to the political ties between all working men. The erotics of male homosocial desire is sublimated into a hunger for the populist community, while images of economic exploitation are often charged with a male dread of penetration and submission.

Although rarely described in these terms, populism offers a melodramatic vision of political and economic relationships. Bruce Palmer argues that populism is characterized by its focus on a tangible reality of immediate experience rather than political abstraction, its emphasis on personal rather than impersonal causation, and its appeal to sentimentality rather than rationality (all traits commonly associated with the melodramatic). As he summarizes the basic axioms of the southern populist movement, "what is most real and most important in the world was that which was most tangible, that which could be seen and touched. . . . People made things move and if some people were moved more than movers, it was because others, more powerful, moved them."[37] American populism sees virtue as originating through physical labor, as a trait possessed by those who are closest to the moment of production (and therefore embodied through manual strength), while moral transgression, particularly greed and ruthlessness, reflects alienation from the production process (often embodied as physical frailty and sniveling cowardice). Populism understands politics through the social relations between individuals rather than between groups, though individuals are understood in larger allegorical categories—the simple farmer vs. the slick Wall Street lawyer, the factory worker vs. the scheming boss, the small businessman vs. the Washington bureaucrat, the American voter vs. the party bosses. Social changes come, within this model, through personal redemption rather than systemic change. A populist utopia would be a community within which individuals recognized their common interests and respected their mutual responsibilities. As Palmer explains, "The only decent society was one in which each person looked out for every other one, a society in which *all* people enjoyed equal rights and the benefits of their labor."[38] Such a movement made common cause between workers and farmers (and in its most progressive forms, between whites and blacks) in their mutual struggle for survival against the forces of capitalist expansion and technological change.

If populism draws on melodramatic rhetoric, populism has also provided the core myths by which the masculine melodrama has historically operated. French melodrama might concern itself with the struggles of the aristocracy and the bourgeois; American faith in a classless society translated these same conventions into narratives about scheming bankers and virtuous yeomen, stock figures within the populist vision. American melodrama, David Grimsted tells us, imagines a democratic universe which rewards a commitment to fraternity and hard work and demonizes appeals to privilege.[39] Michael Denning argues that the sentimental fiction provided by turn-of-the-century dime novels similarly interpreted the economic relations between labor and capital within essentially melodramatic terms.[40] While such visions of American democracy were not automatically populist and often lent themselves to middle-class social reform, melodrama was always available as a vehicle for populist allegory, especially within masculine forms which displace melodrama's characteristic interest in the domestic into the public sphere.

In that sense, melodramatic wrestling fits squarely within the larger tradition of masculine melodrama and populist politics. What is striking about the mythology of WWF wrestling is how explicitly its central conflicts evoke class antagonisms. Its villains offer vivid images of capitalist greed and conspicuous consumption. The Million Dollar Man wears a gold belt studded with diamonds and waves a huge wad of hundred-dollar bills. Magazine photographs and program segments show him driving expensive cars, eating in high-class restaurants, living in a penthouse apartment, or vacationing in his summer house at Palm Beach. What he can't grab with brute force, he buys: "Everybody has a price." In one notorious episode, he bribed Andre the Giant to turn over to him the sacred WWF championship belt; another time, he plotted a hostile takeover of the WWF. Similarly, Ric Flair brags constantly about his wealth and influence: "I'll pull up [to the match] in my stretch limousine with a bottle of Dom Perignon in one hand and a fine-looking woman holding my other. The only thing I'll be worried about is if the champagne stays cold enough."[41] Mean Gene Okerlund interviews him on his yacht, *Gypsy*, as he chuckles over his sexual humiliation of the Macho Man and brags about his wild parties. The Model enjoys a jet-setting lifestyle, displays the "finest in clothing," and tries to market his new line of male perfumes, "the scent of the 90s, Arrogance." Irwin R. Schyster constantly threatens to audit his opponents, while Repo Man promises to foreclose on their possessions: "What's mine is mine. What's yours is mine too! . . . I've got no mercy at all for cheats. Tough luck if you've lost your job. If you can't make the payment, I'll get your car. Walk to look for work, Sucker."[42]

The patriotic laborer (Hacksaw Jim Duggan), the virtuous farm boy (Hillbilly Jim), the small-town boy made good (Big Boss Man), the Horatio Alger character (Virgil, Rowdy Roddy Piper, Tito Santana) are stock figures within this morality play, much as they have been basic tropes in populist discourse for more than a century. WWF heroes hail from humble origins and can therefore act as appropriate champions within fantasies of economic empowerment and social justice. A profile introducing Sid Justice to *WWF Magazine* readers stressed his rural origins: "Sid Justice comes from the land. . . . Born and raised on a farm in Arkansas, imbued with the hardworking values of people who rise before dawn to till the earth and milk the cows. . . . A lifestyle that is the backbone of this country."[43] Justice developed his muscles tossing bales of hay onto his grandfather's truck, and his integrity reflects the simplicity of an agrarian upbringing: "Don't confuse simplicity with stupidity. A man who learned to make the land produce its fruits has smarts." Sid

Justice understands the meaning of personal commitments and the value of simple virtues in a way that would be alien to "people who get their dinner out of a cellophane package from a super market."

Pride in where one comes from extends as well to a recognition of racial or ethnic identities. Tito Santana returns to Mexico to rediscover his roots and takes lessons from a famous bullfighter, changing his name to El Matador. Tatanka emerges as the "leader of the New Indian Nation," demonstrating his pride in his "Native American heritage." He explains, "the tribes of all nations are embodied in me."[44] The creation of tag teams and other alliances cuts across traditional antagonisms to bring together diverse groups behind a common cause. Tag team partners Texas Tornado and El Matador, the Anglo and the Mexicano, join forces in their shared struggle against economic injustice and brute power. "Rule-breakers" are often linked to racial prejudice. The "Brain" releases a steady stream of racial slurs and epithets; the Million Dollar Man visits the "neighborhoods" to make fun of the ramshackle shack where El Matador was raised or to ridicule the crime-ridden streets where Virgil spent his youth. What WWF wrestling enacts, then, are both contemporary class antagonisms (the working man against the Million Dollar Man, the boy from the barrio against the repo man, the farmer against the IRS) and the possibilities of a class solidarity that cuts across racial boundaries, a common community of the oppressed and the marginal.

The rule-breaker's willingness to jeer at honest values and humble ancestry, to hit the proletarian protagonists with economic threats and to shove their own ill-gotten goods in their faces, intensifies the emotions surrounding their confrontations. These men are fighting for all of our dignity against these forces which keep us down, which profit from others' suffering and prosper in times of increased hardship. Big Boss Man defends his mother against false allegations leveled against her by the IRS: "My Mama never had a job in her life. All she did was take care of her children and raise food on the farm down in Georgia."[45] Virgil strikes back not only against the man who forced him to wipe the perspiration from his brow and pick the dirt from between his toes, but also against the conditions of economic subordination which made him dependent on that monster.

COMING TO BLOWS

Such evil must be isolated from the populist community; its origins must be identified and condemned because it represents a threat to mutual survival. This attempt to name and isolate corruption emerges in a particularly vivid fashion when Sgt. Slaughter discusses the Nasty Boys' delinquency:

The Nasty Boys are un-American trash. You know, their hometown of Allentown is a very patriotic town. Its people have worked in the steel mills for years. Their hard work is evident in every skyscraper and building from coast to coast. Allentown's people have worked in the coal mines for years. Their hard work has kept America warm in the dead of winter. But the Nasty Boys don't come from the same Allentown I know. . . . They spit on hard-working Americans. They spit on Patriotic people. And they spit on the symbol of this great land, Old Glory herself.[46]

Slaughter's rhetoric is classic populism, linking virtue and patriotism with labor, treating evil as a threat originating outside of the community which much be contained and vanished.

This process of defining the great American community involves defining outsiders as well as insiders, and it is not simply the rich and the powerful who are excluded. There is a strong strand of nativism in the WWF's populist vision. When we move from national to international politics, the basic moral opposition shifts from the powerless against the powerful to America and its allies (the United Kingdom, Australia and New Zealand, Canada) against its enemies (especially the Arabs and the Communists, often the Japanese). The central match at the 1993 Survivor Series, for example, pitted the "All-Americans" against the "Foreign Fanatics" (a mix that involved not only predictable villains such as Japan's massive Yokozuma but also less predictable ones, such as Finland's Ludwig and the Montrealers). The appeal to racial stereotyping, which had its progressive dimensions in the creation of champions for various oppressed minorities, resurfaces here in a profound xenophobia. Arab wrestlers are ruthless, Asian wrestlers are fiendishly inscrutable or massive and immovable. While America is defined through its acceptance of diversity, foreign cultures are defined through their sameness, their conformity to a common image. This is true for sympathetic foreigners, such as the Bushwhackers, as it is for less sympathetic foreigners, such as Col. Mustafa and Gen. Adnan. At this level, Hulk's long-time possession of the WWF title becomes an issue of national sovereignty, with threats coming from outside not only the populist community but the American nation-state as well; "Foreign Fanatics" are trying to take what belongs always in American hands, and they must be taught that they can't mess with Uncle Sam.

American's foreign relations can be mapped through the changing alliances within the WWF: Nikolia Volkov, one of the two Bolsheviks, retired from view when the Cold War seemed on the verge of resolution but reemerged as a spokesman for the new Eastern Europe, redefined as a citizen of Lithuania. The WWF restaged the Gulf War through a series of "Bodybag" bouts between Hulk Hogan and Sgt. Slaughter. Slaughter, a former

"Restaging the Gulf War": Hulk Hogan and Sgt. Slaughter (accompanied by his attaché, Gen. Adnan) "draw a line in the sand."

Marine drill sergeant, was brainwashed by Iraqi operatives Col. Mustafa and Gen. Adnan. Under their sinister tutelage, he seized the WWF champion-ship belt through brutal means and vowed to turn the entire federation and its followers into "POWs." In a series of staged incidents, Slaughter burned an American flag and ridiculed basic national institutions. The turncoat leatherneck smugly pounded his chest while his turbaned sidekick babbled incessantly in something resembling Arabic. Hulk Hogan, the all-American hero, vowed that his muscles were more powerful than patriot missiles and that he could reclaim the belt in the name of God, family, and country. He dedicated his strength to protect the "Little Hulkamaniacs" whose mothers and fathers were serving in the Gulf. The blond-haired, blue-eyed Hulkster looked directly into the camera, flexing his pythons and biceps, and roared, "What ya gonna do, Sarge Slaughter, when the Red, White and Blue runs wild on you?" Hulk and Hacksaw Jim Duggan incited the crowd to chant "USA" and to jeer at the Iraqi national anthem. Here, the working-class heroes emerge as flag-waving patriots, fighting against "unAmericanism" at home and tyranny abroad.

Yet, however jingoistic this enactment became, WWF's melodramatic con-ventions exercised a counterpressure, bridging the gap between otherwise sharply delimited ideological categories. Humiliated by a crushing defeat, Slaughter pulled back from his foreign allies and began a pilgrimage to various national monuments, pleading with the audience, "I want my coun-try back." Ultimately, in a moment of reconciliation with Hacksaw Jim Duggan, the audience was asked to forgive him for his transgressions and to accept him back into the community. Sarge kneeled and kissed an American flag, Hacksaw embraced him, and the two men walked away together, arm in arm. That moment when one tired and physically wounded man accepted the embrace and assistance of another tired and psychically wounded man contained tremendous emotional intensity. Here, male homosocial desire and populist rhetoric work together to rein in the nationalistic logic of the Gulf War narrative, to create a time and space where male vulnerability and mutual need may be publicly expressed. Here, the personal concerns which had been displaced onto populist politics reassert their powerful demands upon the male combatants and spectators to ensure an emotional resolution to a story which in the real world refused satisfying closure. The story of a soul-less turncoat and a ruthless tyrant evolved into the story of a fallen man's search for redemption and reunion, an autonomous male's hunger for companionship, and an invincible victim's quest for higher justice.

Such a moment can be described only as melodramatic, but what it offers is a peculiarly masculine form of melodrama. If traditional melodrama centers upon the moral struggle between the powerful and the vulnerable, masculine melodrama confronts the painful paradox that working-class men are powerful by virtue of their gender and vulnerable by virtue of their economic status. If traditional melodrama involves a play with affect, masculine melodrama confronts the barriers which traditional masculinity erects around the overt expression of emotion. If traditional melodrama centers on the personal consequences of social change, masculine melodrama must confront traditional masculinity's tendency to displace personal needs and desires onto the public sphere. The populist imagery of melodramatic wrestling can be understood as one way of negotiating within these competing expectations, separating economic vulnerability from any permanent threat to male potency, translating emotional expression into rage against political injustice, turning tears into shouts, and displacing homosocial desire onto the larger social community. Populism may be what makes this powerful mixture of the masculine and the melodramatic popularly accessible and what allows wrestling to become such a powerful release of repressed male emotion.

Laura Kipnis's thoughtful essay "Reading *Hustler*" cautions us against reading popular culture (or working-class ideology) in black-and-white, either-or terms, imposing upon it our own political fantasies: "There is no guarantee that counter-hegemonic or even specifically anti-bourgeois cultural forms are necessarily also going to be progressive."[47] Kipnis finds that *Hustler* "powerfully articulates class resentments" but does so in terms which are "often only incoherent and banal when it means to be alarming and confrontational." Kipnis does not deny the profound "anti-liberalism, anti-feminism, anti-communism and anti-progressivism" which characterizes the magazine's contents; she does not attempt to rescue Larry Flynt for progressive politics. She does, however, see *Hustler* as speaking to an authentic discontent with middle-class values and lifestyles, as a voice that challenges entrenched authority. Kipnis's essay is controversial because it neither condemns nor romanticizes *Hustler* and because its writer struggles in print with her own conflicted feelings about pornography.

WWF wrestling poses this same problematic mixture of the antihegemonic and the reactionary. It is a fascist spectacle of male power, depicting a world where might makes right and moral authority is exercised by brute force. It engages in the worst sort of jingoistic nationalism. It evokes racial and ethnic stereotypes that demean groups even when they are intended to provide positive role models. It provokes homophobic disgust and patriarchal outrage against any and all incursions beyond heterosexual male dominance. But, as Jake the Snake reminds us, "it goes much deeper than that. . . . There's more at stake than just wrestling, man." WWF wrestling is also a form of masculine melodrama which, like its nineteenth-century precedents, lends its voice to the voiceless and champions the powerless. Wrestling allows a sanctioned space of male emotional release and offers utopian visions of the possibility of trust and intimacy within male friendship. It celebrates and encourages working-class resistance to economic injustice and political abuse. It recognizes and values the diversity of American society and imagines a world where mutual cooperation can exist between the races. In short, wrestling embodies the fundamental contradictions of the American populist tradition. The politics of WWF wrestling is punch-drunk and rambunctious, yet it builds upon authentic anger and frustrations which we cannot ignore if we want to understand the state of contemporary American culture. Wrestling makes you want to shout, and perhaps we have had too much silence.

NOTES

1. "WWF Interview: A Talk with Jake 'the Snake' Roberts," *WWF Magazine*, February 1992, p. 17.

2. Roland Barthes, "The World of Wrestling," in Susan Sontag, ed., *A Barthes Reader* (New York: Hill and Wang, 1982), p. 23.

3. Ibid., p. 25.

4. Ibid., p. 29.

5. For useful background on the historical development of television wrestling, as well as for an alternative reading of its narrative structures, see Michael R. Ball, *Professional Wrestling as Ritual Drama in American Popular Culture* (Lewiston: Edwin Mellen Press, 1990). For a performance-centered account of WWF Wrestling, see Sharon Mazer, "The Doggie Doggie World of Professional Wrestling," *The Drama Review*, Winter 1990, pp. 96–122.

6. John Fiske, *Television Culture* (London: Methuen, 1987); Tania Modleski, *Loving with a Vengeance: Mass Produced Fantasies for Women* (London: Methuen, 1982); Jane Feuer, "Melodrama, Serial Form and Television Today," *Screen* 25 (1984): 4–16.

7. Gledhill, pp. 12–13. David Thorburn similarly finds melodramatic conventions underlying much of prime-time television programming. See Thorburn, "Television Melodrama," in Horace Newcomb, ed., *Television: The Critical Eye*, 4th ed. (New York: Oxford University Press, 1987), p. 7.

8. John Fiske, *Understanding Popular Culture* (Boston: Unwin Hyman, 1989), chapter 4.

9. Peter J. Rabinowitz, "The Turn of the Glass Key: Popular Fiction as Reading Strategy," *Critical Inquiry* 12, no. 2 (1985): 421.

10. Norbert Elias and Eric Dunning, *The Quest for Excitement: Sport and Leisure in the Civilizing Process* (New York: Basil Blackwell, 1986), p. 41.

11. Ibid., pp. 64–65.

12. Ibid., p. 111.

13. Ibid., p. 49.

14. Ibid.

15. Ibid., p. 50.

16. Ibid., pp. 86–87.

17. Peter Brooks, *The Melodramatic Imagination: Balzac, Henry James, Melodrama and the Mode of Excess* (New Haven: Yale University Press, 1976).

18. Valerie Walkerdine, "Video Replay: Families, Films and Fantasy," in Victor Burgin, James Donald, and Cora Kaplan, eds., *Formations of Fantasy* (London: Methuen, 1986), pp. 172–74.

19. Ibid., p. 173.

20. Christine Gledhill, "The Melodramatic Field: An Investigation," in Christine Gledhill, ed., *Home Is Where the Heart Is: Studies in Melodrama and the Woman's Film* (London: BFI, 1987), p. 21.

21. Keith Elliot Greenberg, "One Step Too Far: Boss Man and Mountie Clash over Meaning of Justice," *WWF Magazine,* May 1991, p. 40.

22. Brutus was injured in a motorcycle accident several years ago and had his skull reconstructed; he is no longer able to fight but has come to represent the voice of aged wisdom within the WWF universe. Brutus constantly articulates the values of fairness and loyalty in the face of their abuse by the rule-breaking characters, pushing for reconciliations that might resolve old feuds, and watching as these disputes erupt and destroy his barber shop.

23. "The Mark of Cain: Shawn Michaels Betrays His Tag Team Brother," *WWF Magazine,* March 1992, p. 41.

24. "WWF Superstars Talk about Wrestlemania," *WWF Magazine,* March 1992, p. 18.

25. Robert Bechtold Heilman, *The Iceman, the Arsonist and the Troubled Agent: Tragedy and Melodrama on the Modern Stage* (Seattle: University of Washington Press, 1973), p. 53.

26. Brooks, p. 34.

27. "WWF Interview: A Talk with Jake 'the Snake' Roberts," p. 17.

28. Brooks, p. 4.

29. Ibid., p. 41.

30. Robert Bechtold Heilman, *Tragedy and Melodrama: Versions of Experience* (Seattle: University of Washington Press, 1968), p. 76.

31. "Elizabeth Balancing Family with Business," *WWF Wrestling Spotlight,* March 1992.

32. Eve Kosofsky Sedgwick, *Between Men: English Literature and Male Homosocial Desire* (New York: Columbia University Press, 1985).

33. "Meeting of the Minds: Jake and Andre—Psychological Interplay," *WWF Magazine,* August 1991, p. 52.

34. Ibid.

35. Keith Elliot Greenberg, "The Darkness Is in Me Forever . . . ," *WWF Magazine,* August 1991, p. 47.

36. This incident could also be read as a response to a series of rumors and tabloid stories centering on the sexuality of WWF athletes. The Ultimate Warrior was "outed" by one tabloid newspaper, while charges of sexual harassment surfaced on an episode of the Phil Donahue show. Complicating an easy reading of this incident is the strong popularity of wrestling within the gay male community and the existence of gay fanzines publishing sexual fantasies involving wrestlers.

37. Bruce Palmer, *"Man over Money": The Southern Populist Critique of American Capitalism* (Chapel Hill: University of North Carolina Press, 1980), p. 3.

38. Ibid., p. 5.

39. David Grimsted, *Melodrama Unveiled: American Thought and Culture, 1800–1850* (Chicago: University of Chicago Press, 1968).

40. Michael Denning, *Mechanic Accents: Dime Novels and Working-Class Culture in America* (London: Verso, 1987), p. 80.

41. "WWF Superstars Talk about Wrestlemania," p. 18.

42. "Personality Profile: Repo Man," *WWF Magazine*, February 1992, p. 11.

43. "Salt of the Earth: Sid Justice Comes from the Land," *WWF Magazine*, November 1991, pp. 47–48.

44. "Tatanka: Leader of the New Indian Nation," *WWF Magazine*, April 1992, p. 55.

45. "A Talk with Big Boss Man," *WWF Magazine*, November 1991, p. 18.

46. "American Pride: Sarge and Duggan Protect Old Glory from the Nastys," *WWF Magazine*, March 1992, p. 52.

47. Laura Kipnis, "Reading *Hustler*," in Lawrence Grossberg, Cary Nelson, and Paula Treichler, eds., *Cultural Studies* (New York: Routledge, Chapman and Hall, 1992), p. 388.

PART TWO ... *Sports, Race, and Representation*

4 ... *"America's" Apple Pie: Baseball, Japan-Bashing, and the Sexual Threat of Economic Miscegenation*

On December 6, 1991, the eve of the fiftieth anniversary of the Pearl Harbor bombing, Seattle Mariners owner Jeff Smulyan put the baseball team he had owned for two and one-half years up for sale. At the time of his announcement, Smulyan reportedly threatened to move the Mariners from Seattle to St. Petersburg, Florida, where he had a potential buyer, if a Seattle investor did not come forward by March 27, 1992, to purchase the franchise. Smulyan, an Indiana media mogul and resident of Indianapolis, set that deadline after banks encouraged him to put the team up for sale. On January 23, 1992, a Seattle investment group calling itself the Baseball Club of Seattle made a public offer to buy the Mariners and keep them in Seattle. Controversy immediately broke out across the country (with some international ripples) over the fact that majority investor Hiroshi Yamauchi, sixty-three-year-old billionaire president of Kyoto-based Nintendo Company Ltd., would contribute the lion's share of the purchase price.

Although the Baseball Club of Seattle was also composed of four white Seattle investors—John Ellis, president of Puget Sound Power and Light Company; John E. McCaw, Jr., director of McCaw Cellular Communications, Inc.; Frank Shrontz, president of the Boeing Company; and Chris Larson, vice president of Microsoft Corporation—national(ist) criticism arose over Yamauchi's majority investment and the group's plan to make Yamauchi's son-in-law and Nintendo of America president Minoru Arakawa manager of the team. Although at the time of the proposal Arakawa, who would be Yamauchi's proxy, was a fifteen-year resident of Redmond, a Seattle suburb; an employer of 1,400 local workers; and a father of children who attended local schools in the Seattle area, a common perception spread that the proposed purchase and new manager were another sign that the Japanese were "moving in." After a flurry of criticism and racist responses from baseball team owners, baseball commissioner Fay Vincent, his assistant, Stephen Greenberg, sportswriters, newswriters, columnists, editors, and letter writers to editors of local and national newspapers, Smulyan eventually agreed to sell his team to the syndicate on Friday, April 3, 1992, signaling the first time that someone not from North America would own part of a U.S. major-league baseball team.

This particular event took place during a period when the United States was arguably more hostile to Japan than at any other time since the bombing of Pearl Harbor. The national and international press carefully documented the swell of nationalist expression surrounding the anniversary of the bombing of Pearl Harbor; the criticism that U.S. automakers leveled against Japanese trade practices; the visit to Japan by George Bush and CEOs of U.S. automobile manufacturers, during which Bush threw up at a meeting with Japanese prime minister Kiichi Miyazawa (Devroy, January 9, 1992); Los Angeles Metro Rail's much-publicized rejection of a contract with Sumitomo Corporation of America (Jehl, January 23, 1992); and U.S. reactions to the speaker of the lower house of the Japanese parliament, Yoshio Sakurauchi, who said that "American" workers were "lazy" and "illiterate" and that the U.S. was "Japan's subcontractor" (Reid, January 21, 1992).

Press discussions about the fear of Japan's expanding economic power in the Mariners case were not new. In a passage that shows no regret and little awareness of irony, *Houston Chronicle* staff writer David Ivanovich writes, "Anti-Japanese sentiment is sweeping across the nation like a *tsunami,* with both government and business leaders joining in the swell" (January 24, 1992). The representation of Japanese wanting to buy the Seattle Mariners may contribute to the already long history of contemporary portraits of Japanese as greedy, villainous, totalitarian, and selfish opportunists. The media coverage surrounding the purchase of the Seattle Mariners is significant and important because it weaves together issues of nationalism, racism, masculinity, and consumer culture. The narrative constructed through various fragments written in newspapers illustrated, in a very overt, postmodern fashion, the psychological imagination around the metaphor baseball. The discussion of baseball in articles about the purchase of the Seattle Mariners and the Japanese company Nintendo can be said to evoke what I term *the sexual threat of economic miscegenation.*

Less than a week after the syndicate announced its proposal to purchase the Mariners, an article appeared in a Kirkland, Washington, newspaper, *Eastside Week,* that represents the threat of economic miscegenation constructed in discourse in a particularly vivid way. The article, written by Don Varyu, basically supports the sale of the team to the Baseball Club of Seattle, and suggests that the racism in Fay Vincent's opposition to the sale is located within Vincent's character. Varyu's article, "Playing the Race Card: Can Seattle Beat Baseball's Xenophobia?" begins with a bold assertion. He writes:

The birth announcement of the Baseball Club of Seattle came as a surprise. There were rumors, of course, that Seattle was expecting, but no one thought the blessed event would occur so soon. There were the initial oohs and aahs over this perfectly adorable child, then the predictable, back-of-the-hand reference to its mixed parentage. But now, local [sic] spin doctors must somehow find a way to immunize it from the virus of overt racism or it may never leave its incubator. (January 29, 1992)

The "spin doctors" Varyu refers to are the owners of baseball teams, including Smulyan, who, once the syndicate made its proposal, tried to concoct reasons to move the team to Florida. Varyu explains by saying, "But in order for the owners to knock down the deal, they needed to find a way to play on the current anti-Japanese fervor, without stepping over the line to odious cries of nationalism and cultural purity."

Throughout the rest of the article, Varyu depicts the hypocrisy and demagoguery of baseball commissioner Fay Vincent, who waxes nostalgic about "America's" pastime. Varyu quotes Vincent's statement made just weeks before: "There is certainly a conviction that [baseball] is America's game. There is certain identification with sort of the patriotic view of this country, and North America is linked with us in that sense." Varyu then quotes Vincent's response to the proposed sale. Vincent says, "Baseball has developed a strong policy against approving investors from outside the United States and Canada. It is unlikely foreign investors will receive the requisite baseball approvals." Finally, Varyu writes:

> In 1990, he [Fay Vincent] told an interviewer, "the tie between baseball and the soul of America is precious and fragile because we don't understand the nature of the connection. I think of baseball as a quasi public institution. I feel a responsibility to take care of major league baseball, to hold it in my hand and cradle it as if it were to be cherished."

Varyu then goes on to criticize Vincent's stance by saying, "But let's be fair. Could it be that in Vincent's world view there is something sacred about a nation's business and culture, something that precludes the polluting presence of a foreign land?"

Varyu's critical mode illustrates particularly well the sexual dynamics at play in discourse surrounding the sale and purchase of the Mariners, and the combinatory racist, xenophobic, and eugenic strain that flows, in this instance, through the character of Vincent. In this depiction, Vincent represents the authorial white man articulating the pristine nature of baseball, defining rightful ownership, and establishing various lines of difference. While Seattle is feminized within the context of this narrative, ambiguity over the gender of the parents is prominently featured. While this article is suspicious of Vincent's actions, Varyu's characterization of the event nonetheless maintains an ambivalent relationship to the position of race and functions within, not in contrast to, a discourse of the fear of miscegenation. Within the context of his article, Seattle is figured as purely "white," which suggests that, even in protesting the narrative being produced, Varyu's article maintains an essentialist discourse of race that ignores the multiracial make-up of Seattle, and that strict divisions based on biological classification themselves contribute to a system of racial hierarchy and white supremacy. In personifying Seattle as being pregnant, Varyu projects biological characteristics onto the ideograph Seattle. Nonetheless, the nameless and raced father is produced through the enthymeme, through an obviating absence that induces a response in the form of a question about racial origin (e.g., "Is the child's blood tainted?"). Absence promotes curiosity over the racial makeup of the infant; it entertains the possibility that the sexual act that goes undiscussed is nonconsensual, precisely because of Vincent's protective stance against Japanese possession, his feminization of Seattle through pregnancy, and his racist and xenophobic construction of the threatening male. The club is the illegitimate child and the Japanese its absent, and perhaps unsavory, father.

This chapter explores the tension that miscegenation evokes, the fear that the imagined sexual encounter between races produces, and the symbolic embodiment of the racist imagination. Through a critical history of discourse produced in reaction to this political exigence, I will argue that the construction of the debate over whether "Japanese" money can be mixed with a U.S. economy illustrates a racist ideology. This ideology is not unusual in U.S. history. This controversy is no doubt reminiscent of discourse about sexual relations between colonialists and Native Americans, slave masters and African slaves, early twentieth-century eugenics discourse, and discourse resistant to integration in the 1950s and 1960s—that is, the threat of miscegenation. In this case, such discourse takes on an apocalyptic rhetorical posture against "Yellow" conspiracy, a posture which is not new within the long and arduous history of U.S. nationalism.

Varyu's article provides an appropriate skeleton of the issues I will discuss in the rest of the chapter. First I will describe the construction of the pristinity of baseball—its sanctity and its cultural perfection. Then I will discuss the construction of the threat to baseball—the fear of contamination, of occupation, and of colonization. Finally, I will discuss responses to the threat: attempts to deny or avoid the threat, to avenge the threat, and to diminish or rechannel the threat. I will conclude with a careful appraisal of the discourse and a theoretical comment about race-mixing.

PRISTINITY AND THE VIRTUE OF WHITE WOMANHOOD

In Western miscegenation narratives, pristinity is held in nostalgic repose, as an ideal form that the white heterosexual couple must strive to maintain. Man achieves possession of pristinity through his protection and defense of white woman's "God-given" virtue, while woman embodies pristinity through her avoidance of foul things, her carefully chosen social relations, and her lack of intellectual development resulting from her proper domestic training and conduct. Pristinity derives from a complex set of Victorian metaphors: virginity, initial growth, protectedness, naïveté, solemnity, innocence, cleanliness, warmth, eternity, prudery, lightness, comfort, satisfaction, airiness, languor, fragility, youthfulness, and the everlasting ability to flower. Pristinity is definitive of a Victorian sensibility, a figure that is specifically feminine.

But pristinity is also lodged within a history of race-specific discourse. In relation to Native Americans, the protection of white women's pristinity was utilized as a reason to slaughter Native American men. The threat of rape; the genetic pollution of the blood supply and the ruination of patrilineal, colonialist power; the fear of disease; and the spread of spiritual discord mark the pristinity of "woman" as the exigence for racial slaughter, revenge, and masculinist triumph. In these specific examples, white women, who were, along with women of color, at least through the seventeenth, eighteenth, and nineteenth centuries, regarded as men's property, gained unusual prominence within historical discourse as justification for men's desire for competition, power, property, and other possessions.

Caren Deming suggests that white women function in literature as receptacles and preservers. Women maintain culture, but it is white men's duty to protect white women from depravity. It was, as Deming suggests, the inherent nature of women to invite—although not through any specific, conscious intention on their part—rape upon themselves. Their weakness made it necessary for white men to protect white women from Indians on the frontier who threatened to violate them and the culture they preserved. White women lacked courage and were susceptible to capture. Deming writes, "The image of female vulnerability culminates in the white man's defending white women against rape by savages" (p. 92). For Native American women, vulnerability signaled to colonialists their inherent and constant invitation (unspoken desire) to be raped, taken, mutilated, and killed by white men. In my reading of Deming, what white women ultimately protected in these stories was not so much their own innocence and purity but the purity of white culture, the culture they were to preserve through men's protection of their bodies.

Angela Davis and Hazel Carby illustrate how white women functioned, similarly, as justification for killing African American men. The "myth of the black rapist," as Davis suggests, was constructed after slavery to protect white women from the threat African American men posed to them (e.g., a threat constructed as that of the African American male always lurking, always waiting, to descend upon white women), and thus to justify his lynching. Miscegenation laws specifically centered on the fear that white women would be raped by African American males. As Carby writes, "The miscegenation laws thus pretended to offer 'protection' to white women but left black women the victims of rape by white men and simultaneously granted to these same men the power to terrorize black men as a potential threat to the virtue of white womanhood" (p. 307). African American women are anything but innocent in historical constructions. Throughout U.S. history, African American women are constructed as inherently sexual and excessively available. This particular construction is only one of many that depict African Americans as a whole as overly sexualized people. As Sander Gilman writes, "By the eighteenth century, the sexuality of the black, both male and female, becomes an icon for deviant sexuality in general: as we have seen, the black figure appears almost always paired with a white figure of the opposite sex" (p. 228). African American women were, according to Angela Davis, depicted as un-rapable. Moreover, the main construction of African Americans throughout the nineteenth century arguably highlights their sexuality. Sander Gilman suggests that "the detailed presentation of the sexual parts of the black, dominates all medical description of the black during the nineteenth century" (p. 235).

Depictions of women as pristine objects whose innocence could be fouled were not limited to discussions of Native American and African American men as threats. The depiction of men of color, generally, as animals with bad intentions pervades U.S. history. Specific to the focus of this essay, Japanese men are also shown as threats to pristinity and white women's virtue in popular culture. For example, in the case of propaganda posters from World War II and in films such as the *Why We Fight* series, Japanese men are depicted as rapists of white women. One particular poster illustrates this representation. In the poster a white woman, apparently unconscious, is draped over a devilish, crouching, rat-like Japanese man, who carries her off as one of the many baubles of war. This specific World War II image depicts the contrast in hue: the swarthy Japanese man and the pearl-colored skin of the helpless, fully nude, and defenseless white woman. Her languorous posture contrasts with his bestial, sturdy slouch. This particular example of "comic" propaganda illustrates, through the open hand of the woman hanging helplessly as she is carried off, the fear of miscegenation, unrepressed. In his hand is a gun. A drop of blood on her hand can be seen. She is being taken from what looks like a war scene into the dark night. It is the image historically constructed of the bombing of "Pearl" Harbor. Though the United States shows no remorse for bombing "innocent" cities filled with people (most recently in Libya, Panama City, and Baghdad), the construction of the bombing of Pearl Harbor carries with it the onus of the evil Japanese man attacking a helpless and innocent (feminine) military base. Such an image lingers.

In discourse about the sale to "foreigners," the maintenance of the pristinity of baseball begins with a discussion of the "purity" of baseball. Here, unlike in Varyu's description, baseball, not Seattle, is feminized and needs to be protected by masculine armor. On January 28, 1992, an article addressing the issue of purity, titled "Spell Baseball H-y-p-o-c-r-i-t-e," appeared in the *Bellingham Herald.* While this article condemns Vincent's responses to the press, it draws attention to the issues at stake. The article says, "Vincent has been compelled to defend baseball's 'purity' because 60 percent of the $100 million offered to buy the Seattle Mariners is 'Japanese' money." The issue of purity in this instance has to do with the fear of economic miscegenation, the mixing of "foreign" money, and the purity of money prior to being mixed.

An article that explicitly ties together the issue of purity, femininity, and the need for protection of "America's" pastime appeared in the *Herald.* The article quotes Maryland Republican representative Helen Bentley as saying, "This is our apple pie and motherhood [. . .] this is going too far. We are not a colony of Japan" ("Baseball to Wait," January 25, 1992). While drawing specific attention to the maternal role of cultural "pastimes," this particular comment also draws connections to colonization and its implied link with motherhood. As Sam Keen writes in his study of enmity, "As the destroyer of motherhood, the enemy threatens the sacred Madonna-and-Child. Here it is not the woman as sexual object who is threatened, but as nurturer, the guardian of home, hearth, and family" (p. 58). Moreover, Bentley's statement indirectly references Sakurauchi's comment that the U.S. is Japan's subcontractor by articulating the fear of what is implied by colonization. Ironically, the comment seems to suggest that if the U.S. were a "colony of Japan," the threat to femininity that Japan now poses would no longer be something to resist.

A third article invokes eugenics discourse and the prospect of outside forces causing miscegenation. Ron Judd begins his article by saying, "A forced marriage between Seattle and Mariners owner Jeff Smulyan is not a suitable solution to the city's baseball ownership crisis, local leaders have warned baseball Commissioner Fay Vincent" (February 6, 1992, p. B1). Here the white owner trying to sell the team becomes the man to be avoided, even though Seattle is once again feminized as powerless, acted upon, and unable to protect herself. The ownership crisis figures as the cause of the pregnancy. Why else would a marriage have to be forced? The article goes on to cite Smulyan addressing the issue of mixed blood directly: "But enough blood has been spilled in this situation. I want to sell this team. This has been a nightmare" (p. B2). Reference to spilled "blood," not milk, suggests a mysterious focus on sinister forces and genealogy. Whose blood was spilled remains a mystery in this passage, but the threat to genetic line remains a palpable consequence of the unwanted pregnancy, a pregnancy Smulyan may wish to abort.

A fourth article sees miscegenation as producing something positive, as reversing the role of pristinity in sustaining patriarchal rule. The *Olympian* ran an article pleading for "Baseball" to rethink the offer, supporting Arakawa as a "community [. . .] resident," and defending U.S. business partnerships with Japanese companies. The article supports the sale and purchase and says, "These problems will be worked out. But we need something to tie these two disparate cultures together. Baseball might just be able to forge that link. What a benefit that would be to both nations" ("Mariner Deal," January 30, 1992). The merger between Japan and baseball figures here as an international "benefit." Nonetheless, the article does not address pristinity specifically as an issue. The issue of the sanctity of baseball is repressed in favor of vague commentary about the benefits that a "tie" can bring. Interestingly, this article does not suggest how a consensual marriage might bring greater power to both through a combination of forces.

Perhaps the clearest example of the construction of pristinity appears in an article by Joey Reaves of the *Chicago Tribune*. This article focuses on the cultural constitution of what is "American" and how what is "American" is threatened. To some degree, it helps to explain the repression of a discussion of pristinity and the focus on the profits of miscegenation in the *Olympian* article. Reaves begins the article by saying, "Sure, President Bush wants the Japanese to 'Buy American.' But hold on. Buying American is one thing. Buying the American national pastime is another" (January 15, 1992, p. 1). Reaves distinguishes between something consensually bought and what he characterizes as an undesired purchase, a purchase struggled against. Then he suggests that Bush's desires are generalized to the public as a whole. He says, "That, essentially, was the reaction nationwide Friday to news that a group of Japanese investors, headed by the chief of the Nintendo video game company, planned to make an offer for the star-crossed Seattle Mariners baseball team" (p. 1). Reaves says the Japanese appear to be "throwing their money around," which "no one likes to see" (p. 1). "But," Reaves writes, "the bulging wallets of the Japanese were only part of the problem. The truth is, these days, the Japanese can't seem to do anything right in the eyes of many Americans. And vice versa" (p. 1). What initially begins as a story characterizing reactions to Japanese actions now shifts to a story about Japanese-U.S. relations. Reaves details events that have led to U.S. criticism of Japan (e.g., Sakurauchi, Sumitomo). He cites Charles Morrison (a "specialist" in U.S.-Japanese relations), who says, "I think baseball is one of these areas that is sort of seen as quintessentially American—or, at least, American and Canadian. And to have foreigners buying American baseball teams reminds us of our vulnerability and makes us sort of neo-nationalistic" (p. 8). What begins as a description of social/cultural relations now takes on a more personal tone. Morrison's shift from "American" in the third person to "us" in the first person authenticates his own, personal opinion as speaking on behalf of America, as "American" rhetoric, an American rhetoric feminized by its "vulnerability."

Reaves goes on to discuss purchases by Japanese companies in the U.S. (e.g., Sony's purchase of Columbia Pictures, Matsushita's purchase of MCA, Toshiba's investment in Time/Warner). He says, "Hollywood. The recording industry. Time Magazine. All sold or going into partnership with people the United States defeated and then helped climb out of the rubble of World War II. And, now, they want to buy baseball" (p. 8). The progression in logic here from Japanese investments in entertainment companies to what is distinguished as the ultimate purchase—baseball—occurs only in metaphorical relation to U.S.-Japanese relations during World War II. Moreover, the contrast with helping "people" who then "want to buy baseball" creates a dichotomy between what is to be seen as genuinely giving and philanthropic and what should be seen as its opposite—taking and harmful.

After detailing how the purchase is unlikely to fly and driving home the fact that Yamauchi speaks no English, Reaves's article suddenly shifts. He says, "As for the national sanctity of baseball, that was shattered long ago when Toronto and Montreal joined the major leagues" (p. 8). He explains how Japanese have already invested in minor-league baseball teams, and while Nintendo has been labeled an unfair marketing company, Reaves ends the article by saying, "Toy retailers, many of which get most of their profits from Nintendo products, are leery of alienating the Japanese games giant and go along, competitors say" (p. 8).

The article ends ambivalently: while there are many reasons to fear Japanese economic ventures, Reaves suggests, U.S. companies are resigned to letting them invest. Because unwanted miscegenation cannot be avoided, it is therefore a product of masculine competition, and because pristinity has already been soiled by other countries in the past, in this instance its re-soilage by Japan is no longer to be feared. This ambivalence and resignation maintains a resentful focus on Japan's unthankful choice to invest in U.S. companies that have a specifically "American" identity. While the article struggles to get beyond the fears of Japanese investment in the Mariners, it ultimately ends up affirming such a fear, while resigning itself to the loss of pristinity.

The inability of U.S. companies to protect the virtuous, authentic, and pristine "America" and her "pastime" leaves the fallen victor bitter with envy but willing to step aside, in hopes of a possibility of regaining his competitive place in the world economy. Pristinity, still idealized in the article, although not necessarily feminized and sexualized as in most of these articles, cannot be maintained in the face of such overdetermining forces, the forces of masculine competition, forces that the article suggests grow beyond U.S. control.

PEARL HARBOR II: THREAT OF A SEQUEL

The heading of this section highlights the fact that the narrative construction that focuses on the threat of the Japanese to the sanctity of what is purely "American" is really a sequel to historical events of the past. The ghost of World War II haunts the discourse surrounding the purchase of the Mariners in a mythological way, in the same way that the dark man haunts the images of white women in racist, colonialist propaganda. As I have already suggested, however, this discourse is not limited to the sensationalistic and extreme propaganda spread during wartime. It exists in daily discourse, in the very mundane words of the day. During 1995, the *Sacramento Bee* even ran a "World War II Watch" column regularly. It is as if World War II were the last war the U.S. fought, as if fifty years of history had not altered the basic, and biological, determining fact of interracial and international difference. The Japanese, the story goes, were not defeated during World War II. The fact that they were spared, ultimately, explains the resurrection of their treachery. Had they been completely exterminated, then, this narrative argument goes, there would be no fear of an economic invasion now.

An article in *Eastside Week* (an east Seattle suburban newspaper) begins by questioning the ulterior motives behind reported Japanese investments in the Mariners, but then goes on to reproduce the apocalyptic and paranoid rhetoric endemic of World War II U.S. discourse. The title is: "Nintendo's Game Plan: Are There Strings Attached to the Mariners Deal?" Similar to the article by Reaves, this article focuses on the opinions of a U.S.-Japan expert. Ted Kenney writes:

> Trade expert Pat Choate thinks major league baseball should turn down Nintendo Corp. president Hiroshi Yamauchi's offer of $75 million for a controlling interest in the Seattle Mariners. Choate, author of an influential book on US-Japan relations, thinks Yamauchi has an ulterior motive: he wants to bring major league baseball to Washington [D.C.]. (February 5, 1992, p. 9)

The ulterior motive behind Yamauchi's investment, not unlike Roosevelt's fear of a Japanese invasion of the West Coast that would spread all the way across the country to Washington, D.C., is eastward expansion and inevitable colonization of the Americas. Kenney writes:

> The next logical step would be for other Japanese tycoons to fund a franchise in the nation's capital, which hasn't had a major league team since the Washington Senators folded in 1961. In his mind's eye, Choate sees Japanese lobbyists dangling game passes in front of frothing government officials. "You'd be surprised at the leaders who would suck up to the owners to get season tickets," he says. (P. 9)

The melodramatic and paranoid story grows as Choate begins to see pollution of baseball as the harbinger of the pollution of U.S. government, and no doubt its driving ideology. Here politicians are feminized, because of their unknowing collusion in pleasure politics. Their selfish decisions to take baseball tickets from Japanese for political favors makes them particularly vulnerable to becoming subjects of Japanese ideology. Apocalyptically, Kenney writes:

> Choate's take on the Mariners deal is thought-provoking because it cuts through the rhetoric about racism and asks what might be asked of any prospective sports-franchise owner: What's in it for them? In the elation over a viable plan to save the team, Seattle seems to have foregone any examination of the motivations behind the deal. (P. 9)

Kenney sees the discussion of "racism" as a foil to send watchdogs like himself off on errant paths. Moreover, Kenney uses "rhetoric" figuratively as the antithesis to what is "thought-provoking." In doing so, he misrecognizes his own narrative as somehow devoid of rhetorical style. "Seattle," in this depiction, is feminized through its inability to see the ulterior motives behind the Japanese offer to buy the team. Kenney builds his case further by detailing Nintendo's disreputable character in other business dealings. He writes:

> But Nintendo's success has brought with it repeated allegations that the company bullies its way to illegal control of its market. Judging from the complaints of competitors, Nintendo seems more intent than most companies on controlling the sphere in which it operates. (P. 10)

Kenney highlights "Nintendo's" masculinity. The construction of Nintendo's gender produces a personification of physical power and intellectual manipulation. Kenney supports his rhetorical strategy to link Japan's present actions with those of its suspicious past with a reference to World War II. Then he goes on to cite someone who really has a reason to agree with him.

> "They ruthlessly took over the market. The more they captured the market, the more they locked in their game makers," says Stan Friedman, a San Francisco lawyer who has brought a class-action suit against Nintendo on behalf of game-cartridge buyers in California. (P. 10)

Finally, Kenney closes his article by tying the motives behind Yamauchi's interest in investing in the Seattle Mariners to motives of Japanese government officials. He writes:

> But it is even more unlikely, [Bill] Asbury and other experts say, that Yamauchi did not consult with Japan's Ministry of International Trade and Industry, and with leaders of the Keidanren, an extremely powerful Japanese industry group, before making the offer. Americans have trouble understanding the extent to which Japanese companies view their success in America as a collective endeavor, he says. (P. 10)

This last depiction shows Japanese companies as no better than the Borg on *Star Trek: The Next Generation*. As in World War II discourse depictions of them, Japanese, unlike "Americans," are not individuals with motives of their own. They act collectively, in the interests of the greater good of Japan. According to Kenney, Yamauchi's investment in the Seattle Mariners takes on greater significance if seen in the context of Japanese culture, where collective behavior, suppression of individual desire, and greater political power are supposedly revered. "Americans" in this scenario are gullible and naïve, because they are so sure the person they are dealing with has as much good will as they have that they overlook Nintendo's motivations. For Kenney, normal daily business transactions suddenly threaten in geopolitical dimensions.

Not all articles depicting the current events surrounding the Seattle Mariners' purchase are apocalyptic and paranoid in the way that Kenney's is. In an article in the *Sporting News,* Dave Kindred justifies the need for the Baseball Club of Seattle to buy the Mariners. But even in justifying the purchase, Kindred plays on the fears of a return of World War II Japan to evoke the opposite response. He begins his article with a story about a paranoid person he knows. He writes:

> I have a friend in the journalism business who flew bombers over Japan in World War II. To write his sports column, he uses a laptop computer made in Japan. He does this with a certain reluctance and tells me the computer

is Japan's revenge for the atomic bomb. "We'll wake up dead someday and it'll be because the Japs built tiny death rays into the computer screen we stare at all day," he said. He laughed at his little joke, but the message was clear. He could never trust Japan. (February 10, 1992)

This narrative construction shows how criticism of Japan, through the ironic use of economic choice, is hypocritical. The apocalyptic tenor of the passage does not diminish the familial relationship constructed between the narrator and his "friend." Kindred goes on to discuss the way Fay Vincent's attitude toward the Japanese, like that of his friend who bombed Japan, maintains a racist posture that makes better relations with Japan impossible. Kindred writes:

Vincent's stand seems built on distrust, fear and discrimination by race. If not built on those foundations, then how does baseball explain its problem with the Japanese ownership of an American baseball team? And if baseball's problem is built on those attitudes, shouldn't the commissioner, by his position as the game's conscience, be issuing not a call to racism but a call for the wisdom and tolerance that would create partnerships with the Japanese to help Americans?

The equation of "baseball" with "Vincent" here is endemic of baseball discourse largely found on the sports pages. The merging of a "pastime," an "event," and a "game" with the institutional actors and decision makers seems an interesting confusion of terms. This discourse functions, so far, through a topos of tolerance, which stands as the idealization of the political arena in which skirmishes over baseball begin. Kindred continues his article by discussing things that he thinks *would* be cause for fear, mistrust, racism, and avoidance of a tolerant partnership. He writes:

To judge by baseball's first reaction, you'd think the Japanese intended to move the Mariners to Tokyo. Or you'd think they wanted geisha girls on the foul lines. Or maybe American players thought they'd be required to endure the militaristic, theologic, psychological training imposed on Japanese stars. Good heavens, you'd have thought Godzilla was about to drop Fay Vincent from the Empire State Building.

Thus, Kindred sets arbitrary limitations on how far the relationship should be allowed to go. In justifying his critique of Vincent, Kindred ultimately ends up reaffirming the racist discourse he initially sets out to discredit. Moreover, interestingly enough, Kindred puts his finger on the thesis of my essay: that the discourse itself relies on imaginary relations of appropriating symbols, femininity as receptacle of culture, and resurrects the fear of military occupation and perhaps torture in order for such reactions to gain force and legitimacy. Moreover, through Kindred's use of the Godzilla metaphor, the fear of the dark, masculine "other" colonizing, overpowering, and capturing white women becomes a signal for humor. This humor is predicated on associating Fay Vincent with pristine womanhood. Thus, Kindred takes two metaphors of baseball—as innocent and sanctified cultural object and as an embodiment of the institutional and political management of the game—and combines them so as to represent Vincent himself, who stands in for "baseball" throughout sports discourse, as site of vulnerability. However, this combined metaphor cannot be sustained unless Kindred appropriates the masculine perspective he cites Vincent as maintaining. Only through Vincent's feminization does this particular anecdote make sense. The humor is based on irony, the inappropriate comparison or contrast of discordant metaphors.

In the rest of the article, aside from confusing Arakawa with Yamauchi (which rarely happens in the discourse), Kindred argues that baseball is as Japanese as it is American. However, he ends with an anomalous statement reasserting the inherent nationalism of the Japanese race. He writes, "Japan baseball expert Robert Whiting wrote: 'Baseball's grip on Japan's collective psyche is due, ultimately, to the fact that it suits the national character.' It involves group action, a test of one-to-one wills, a slow pace and a fanatical attachment to statistics" (February 10, 1992, p. 6). Here the way they play baseball is constructed in parallel to the Japanese attitude toward political judgments. Japan becomes one giant homogeneous machine, operating because Japanese deny their own inherent individuality in favor of the collective will of the nation.

Parallels between Japanese wanting to contribute to the purchase of a baseball team and Japanese government wanting to take control of "America" are a central rhetorical device operating in apocalyptic stories of Pearl Harbor II. In a particularly crotchety article from the *Tampa Tribune,* a newspaper from Seattle's rival part of the country, Tom McEwen explicitly draws a connection between Nintendo and the Japanese government. He begins his article by writing:

> "Toy! Toy! Toy!" That's the suggested title for the movie later recounting the drama of the sudden Japanese attack on American baseball Thursday. Difference between "Toy! Toy! Toy!" and "Tora! Tora! Tora!" appears to be Admiral Fay Vincent's forces were ready and may deny even temporary victory. (January 24, 1992)

Here history is retold for a present audience, but in this story the Japanese are not able to gain even a temporary victory. The goal, McEwen suggests, is to avoid a repeat of the victory *this time,* which Fay Vincent has already accomplished.

Even though McEwen assures the reader in the opening paragraph that victory this time is imminent, he devotes the next section of his article to developing reasons to fear the Japanese in typical war imagery. He writes, "The announcement [of the proposed purchase] hit Seattle with a financial bomb that shook St. Petersburg. The battle plan was designed to keep the Mariners in Seattle and prevent their possible move to the Florida Suncoast Dome in St. Petersburg, if not in 1992, certainly in 1993" (January 24, 1992, p. 1). The strategy of assigning intent makes the story easy to understand in Florida. The "battle" lines are clearly drawn. No room for other reasons for the announcement seems possible. McEwen goes on to call this a "sports war that puts offensive-minded St. Petersburg on the defense." He writes, "When the attack began with the support of Seattle leaders but no consort with Mariners owner Jeff Smulyan, it appeared the conflict may not be quickly settled." The intent that he suggests is behind the proposed purchase here is affirmed. At least he makes evident that the Japanese are cunning enough not to make the offer in the presence of the owner.

His article goes on to give background for the purchase, information that details the threat to Floridians. He concludes, however, by drawing attention to the implied parallel between these actions and Pearl Harbor, again using war imagery to effect this end. He writes:

> This is a big-time controversy. And while at first glance Vincent's quick reaction seems to shoot down the Sino-Seattle attack, it may be just beginning the reparations the way Seattle will go if this war is lost. St. Petersburg's long-range success in this war has to be winning baseball over its alliance on the nationalistic theme, and clearly there is a progress there if Vincent remains committed. Surely the painful cry around Tampa Bay on Thursday, at least for while, was: Not Again!

The lines of battle shift in this paragraph from U.S. baseball to St. Petersburg versus Seattle. The final sentence ties the fear of Japanese invasion to the fear of St. Petersburg's baseball loss.

The discourse is about national identity, the sum qualities of being "American," and how commitment to a particular conception of a collective body is marked within the symbolic imaginary. The fear of miscegenation takes root in the realization of World War II fears of totalitarianist Japanese expansion. The fear of the return of the imperialist evil demon allows for public discussion of the role that identity plays. Racism is tied to the postmodern angst about national identity. The fear that the identity of pre-World War II America, in which baseball had a significant part, has been altered through miscegenation to become something very different from what it was, is an anxiety over racial purity. Postmodernism harks back to a time when questions of identity reach the fore, but also a time when that identity is interminably questioned.

Postmodernism is not so much allowing for change, but rather rethinking the question of whether change has happened, whether something has evolved, whether something can be said to have happened, not to say that it should happen. Equally strong is the fear that change has not occurred, that miscegenation has not produced the offspring necessary, that the luxury of exoticization of the Orient has not been legalized.

SUBMISSION AS REVENGE

As in McEwen's article, many articles suggest that while "America" won World War II, Japan is winning the trade war. Within the context of this war, the offer to purchase the Seattle Mariners, fraught with fear of miscegenation, manifests itself symbolically as something that can be reversed, that can one day be dissolved. While this is a rhetoric of resignation, it also functions by transference, by locating frustrations over loss within the realm of the imaginary. The imaginary in operation is that of avenging the loss of sanctity, of fulfilling the promise of protection, by doing to Japan what Japan has done to the U.S.

In an article published in the *Philadelphia Inquirer,* Frank Dolson ostensibly argues in favor of the purchase. He writes, "But this is 1992, not 1984. And this is baseball, the sport that used to be our national pastime until a new pastime—Japanese bashing—moved ahead of it" (January 27, 1992). He downplays the apocalyptic nature of the purchase in favor of a condemnation of hypocrisy. He continues by describing the racist environment in which the proposal was made. He writes, "'Buy American!' has become the battle cry on the political front this presidential election year. Fine. That's precisely what Nintendo is trying to do." Dolson admits, "Frankly, it's hard to get upset over foreign investment in our teams when you look at some of the Americans who own franchises and run them so ineptly that the Big Three automobile manufacturers look good by comparison." What is recognizably a defense of the proposal suddenly becomes a story of retribution, of revenge. The conciliatory and resolving understanding of the situation becomes a strategy for payback:

> Frankly, if running a big-league baseball team in Seattle is as difficult an economic proposition as we've been led to believe, Japan-bashers should welcome the idea of Japanese ownership of the Mariners. Instead of Amer-

ican investors losing money, here's an opportunity for Japanese investors to lose their shirts by paying the inflated salaries American owners brought on themselves. Just think of it as sweet revenge.

Having stated opposition to xenophobic logic regarding the purchase, here Dolson plays on the very fears of miscegenation that he purportedly attempts to unravel. He relinquishes his fuller focus on change for a rationale that makes sense to the people whose logic he condemns. His own rationale functions around the notion of revenge, which goes unqualified. He makes no statement to undermine the possibility that revenge may be a warranted and acceptable outcome. Nor does his logic leave room for any other response.

In a similar article, "Baseball's Being Merciful to Japan," Bernie Lincicome of the *Chicago Tribune* begins by addressing the illicit sexual nature of the offer and potential purchase. He writes, "Due to the fog of the modern marketplace, the American pastime has long ago crawled under the slipcovers with foreigners" (February 4, 1992, p. 1). Here the reference to miscegenation as an illicit sexual act is only slightly veiled. Such illicit acts, Lincicome suggests, are naturalized within this specific economic context. Once again, "baseball's" pristinity is at stake. Because "baseball" cannot see the intentions of "foreigners," it continues to crawl under their "slipcovers." Not unlike general discourse about the subject, however, baseball, and its feminizing influence, naïveté, parallels governmental innocence with regard to Japan. Lincicome writes, "I don't believe anyone in our government could look his waiter in the eye if there were a Hiroshima Carp in the American League before another Washington Senator" (ibid.). The fear that the team's name creates hinges on the historical legacy of World War II. Once again, the fear illustrates the haunting nature of U.S.-Japanese relations.

Lincicome goes on to admit the racist logic behind "baseball," referring to the management and organization. He writes, "Baseball is resistant to native-born managers if they are the wrong color and frightened of potential owners with suspicious surnames. So, it is not likely that the folks from Nintendo will be buying the Mariners any time soon. That is too bad" (ibid.). However, this supposed support for the sale, as in Dolson's article, ends up reaffirming the racism behind the discrimination being criticized. Lincicome ends his article by saying:

> The Seattle Mariners are a wonderful revenge. Let the Japanese try to squeeze only the second winning season out of the saddest franchise in baseball. Let them wrestle with free agency, injured reserve and player agents. Let the Japanese share the extortion that has become the business of baseball. Never mind paying for Griffey, who at least has some talent.

> Anyone seriously into Japan-bashing ought to love to see them squirming
> in an arbitration hearing with a third-string catcher. Nah, that would be
> too cruel. (February 4, 1992, p. 2)

The innocence and naïveté of feminized baseball and the consequent loss
of control by "baseball" are avenged inevitably here when the "naïve" Japanese fail to recognize the danger in possessing. The very act of owning has
its drawbacks, according to Lincicome, but seeing the Japanese squirm,
albeit to the delight of Japan-bashers, would ironically be "too cruel" an act
to wish on anyone. This construction could be said to be the flip side of
the "myth of the black rapist." Here the Seattle Mariners, as white womanhood, willing to lie down with the "other," deserve to be sacrificed. In the
process of this narrative logic, both white women and Japanese men lose,
but who wins? The ambivalence of the final statement admits the insecurity
of the subject position constructed around the author. While articulating
the need to condemn racism, xenophobia, and discrimination, the author
legitimizes racist pleasure through the act of revenge, a vengeful pleasure at
the expense of Japan, the feminine, and the Seattle Mariners. The narrative
concludes with the masculine author and presumably his cohort, the preferred racist reader, ultimately saving feminized baseball and government
through vengeful acts. The superiority of position and of perception ultimately allows for victory over conditions beyond control. The author ele-
vates those whose innocence will be lost above the act of possession in a
final act "that would be too cruel."

The logic of revenge can be seen perhaps most vividly in an article that
ran in the *Anchorage Daily News* by Donald Kaul, a *Des Moines Register*
columnist. The article is titled "Revenge on Japanese! Sell 'em Mariners!" In
this unusual, even strange, article, Kaul begins by saying, "You're probably
not going to believe this, but there are things I don't understand" (February
8, 1992), a humble cue to the ironic position that the author, as subject, will
take in the article. Kaul goes on to say that he cannot understand "why they
won't let that Japanese fellow buy the Seattle Mariners." His incredulity stems
from his personal knowledge that it is a bad team. He writes, "Peddling these
misfits to foreigners would be an act of patriotism, but it would be especially
sweet to sell them to Japanese interests, in revenge for the trade deficit." Kaul
goes on to tell an anecdote about how Japanese owners would be less likely
to pay players a lot of money for not playing well. However, he concludes
this article with other things he does not understand, which ostensibly is a
cue to humor, but the issues in play in this article suggest an imaginary world
particular to the realm of masculinity. He writes, in a rather lengthy passage
that I must quote in its entirety:

And speaking of crazy, I don't understand the Jeffrey Dahmer trial in Milwaukee. I don't see how his defense attorneys can argue that he's insane. He seems like a perfectly normal necrophiliac-serial killer-cannibal to me. And while I'm at it, I might as well admit I don't understand rape trials. The Mike Tyson trial brought it to mind. The defense always takes the position that the woman is a person of easy virtue and asked for what she got. Failing that, she is emotionally unhinged, a walking "Fatal Attraction" case who is obsessed with the accused rapist. (This is also the strategy in sexual harassment cases: see Thomas vs. Hill.) That's not the part I don't understand; the defense has to say something, after all. The confusing part is that juries so often believe it, women jurors as well as men. Do they really imagine that there are all of these half-crazed sluts walking around loose, waiting to pounce on innocent males? I don't get it. But all the rest of it, I understand.

While the article begins with a discussion of how Kaul does not understand why the Mariners are not sold to Yamauchi, the rest of his examples show that he does not understand the logic of Jeffrey Dahmer's plea of insanity, what is wrong with defense attorneys' characterizations of rape victims as wanting to be raped, and finally why juries believe that women want to be raped. Although this article, through self-referentiality to authorial voice, anticipates its own enaction of humor, the combination of sports, race, mass murder, sexual harassment, and rape functions within the symbolic construction of the imaginary here within a logical system that may be said to characterize the repressed threat of economic miscegenation. Moreover, the juxtaposition of Yamauchi's investment in baseball with women being raped for their lack of virtue fits well within the masculinist discourse surrounding the offer and purchase of the Seattle Mariners.

Kaul's essay functions within the sexual imaginary that narratives about the Seattle Mariners construct. The place of feminine virtue, which is deflowered, through the economic war that Japan is waging against the feminized "America," itself revenge for World War II, must be avenged in order for the patriarch to rise once again to his calling to save the endangered woman—a modern-day *Last of the Mohicans* narrative. That Kaul positions himself as unable to understand how male *and* female jurors buy defense testimonies that women want to be raped affirms the patriarch's role as all-knowing and all-powerful actor.

Through a review of public discourse about the purchase of the Seattle Mariners, we can see the extent to which present-day ideology reproduces rhetorical assumptions about racial and sexual difference in ways similar to the contemporary discussion of AIDS, the U.S. war against Iraq, and the threat of environmental extermination from an ever-expanding hole in the ozone layer. This mutant racist ideology bears a new threat of the extermination of racial difference, similar to the way depictions of Japanese as bubonic-plague-infected rats during World War II influenced those who bombed Hiroshima and Nagasaki.

From the beginning of colonialism to the present, the repressed desire of U.S. racist ideology represented itself in the form of romanticization, exoticization, and scopophilization of the "Orient" and other racially, geographically, and politically ethnic peoples as feminine Other, to be dominated and made subservient to masculine, primarily corporate, enterprises. Because of economic and political transformations, Japan is presented in discourse about the Mariners as newly masculinized Other, attempting to dominate, control, and take over feminized baseball, Seattle, and the U.S. government. The gender-reversed paradigm is more precisely a biologically based rhetoric that sees Japan as a plague or disease, spreading across the body and land of a helpless U.S. economy, producing Other Japanese-controlled baseball teams, and thinning the blood of "America" or allowing America to be completely dominated. The absence of the woman of color in the discourse about baseball and apple pie suggests that women of color generally have no place within the narrative about white men saving white women from dark-skinned men. This absence also refers to the masculinist nature of the discourse that restricts the representation of women, but also to the repressed feminine, the fear that femininity—inaction and vulnerability—is the real reason for colonization. Femininity, in this equation, causes men to conquer. As a casualty of war, femininity also functions as its *raison d'être*—the stake men have in fighting in the first place.

REFERENCES

"Baseball to Wait, See on M's Deal: Ownership Panel Says Smulyan Pact First Issue." *Herald,* January 25, 1992.

Carby, Hazel V. "On the Threshold of Woman's Era: Lynching, Empire, and Sexuality in Black Feminist Theory." In Henry Louis Gates, Jr., ed., *"Race," Writing, and Difference,* pp. 301-16. Chicago: University of Chicago Press, 1986.

Davis, Angela Y. "Rape, Racism and the Myth of the Black Rapist." In *Women, Race and Class,* pp. 172-201. New York: Vintage, 1983.

Deming, Caren J. "Miscegenation in Popular Western History and Fiction." In Helen Winter Stauffer and Susan J. Rosowski, eds., *Women and Western American Literature,* pp. 90-99. Troy, N.Y.: Whitston, 1982.

Devroy, Ann. "America's First Image of a Stricken President Bush: George Bush's Health Problems on His Visit to Japan." *Washington Post,* January 9, 1992, p. A1.

Dolson, Frank. "Give Nintendo Owner a Shot in Seattle." *Philadelphia Inquirer,* January 27, 1992, p. C10.

Gilman, Sander L. "Black Bodies, White Bodies: Toward an Iconography of Female Sexuality in Late Nineteenth-Century Art, Medicine, and Literature." In Henry Louis Gates, Jr., ed., *"Race," Writing, and Difference,* pp. 223-61. Chicago: University of Chicago Press, 1986.

Ivanovich, David. "Anti-Japanese Feelings Erupt into Fury of Americanism." *Houston Chronicle,* January 24, 1992, p. A1.

Jehl, Douglas. "Japanese Remarks Upset Bush: United States Trade Talks with Japan, Criticism of the American Worker." *Los Angeles Times,* January 23, 1992, p. A4.

Judd, Ron. "Seattle Leaders Spurn Smulyan." *Seattle Times,* February 6, 1992, pp. B1-B2.

Kaul, Donald. "Revenge on Japanese! Sell 'em Mariners!" *Anchorage Daily News,* February 8, 1992.

Keen, Sam. *Faces of the Enemy: Reflections of the Hostile Imagination.* San Francisco: Harper and Row, 1986.

Kenney, Ted. "Nintendo's Game Plan: Are There Strings Attached to the Mariners Deal?" *Eastside Week,* February 5, 1992, pp. 9-11.

Kindred, Dave. "Baseball Flunks Its Course in Foreign Affairs." *Sporting News,* February 10, 1992, p. 6.

Lincicome, Bernie. "Baseball's Being Merciful to Japan." *Chicago Tribune,* February 4, 1992, pp. 1-2.

"Mariner Deal Gets Boost from Gardner: The Governor Strikes Out at Critics of the Purchase Plan, Saying It Has Regional Support," *Olympian,* January 30, 1992.

McEwen, Tom. "Seattle Playing a Serious Game with Nintendo." *Tampa Tribune,* January 24, 1992, p. 1.

Reaves, Joey. "Bid to Buy Ballclub Draws the Boo-birds." *Chicago Tribune,* January 25, 1992, pp. 1, 8.

Reid, T. R. "Tokyo Leader: U.S. Is 'Japan's Subcontractor.'" *Washington Post,* January 21, 1992, p. A1.

"Spell Baseball H-y-p-o-c-r-i-t-e." *Bellingham Herald,* January 28, 1992.

Varyu, Don. "Playing the Race Card: Can Seattle Beat Baseball's Xenophobia?" *Eastside Week,* January 29, 1992.

5 . . . *Mike Tyson and the Perils of Discursive Constraints: Boxing, Race, and the Assumption of Guilt*

And anger is what drives a boxing champion. . . . That's an emotion that comes from the gut of every successful fighter, and he can't displace that. He cannot rid himself of that any more than he can rid himself of the color of his skin or the way he looks.

— Gerry Spence

Gerry Spence, the Wyoming trial lawyer who defended Imelda Marcos and represented the family of Karen Silkwood, made the above observation in the context of a daily newspaper's attempt to understand the different outcomes of the prosecutions of Mike Tyson and William Kennedy Smith. His claim is revealing in more ways than one: it not only serves as a crystallization of claims I will make regarding the discourse surrounding the Tyson trial in specific, but it also serves as a representation of the ways cultural discourses and mass-mediated representations work to discipline subjects to fit within the constraints of dominant cultural ideology. While I do not, indeed cannot, presume to know the ultimate guilt or innocence of Tyson and am attempting neither to exonerate nor to condemn him, I will argue that the multiple rhetorical positions provided for, and occupied by, Mike Tyson as an African American man in general, and as a boxer who rose from poverty specifically, worked to position him as likely to be guilty of rape, even prior to the public airing of the charges of this particular case. Moreover, during the trial itself, Tyson's representation in dominant mass-media reports as an African American boxer, as well as the persistent description of the trial through the metaphor of a prizefight, worked to encourage the assumption of Tyson's guilt and, perhaps more important, to reify those very assumptions.

While there is truth to Spence's claim to the degree that one cannot easily change the color of skin or other physical features, a more important point that Spence does not touch upon is that the subject position a person embodies as a result of the cultural discourses of such factors as skin color and body shape is itself fairly resistant to change, malleable only over long periods of time—only in particular historical moments does it seem objective, reified, or structured. Indeed, while Spence errs theoretically in essentializing boxers as driven by anger, the fact that such a claim can be made without provoking an astonished reaction (or any reaction at all) from readers reveals its social materiality, its reification, within the confines of our culture. Spence's claims, along with multitudes of others, create a discursive situation in which Tyson, as boxer, as African American, and as himself, is constructed rhetorically as naturally angry, persistently dangerous to all who enter his domain.[1]

This study is personally compelling because my own life history precludes me from pleading innocent to the same faults of which I am accusing cultural discourses as a whole. In 1975, for my twelfth birthday, I received a copy of Muhammad Ali's autobiography, *The Greatest*. In the wake of his defeat of George Foreman the previous year, Ali had captured my imagination and my heart. For the first time, I had a hero located not in pop music but in athletics, and while I recognized this, I did not recognize the perhaps more dramatic shift of myself as a white child from a small town in North Carolina not only taking on a black athlete as a hero but taking on Ali specifically, and what he had come to represent, as a hero. The defenses I had to make of Ali against rather naive racist attacks provided me, in addition to something of a learning experience, many moments of pride for my "lack of racism" in having chosen such a hero. It is not surprising, then, that I never recognized the problematic nature of my reading of *The Greatest*. Reading in the living room of my parents' house, I was particularly taken by Ali's recounting of his visit to a prostitute during a Golden Gloves contest (91–107). Taken by a fellow boxer, Ali claims to have been completely confused by the entire process, from the "pricing strategies," to the terminology, to the sexual act itself. As I read the passage and imagined my own future sexual encounters, I didn't believe a word of what Ali had to say about this particular experience. What he said, I thought, he said in order to please the Nation of Islam. While I could not articulate the basis of my disbelief (and indeed saw no reason to investigate that disbelief), it emerged from my understanding of Ali as not only a boxer but a black boxer, a black boxer who proudly claimed his blackness. When I defended Ali to my friends, I was defending the sexual prowess, the primitivism, that he wore so loudly. His denial of sexual know-how couldn't possibly be true; it was part and parcel of what my hero worship was built upon, part and parcel of what I was defending.

The story of my worship of Ali and the public conviction of Mike Tyson meet in culture, in particular in the dominant discourses that offer definitions of the African American boxer, the African American athlete. In that I am assuming that discourse has a materiality within culture, my investigation of the discourse surrounding the Tyson trial concerns the representation of boxers and African Americans in general, Mike Tyson in specific, and of the trial as a boxing match—each of which worked to create a specific discursive/subject position that virtually precluded his innocence.

I should be clear that my focus will not be on Desiree Washington, the rape victim, although I will comment on her representation as it pertains to Tyson. Jointly, I should emphasize that this is a study of dominant cultural representations rather than "marginal ones," a study of complicit representations rather than resistant ones, a study of cultural discourse rather than its reception. However, even a surface investigation of the dominant public address surrounding the case makes it quite evident that Washington's representation was/is itself heavily imbued in a cultural mix that limited how she could be read. That is, in that Washington was positioned as the victim of rape, her representation removed her from the stereotypical representation of the African American female. As the case unfolded, Washington was transformed from an anonymous African American "alleged" rape victim to, through the intermingling of cultural signs, an "almost white" female, victim of rape at the hands of the black athlete.[2]

BRICKS, MORTAR, ENERGY

In order to make my assumptions clear, I want to begin by first discussing the force of rhetoric in history, the ways in which cultural discourses, once taking on a material presence, constrain the subjects who "take on," or are posited within, those particular positions. What does one mean when one speaks of the "materiality" of culture? In short, my assumption, certainly a common one, is that rhetoric is an extraordinarily powerful and historical basis through which cultures and "individuals" come to know and understand themselves. In noting that culture "is the very material of our daily lives, the bricks and mortar of our most commonplace understandings," Paul Willis provides a definition of culture that works in a double-edged fashion. While culture is positive in the sense that life cannot be experienced without the bricks and mortar that give it shape and substance, it is also negative, or constraining, in that bricks and mortar have a discursive materiality that privileges existing discourses, existing ideology. As discourses and definitions become generally accepted within culture, they become assumed and hence act as "sedimented practices." They must exist if humans are to have consciousness of themselves and the world around them. On the other hand, the human desire for stability and the ability to understand the world in which they are located gives such discourses a "solidified" nature in which change and transition are difficult.

If culture is the bricks and mortar of everyday understandings, rhetoric is the "energy" of culture. That is, just as energy in the material world represents the "work" of material objects, rhetoric is that which is the energy of the symbolic or cultural world.[3] The implications of this reading of rhetoric and culture are twofold. First, rhetoric and culture cannot be studied separately. When we study the movement or "work" of bricks and mortar, we necessarily investigate the bricks and mortar themselves. When we investigate culture, we are necessarily making comment on the ways culture works to gain acceptance.

Secondly, just as with energy in the material world, rhetoric is easiest to see, and is hence less dangerous, when it is most exposed. It is at its most dangerous when we do not know it is there. If we watch a fundamentalist preacher on television, his energy, his rhetoric, is most exposed, and we know to stay away from it. However, in sincere conversations with family members and best friends, we are less likely to see rhetoric exposed and are more likely to be persuaded. In the Tyson case, cultural discourses come in a wide variety of strengths, a wide variety of exposures, from the explicit calls of his defense attorneys that we attend to the size of his penis and his reputation as a womanizer, to the more subtle, and hence more effective, parallels of the court case to a boxing event and the placement of Tyson into a lineage of other boxers, many of whom were convicted of various crimes. The task here is to magnify the subtle energy of the cultural bricks and mortar of everyday assumptions.

In some sense, this study emerges in the interstices of Foucault's archaeological and genealogical methods. In Foucault's explication of his archaeological method, *The Archaeology of Knowledge,* he claims that his studies "belong to that field in which the questions of the human being, consciousness, origin, and the subject emerge, intersect, mingle, and separate off" (16). He also promises to accept the historical groupings of discourse already suggested by historians only long enough to "subject them at once to interrogation; to break them up and then to see whether they can be legitimately reformed; or whether other groupings should be made" (26).

Foucault is arguing in effect that the discourse and knowledge that can be articulated at any given time and place are open to human subjects only to the degree that social conventions and "discursive rules" allow. As a result, we need only look at what has actually been said—statements, words in action, relations among statements, and the knowledge that is created within these relations—not at the authors or the intent of the authors' production, in order to understand the contours of subject positions and actions available to actors within a given culture (26–30; see also "What Is an Author?"). Such assumptions tie back into an understanding of discourse as the bricks and

mortal of culture. While knowledge is relative to different discursive formations, it nonetheless constrains each of us within the layered and shifting
rules of our culture. Hence, for example, a homosexual cannot simply deny
the discursive space created for him/her and move to a less constraining one.
The weight of the subject position, as embedded in the reactions of others
to homosexuality and to the particular homosexual individual, precludes this.

The task of those taking on such assumptions is to unearth the rules by
which different objects are created and various subjects constituted in different cultural formations. A critic performs this task by asking a series of
questions directed toward understanding a culture's discursive rules and the
relations of knowledge and power (*Archaeology* 41–44). A project of this
nature, then, traces out the changes in discourse and cultural rules over
lengthy periods of time. Such histories force their audiences to reflect on the
rules and constraints faced by their own culture as well as providing them
with an understanding of past discourses.

The axiom for this stance is "X is as X does"—an axiom succinctly
suggesting that if we are to understand the meaning of, for example, "boxer"
in a given historic juncture, we must know how the term is enacted, embodied, and given meaning within public discursive boundaries. We cannot
understand the enacted meaning of the term by looking only at what a
sociologist of sports means when she or he utilizes it unless or until s/he has
taken her or his discourse into the public forum, staking a claim in the
ideological struggle over its meanings.

My analysis is based on such assumptions about discourse but differs in
that rather than a project that traces out the "rules" of cultural discourse
diachronically, over long periods of time, what I want to do here is engage in
a more limited "snapshot" of dominant cultural rules, a synchronic archaeology.[4] If we parallel a Foucauldian archaeology to a documentary, say, of a foot
race, then this analysis would be a frame from that documentary. While the
documentary would be capable of showing the individuals changing their
relative positions in the race, changes in scenery, changes in the appearance of
individual racers, and so forth, a snapshot will reveal the race as it is at one
specific temporal and spatial point. Moreover, in this case, it is only a snapshot
of one particular aspect of culture—dominant culture. While it does not show
how the positions of the racers or the scenery changes, it does illustrate the
racers' current relations to one another, their current individual dispositions,
and the current context of the race. In effect, I am making the assumptions
of the archaeologist but focusing on situations and events that are temporally
local, occurring in the present in a relatively short period of time.

In such an analysis, I attempt to enlighten the general contours of a
particular topic by outlining the relations of different subjects to one another,

the position of a topic within the interstices of race, gender, and so forth. While a snapshot perspective cannot provide a view of how a particular subject changes as an object of discourse over time, it does allow a frozen picture of the scene at a particular historic juncture and thereby allows insights into the general structure of knowledge at that juncture. In the case of the Mike Tyson trial, we receive a more cogent understanding of how Tyson was positioned rhetorically as "Mike Tyson," as a boxer, and as an African American. We are provided with a more insightful glance at how a vote of not guilty would have been difficult to conceive of on the dominant public level, even had there not been a trial. The discursive rules uncovered reveal it to be entirely feasible, indeed probable, that an African American boxer, especially Mike Tyson, would have committed this act. While the particular discourses viewed in this snapshot may not have been read by the jury at his trial, they would ring true to that jury in that their publication within our culture reveals their common acceptance, the low voltage of their rhetoric.

MIKE TYSON: BOXING AND THE MAN-BEAST-MACHINE

While I of course have no knowledge of the absolute guilt or innocence of Mike Tyson or of the validity of the jury's verdict, I am assuming that members of the jury, like all members of culture, understand Tyson by virtue of his multiple cultural representations—"Tyson" emerges for each of us in the accumulation of discourses concerning African American men, boxers, sports figures, and so on, as well as in representations of Mike Tyson as an individual. To the degree that such discourses and representations work on the basis of cultural familiarity with their stereotypes, it is irrelevant that jurors were kept away from these specific representations. That is, the representations of Tyson were ones that had to "ring true" to the general public if they were to be accepted; to the degree that jurors are participants in culture, the representations of Tyson that I am investigating here are ones that were already acceptable to, and expected by, members of the jury. Hence, when Sonja Steptoe criticized Tyson's original defense lawyer for characterizing Tyson as a naturally brutal animal, she was right to do so ("Fallen Champ"). However, this characterization rang true only to the degree that his blackness and his position as an athlete already dictated this meaning culturally.

The representations of Tyson are also ripe for study because they work to reify the problematic stereotypes of African American men and boxers in general as the trial, and its characterizations, played out in the drama of mass-mediated reports. As I will illustrate, the representation of Tyson worked on a number of axes, most dealing with the relationship of boxing and boxers to particular forms of behavior. Ultimately, these representations culminated in the "bending in" of the metaphors of the trial onto itself—when the trial metaphorically becomes a boxing match, Tyson is imbued with the cultural characteristics of the boxer, and his persona collapses under the weight of past discourses, the energy of culture.

Tyson, Boxing, and the Predatory Instinct

Reports before, during, and after the trial persistently focused on Tyson's skill as a boxer and his inherent instincts as a "pure" fighter, a predator. Comments in the dominant media during the trial constructed an especially menacing fighter who utilized the same style of deception in the ring as he did in his interactions with women in general and Desiree Washington in particular. For example, in August 1991, when Tyson was first accused of rape, Richard Corliss provided the following description and commentary about him in *Time:*

> Tyson may plead that he was only doing what is expected of a top dog in a vicious sport. A fighter's business, which may also be his pleasure, is hurting people; because it is the public's pleasure too, he is paid for his work. It would be nice if this *walking keg of testosterone* believed that what he does is just a job, a dispassionate display of skill, and that his ferocious aggression is merely an attitude to be shucked along with his mouthpiece after the final bell. Nice, but not likely. ("Tragedy" 67; emphasis mine)

Corliss goes on to note that "a killing machine knows no scruples" (67). Tyson is represented not only as a fighter, but as a person unable to behave in any but an animalistic fashion both in and out of the ring. Not only is he the "top dog," but he is "evil incarnate" with "ferocious aggression" (Leerhsen and Blum 63). Not only is he unable to control his aggression, but he is also mechanistic, a killing machine that cannot be unplugged. Indeed, Tyson has no heart; he punishes without guilt, and this predatory instinct has links to his idea of romantic relationships: "This is atavistic manhood, stripped of all weapons but fists, guile and will. A man-beast-machine: hunter, warrior, conqueror, terminator. Even lover. . . . A fight with Tyson at his physical and emotional peak is like a brisk courtship that ends in slaughter" (Corliss, "In Judgment" 77). In Barbara Kopple's documentary about Tyson, sportswriter Robert Lipsyte noted that Tyson was an "American pitbull," trained to be a killer in the ring ("Fallen Champ"). The Mike Tyson that emerges from this axis works to create and/or reinforce the assumption that Tyson's behavior, based on race, class, and career, is likely to lead to dangerous and violent relationships.

Further, Tyson's fighting style, as described in *U.S. News and World Report's* pre-trial coverage and elsewhere, is linked with his interpersonal interactions—his fighting style and his actions in daily life merge. Tyson is observed noting that he uses his fists with "murderous intentions," wishing he had "driven Jesse Ferguson's nose back into his brain." He is a "primitive without stockings" who noted of his upcoming fight with Razor Ruddock, "If he doesn't die, it doesn't count" (Callahan 53). In a concurrent televised interview with Ruddock, Tyson promised to "make [Ruddock] into my girlfriend," prompting Joyce Carol Oates to note in *Newsweek* that his claim is the "boast of the rapist" (61).

One of the most fascinating links of Tyson's boxing style to the predatory instinct, both within the trial and in the larger public domain, was that posited by J. Gregory Garrison, the special prosecutor for Indiana in the rape case. Garrison, in an attempt to parallel Tyson's boxing style in the ring with that of his interactions outside the ring, asked Tyson to describe his boxing style while on the witness stand. The *Indianapolis Star* reported that Tyson noted that a boxer needs to be elusive, that "an opponent shouldn't see a punch coming" (Albert, "Boxer"). In his closing arguments, Garrison instructed the jury to "remember what he does when he want to deceive—move in" (Albert, "State"). After Tyson's conviction, Garrison again noted the similarity between Tyson's style in and out of the ring by asserting that Tyson used deception to gain an advantage, then went straight ahead at his opponent: "Tyson is a *predatory person.* He stalks his opponent. *Like a wild creature,* he senses an opening and goes for it" (Gelarden, "Low Key"; emphasis mine). Again, Tyson as predator is uncontrollable, working with an instinct that he cannot himself control or necessarily understand.

Follow-up stories after the trial (during the appeals process) and reports on Tyson's early days in prison served to maintain the link between boxing and predatory/violent instincts. Hence, Tyson was highlighted as noting during the sentencing phase of the trial, "I didn't hurt anyone—no black eyes, no broken ribs. When I'm in the ring, I break their ribs; I break their jaws. To me, that's hurting someone" (Berkow, "It Seems" B13). Here, Tyson is unable to envision injury or pain in any form outside of physical violence. Imprisoned, Tyson was reported to be unable to control his violent instincts. The *New York Post* reported that while Tyson was imprisoned at the Indiana Youth Center, a guard told him to "shut up," and Tyson responded by threatening to "whup the guard" and his eight colleagues (McDarrah and Anthony). Even though he was imprisoned, his move to destruction, violence, and the predatory instinct cannot be squelched.

Tyson, Boxing, and the Inarticulate and Impoverished Athlete

In an attempt to anticipate the defense's tactics in the trial, the *Indianapolis Star* asked Roy Black, William Kennedy Smith's defense lawyer, to delineate the advantages and disadvantages of having Tyson testify at the rape trial. After noting that testimony from the defendant is always a risky tactic, Black asserted that this was especially true in the case of Tyson, a man whose physical appearance would serve only to emphasize his career as a boxer and his overall persona, that of a "clearly not well-educated, well-spoken person" (Albert, "Formidable"). One of the recurring themes of the trial and the media coverage of the trial hinged on the link between Tyson as a boxer and Tyson as an uneducated brute. "Fallen Champ," the documentary of Tyson's life, repeatedly asserts that, while "tough physically," Tyson was easily duped, easily misled. Not only was he easily misled by classmates early in his career, but as an adult he was manipulated in his relationships with Robin Givens and later with Don King.[5]

In addition to being represented as inarticulate and unintelligent, Tyson is repeatedly positioned as having risen from poverty, and it is this dual link between impoverishment and his inability to speak articulately that marks him in direct opposition to Desiree Washington. In "Fallen Champ," former neighbors of the young Tyson observe that he grew up in impoverished surroundings with a mother on welfare, that he was always so dirty from playing in filth and abandoned buildings that he was called "Dirty Mike," and that his petty thievery and robbery landed him in the Spofford Youth Center and Tryon Youth Camp. On the other hand, in the film and in virtually all other representations, Desiree Washington is primarily and notably a wide-eyed college student, had visited Russia on an O'Brien scholarship, and had a loving family complete with a father who repeatedly spoke of his "little girl" ("Fallen Champ"). In multiple instances, we are confronted with the specter of Tyson, the ex-champion, "high school dropout raised in Brooklyn, NY" (Albert, "Remorseless"), being squared off with Washington, the "Sunday school teacher and model student" ("Mike Tyson Convicted" 18; Stepp), the sophomore (or junior) from Providence College in Rhode Island (Albert, "Appeal Rests"; Albert, "Crude"; Albert, "Prison or Not"; Albert, "State"; Albert, "Tyson to Fight"; Albert, "With Tyson"; Steptoe 92). It is in the contrast of Tyson and Washington, black athlete vs. naive college student, that the representation of Tyson has its greatest strength.

It should not go without comment that while representations of Tyson's background position him as the stereotypical African American athlete who rises out of the poverty and trials of a single-parent welfare background, the representations of Washington continually move her in a different direction. In "Fallen Champ," the dirty parks and abandoned buildings of Tyson's youth are visually set off against literal picket fences in the yards that make up Washington's hometown. "Fallen Champ" introduces viewers to Washington through interviews with two of her high school friends, both white, and then with a peek into her high school annual. As the camera scans the page of the yearbook, we find Washington's picture positioned between two Caucasian classmates and under a group shot of four more of her classmates, all Caucasian. In two more pictures from the annual, she stands playfully next to yet two more white classmates. Indeed, save the shots of her attendance at the "Miss Black America" contest, one cannot help but think of her growing up upper-middle-class in an almost exclusively white neighborhood with an almost exclusively white set of classmates.

In a discussion of race and gender in contemporary film, bell hooks notes the following of white racist/sexist stereotypes in mass-media representations: "Scratch the surface of any black woman's sexuality and you find a 'ho'— someone who is sexually available, apparently indiscriminate, who is incapable of commitment, someone who is likely to seduce and betray" (57). While this stereotype was certainly used by some defenders of Tyson and by his legal defense, dominant media representations of Washington counterposed this stereotype, configuring her rhetorically in a role that made Tyson's crime appear more heinous in the terms of dominant culture. That is, on one level, because of the history of cultural discourse about race and social status, these representations served to emphasize the position of Tyson as impoverished and inarticulate and of Washington as a child of American values, and this configuration raises the stakes of the trial. No longer do we have a rape case involving two stereotypical African Americans, but instead we have something much different—the rape of a child of privilege by the primitive black man.

Tyson, Boxing, and Sexual Prowess

Sonja Steptoe noted of the Tyson defense in *Sports Illustrated* that Tyson was constructed by his own defense team as "your worst nightmare—a vulgar, socially inept, sex-obsessed black athlete" (92). Tyson's defense, she remarked, less than subtly affixed him with the warning tag: "Beware—Dangerous Sexual Animal" (92). Tied together with the images of the inarticulate predator, Tyson fits comfortably in the cultural stereotype of the sexually insatiable black with an appetite that demands attention at any cost. The influence of these representations is ensured to the degree that both Tyson and African Americans in general have been preconstructed in such a fashion. While Tyson is constructed within the myth of the black male, this is strengthened by his placement as a boxer. Hence, defense attorney Vincent J. Fuller is reported to have argued during the case that "it was regrettable that Tyson never learned how to treat women and didn't interact with them when he was growing up because 'his whole world was boxing'" (Albert, "Remorseless"). In *Jet,* World Boxing Association president Elias Cordova asserted that the case should act as an example to other professional athletes, noting that this "isn't the first time this has happened to a professional boxer" ("Mike Tyson Sentenced" 51-52; see also Boyer).

Tyson's treatment of women itself is tied to his role as a boxer, again suggesting guilt in the rape charge. His reportedly volatile relationship with former spouse Robin Givens was predictably highlighted throughout the portrayals of the case, and these reports included depictions of numerous run-ins with police officers called out for domestic disputes between Tyson and Givens (Ziner). More to the point, former Tyson confidant Jose Torres asserted in *U.S. News and World Report* that Tyson once bragged that "the best punch I ever threw" was one thrown at Givens, and that "I like to hurt women when I make love to them. I like to hear them scream and see them bleed. It gives me pleasure" (Callahan 53). More blatantly, *Time* reported that "for [Tyson], romance is boxing with the gloves off" (Corliss, "In Judgment" 77).

As if in cahoots with the mediated constructions of Tyson, the defense's case, structured by attorney Vincent Fuller, portrayed Tyson "as a crude-man-nered punk who paws, fondles and gropes every woman he sees" (Treen and Shaw 36). Richard Corliss noted in *Time* that, as the "most dangerous man in sport," Tyson is said to number among his conquests "countless women" ("The Bad" 25). Finally, when lawyer Alan M. Dershowitz attempted to mount an appeal for Tyson, he swore that Tyson could be allowed to remain out of prison during the appeal procedure, as Dershowitz would personally vow to keep him away from women, Tyson's sexual prowess to be held in check by a more collected and rational (white) male (Shipp A10).

Playing into the myths of the black male and the black athlete, it becomes only logical that Tyson is guilty. Again, the crime is seen as all the more unforgivable once we consider the repositioning of Desiree Washington as something other than the stereotypical black. Washington, given the subject position of the college student and Sunday school teacher, is able to effectively shed the myths of the stereotype of the promiscuous African American female and is enabled to become the sexually naive and innocent debutante, whitened to such a degree that Tyson's inevitable rape is both more predict-able and all the more unforgiving.

The Boxing Tradition, the Boxing Lineage

Utilizing a theme sprinkled throughout the discourse concerning the trial, Joyce Carol Oates notes that boxing and "women's rights" are symbolically opposed because "boxing is the most aggressively masculine sport, the very soul of war in microcosm. . . . Its fundamentally murderous intent is not obscured by the pursuit of balls or pucks" (60). Oates goes on to note that boxing "imitates our early ancestors' rite of bloody sacrifice and redemption" and encourages behaviors that would outside the ring be considered aggravated assault or manslaughter (60). Boxing, in Oates's discourse and that of most of those who discuss its tradition in the context of the Tyson trial, is the model par excellence of violence, masculinity, and immorality. As African Americans have clearly been the most praised and celebrated of boxing participants in contemporary American culture, the discourse by necessity is linked to them. While boxing may have been a "sweet science" when its champions were Dempsey, Tunney, and the anomalous African American such as Joe Louis or Sugar Ray Robinson, it is a "sacrificial rite" when its champions are Jack Johnson, Sonny Liston, and Mike Tyson. Hence, boxing, a sport that has been constructed in various fashions, coheres during the trial as the most brutal of sports, its participants the most brutal of men, and Tyson perhaps the most brutal of all.

In his attempt to discuss the upcoming Tyson trial, Richard Corliss quotes A. J. Liebling's classic boxing text *The Sweet Science* to note that boxers with exemplary moral quality are bores: "The good guys get married. The bad guys get into jams" ("Tragedy" 67). Corliss is not alone in emphasizing repeatedly that boxers are infamously immoral: they are not expected to be "choir boys" (Gelarden, "Lawyer"); they have "made their share of appearances in courtrooms" (Nack 46); and they often end up behind bars (Anderson, "The Humiliation"). Boxers are positioned with the expectation of immoral behavior, of nonexemplary citizenship.

One often finds a roll call of boxers and their transgressions in accounts of the Tyson trial. A narrative telling of the history of boxing that places Tyson at the end of a history of convicted drug abusers and murderers dresses him in the clothes of the convict. For example, as Dave Anderson noted in the *New York Times:*

> More than other sports, boxing has a long rap sheet. Sonny Liston did time before winning the heavyweight title. Rubin (Hurricane) Carter did nearly 20 years before a Federal Judge overturned his triple murder conviction. Tony Ayala is in Rahway for rape. James Scott is in Trenton for violating parole on an armed robbery conviction. As a teen-ager, Frankie De Paula was in a reformatory, just as Tyson was before he found boxing. ("The Humiliation"; see also Berger)

In a strikingly similar line of reasoning, and one that ties Tyson directly into the narrative sequence, Playthell Benjamin asserted in the *Village Voice* that while one can point to boxers who would "still have been solid citizens" had they not been boxers, "there is another type of fighter who is basically a sadist with a criminal disposition. Among these guys are Sonny Liston, Carlos Monzon, Dwight Muhammad Qawi, James Scott, Big Art Tucker, and Tony

Ayala—and, based on his own testimony, 'Iron Mike' Tyson" (103). Again, "Fallen Champ," the documentary, pointedly identifies the criminal "element" of Tyson's life by placing him in the ghetto, highlighting his career as a thief through the testimony of his former cohorts, and by reviewing his career in reform school for committing crimes that "would have counted as felonies" had he been over sixteen. Like a campaign film for a political office that sets the candidate in the lineage of past political heroes and provides the assumption that the candidate will assume the mantle, such testimony places Tyson at the end of the line as the latest in a line of "sadists with criminal dispositions."

The specter of Sonny Liston in particular haunts discussions of Tyson during the trial. It is a specter that reifies the criminal nature of the boxer while working to solidify Tyson's guilt. Hence, a *U.S. News and World Report* discussion of the trial and the reasons why a heavyweight champion might have committed such an act began with a quotation from Sonny Liston asserting, "Not that many archbishops become world champion" (Callahan 52). In Joyce Carol Oates's *Newsweek* account of the trial, she noted that

> Tyson seems to have styled himself at least partly on the model of Charles (Sonny) Liston, the "baddest of the bad" black heavyweights. Liston had numerous arrests to his credit and served time in prison; he had the air, not entirely contrived, of a psychopath; he was always friendly with racketeers, and died of a drug overdose that may in fact have been murder. (61)

Tied to Liston, Tyson takes on the full persona of the "black thug"; not only guilty of the rape with which he is charged, then, Tyson becomes a psychopath, friendly with racketeers, a drug abuser. In effect, Tyson not only is working against a prosecution that argues toward his guilt, but he is also in a losing battle against an entire set of cultural discourses that frame him with the characteristics of the "black heavyweight champion." It is with great difficulty that he might throw off the materiality of these characterizations. Again, the dialects of such constructions with the cultural discourses at large ensures that boxers, and by association and cultural precedent African Americans, are identifiable by their immorality and violent nature. Hence, Tyson is faced with the specific legal charges against him as well as the charges brought on by a miasma of cultural stereotypes.

Trial as Prizefight

With headlines reading "With Tyson Jury Selected, the Sparring Can Now Begin" (Albert), "Lawyers to Their Corners: Former Heavyweight Champion Mike Tyson Faces the Most Crucial Fight of His Young Life" (Callahan),

"Experts Say Jurors' Doubts Won't TKO Tyson Conviction" (Albert), and "Low-Key Garrison in Spotlight after Tyson KO" (Gelarden), readers are presented with the trial through the metaphor of a fight and hence find further emphasized Tyson's position as a heavyweight fighter, reifying the attributes associated with fighters. That is, while the metaphor may have provided the prosecution and the defense different perceived strengths with the public readership, it also, combined with discourses questioning the feasibility of staging Tyson's championship bout with Evander Holyfield despite the trial, yet again reifies the constructed personality traits of Tyson as an African American boxer (Glauber). Moreover, in that many of the articles about the trial appeared in the sports section of newspapers and during the sports portion of news broadcasts, the case itself was positioned as a sports event.[6]

The metaphor of boxing was pervasive. During the booking proceedings, for example, the *Baltimore Sun* reported that "the hearing . . . lasted one minute longer than a fight round" (Glauber). *Newsweek*'s Charles Leerhsen and Peter Blum made the connection between the trial and a fight more overtly in noting that "Tyson's lawyers thus will have to spar and parry, and not brawl their way through the case. It's one approach that has never suited their client's style" (63). Moreover, the entire scenario of the trial was given in "blow by blow" terms; the lawyers and principals, for instance, were introduced in terms more befitting the opening of a championship bout: "In this corner, weighing . . ." (Callahan 52). Such discourse situated Tyson not as a man accused of rape, but as more specifically a boxer accused of rape—a boxer already positioned within the tradition of Sonny Liston—and hence far less likely to be viewed as innocent until proven guilty.

After the guilty verdict was read, the description of the trial as a fight persisted, with Tyson squaring off against and ultimately being defeated by a number of "great white hopes," including Superior Court judge Patricia Gifford, prosecutor J. Gregory Garrison, and the redrawn Desiree Washington. Hence, the *Indianapolis Star* noted that J. Gregory Garrison "whipped the former world heavyweight boxing champion," putting Tyson "down for the count" (Gelarden, "Low-Key"). A *People* essay titled "Desiree Washington—She KO'd Iron Mike but Remains More Victim Than Victor" claimed that "with her unwavering accusations, the shy former beauty queen courageously toppled the ex-heavyweight champion, doing in an Indianapolis courtroom what few could do in the ring" (90). His opponent was not just the opposing law team or Washington, however. As *Jet* described the sentencing procedure: "Boxer Mike Tyson never liked to leave decisions in the hands of judges, preferring instead to settle matters with a knockout. But Indiana Superior Court Judge Patricia Gifford delivered a knockout blow to Tyson, sentencing him to six years in prison for raping a teen-age beauty queen in Indianapolis last July" ("Mike Tyson Sentenced" 16). The conviction left Tyson with the option of awaiting his appeal, what the *Indianapolis Star* referred to as his "second round" (Gelarden and Albert). Finally, Ira Berkow noted in the *New York Times* that while Tyson may be accustomed to winning in the ring, the reason for his difficulty in this case was that it was indeed taking place not in a boxing ring but in an appeals court ("It Seems" B13). As a boxer, Tyson achieves his sole successes in the ring. The trial itself, then, is represented in such a way that it is consistent with the rest of the coverage of the case. Tyson, the immoral and inarticulate African American athlete, finds himself in a boxing match with that rare enemy he cannot defeat, the system of justice. Against the virtues of "shy Sunday school teachers," the prowess of the man-beast-machine is in a problematic position.

The Men Who Delivered Him: Tyson's "Release"

On March 25, 1995, after three years of imprisonment, numerous unsuccessful appeals, and a refusal to admit to, and apologize for, the rape, Mike Tyson was released from prison. As the conditions of his probation were structured around full-time employment, he returned to a career in professional boxing. While I had left an earlier draft of this essay in a pessimistic mood nearly two years ago, it was with some optimism that I began to investigate the discourse surrounding Tyson's release. If I come away with any particular thought as a result of the continuation of this drama, however, it is that Tyson's release from prison, and the discourse surrounding that release, serve as a powerful testament to the strength and materiality of the cultural prison. Tyson steps through the bars of the Indiana Youth Center in Plainfield and into the symbolic bars of cultural discourse, a discourse none too favorable to his position within culture, and that of many others who fall along the same lines of class and race. While imprisonment may rehabilitate and influence some "individuals," the cultural prison itself remains relatively untarnished. Returning to boxing, Tyson remains the man-beast-machine, hunter-boxer-warrior—perhaps he returns even more so.

The news concerning Tyson's release was highlighted by three factors: his conversion to Islam, the recovery of professional boxing, and the battle for control over Tyson's career and soul. In each case, Tyson is reinscribed as the warrior African American athlete. First, and as numerous reports note, Tyson, under the direction of a local junior high school teacher named Muhammad Siddeeq, had converted, at least in part, to Islam (Wulf 56). Indeed, upon his release, Tyson immediately visited a local Indiana mosque with a number of other Muslims, including Siddeeq and Muhammad Ali. As the story was told and retold in accounts of his release, I found myself wondering, and asking of others, "What type of Muslim is Tyson? Has he joined the Nation of Islam or a more traditional form of Islam? Does the attendance of Ali, who is not a member of the Nation of Islam, signify a link with more traditional Islam?" This question, and the lack of specificity in the answer, seems to me significant. The degree to which a large percentage of the public holds an image of "black Muslims" as black nationalists, linked to the popular cultural image of Minister Farrakhan, is the degree to which this becomes a vital question in the ongoing struggle for, and representation of, Mike Tyson. Since the Nation of Islam has been revived so recently in popular media reports as a result of Spike Lee's *Malcolm X,* death threats against Minister Farrakhan, and a very real growth in membership, the assumption may well lie toward Tyson's conversion to the Nation of Islam, regardless of the actual direction of his conversion and orientation. Tyson, as Black Muslim, is an intensified version of the Tyson imprisoned to begin with—a natural warrior, "pure in the ring," "the absolute essence of competition" (Hoffer, "Up" 53).

At the time of Tyson's release, Richard Hoffer noted in *Sports Illustrated* that "the awakening will happen around the world. Boxing comes back on March 25" ("Up" 53). Centering his article on the languishment under which boxing had suffered during Mike Tyson's imprisonment, Hoffer offered Tyson up as the whole of boxing. As Tyson reemerges from prison, boxing reemerges "up from the canvas." And in this regard Hoffer was not alone; numerous commentaries equated Tyson with boxing itself, maintaining his inscription as a particular type of African American athlete. For example, Dave Anderson observed the appearance of T-shirts with Tyson staring up at the viewer, boxing gloves affixed, and red, green, and gold lettering reading "March 25, 1995," "as if yesterday's date of his release from an Indiana prison will live in history" ("Tyson Faces" S9). Similarly, another description of his release from prison claimed that "Tyson's departure at 6:15 AM, with his retinue encircling him, was reminiscent of his scenes from the ring" (Berkow, "After Three" S1). Even leaving prison, Tyson appears as boxer and boxing as Tyson—a link frozen in culture.

The most obvious and troubling characterization of Tyson, however, emerges in the discussion of the anticipation over who will "control" him. On the day of his release, numerous reporters noted the desire to see if Tyson, after having been courted by every major fight promoter in the business and after having converted to Islam, would fall back into Don King's "clutches" (Wulf 56). In a *Sports Illustrated* report, Richard Hoffer noted of Tyson's release into the hands of Don King: "Except for the white knit skullcap that Tyson wore—it reflected all the available light, and you could see him easily in the middle of the moving huddle—it seemed that he was not much changed by three years in jail. It was a gloomy and quickly arriving idea: Weren't these the same men who, more or less, delivered him here?" ("Out" 45). The irony of the statement is staggering—rather than investigating "Tyson" in order to understand how Tyson had changed, Hoffer observed that, regardless of other changes in Tyson's spiritual beliefs, his connection with King was enough to signify an obvious lack of change. One cannot help but reflect back onto Hoffer's question—"Weren't these the same men who, more or less, delivered him here?"—and answer that indeed it is the same men delivering him again to the representations of cultural discourses who, more or less, delivered him in the first place. These "men" are not Don King and company, however, but all of us who work to maintain dominant discourses through our lack of critical reflection. In placing the entire burden on association, on allowing Tyson to remain an appearance, Hoffer and others (i.e., "culture") redeliver Tyson to the very cultural norms and stereotypes from three years earlier, negating any personal change by stressing his links with King. In a particularly telling *New York Times* account of the release, Ira Berkow recounted that "as the cars pulled away from prison in the growing light of day, people shouted well-wishes after Tyson. Someone, perhaps lost, shouted, 'Free the Juice!'" ("After Three" S9). With the reinscription of Tyson as the African American athlete, it is not surprising that one well-wisher was so lost as to fit Tyson so snugly within the caricature of Simpson. It is perhaps more surprising that others did not.

And what of Desiree Washington? While she appears sporadically in the news reports about Tyson's release, it is only to recap the reason for his imprisonment, the rape of a "then 18 year old beauty pageant contestant . . . and now a fifth grade student teacher" (Berkow, "After Three" S1). Other than cursory mentions, Washington disappears from the scene of the crime. In the discourse of popular culture, Tyson is reinscribed into discourses about the African American athlete that his case, and the discourse machinery surrounding it, served only to reify. Washington, on the other hand, is symbolically silenced, disappearing from the popular cultural landscape.

This spring, I taught a course that attempted to introduce students to some of the themes of cultural studies. At one point in the semester, we watched scenes from "Fallen Champ" and discussed the representations of Tyson and Washington, and I asked the students to write up brief responses to the film. In what I see as a very fitting commentary, a student in the course noted of the discourse in the case and its configuration of the rape victim: "When the effects [of discourse] are discussed, it is usually after someone has been raped or killed—and then the individual can be blamed. And the victim/survivor is almost inevitably lost in the process. One person in our group asked at the end of our discussion whether Desiree died. Indeed."

While Washington's construction is key to understanding the representation of Tyson during the trial, she disappears in his imprisonment and thereafter. While Tyson reemerges "unchanged," realigned with "the men who . . . delivered him," Washington is absent altogether.

I want to reassert that I am not arguing that the discourse delineated here directly influenced the jury or the outcome of the trial. I would assume, in fact, that if the jury was sequestered properly and none of its members found the means to review news reports during the trial, the reports I have studied would have no direct influence on the jury. This is a cultural, not a causal, argument. By taking a snapshot of a particular type of discourse, that concerning this trial, and seeing culturally not only how Tyson is portrayed but, perhaps more important, how boxers in general are portrayed, I am attempting to underscore that the way in which Tyson is culturally portrayed significantly influences our chances of seeing him as capable of rape and other crimes. The jury and the culture at large had no need of seeing the specific discourse surrounding this trial to reach the conclusions it leads one to make. This discourse can emerge only from speakers and a culture in which they resonate, in which a discursive background has already made them acceptable.[7] In short, the construction of Tyson and of boxers in general had to have been in line with the already existing cultural discourses on these topics for at least two reasons. First, as members of the culture, the writers and reporters who discuss Tyson and boxing in general inherently share the culture's constructions of Tyson, African Americans, athletes, and boxers. Secondly, because news outlets, like all moneymaking enterprises, must satisfy their consumers, the discourse and ideas they espouse cannot stray radically from those of their consumers if a strong consumer base is to be maintained (Condit 105).

As a result of the discourse's resonance with cultural beliefs, we can assert not only that it reflects dominant cultural representations of Tyson but also that it advances, solidifies, and transforms the representations of boxers, Tyson, and African American athletes in future intracultural conversations. It is irrelevant whether the jury received the information or not because culturally, all of those who took part in the larger public conversation of Tyson's guilt engaged in the construction, deconstruction, and reconstruction of positions for Tyson, African Americans, and boxers. The conversation concerning Tyson and the trial sets the stage and drafts the scripts that frame our cultural understanding of future actors walking onto the stage.

This is not to say, however, that there is no room for movement or change; it is to say only that such change comes very slowly—the "bricks and mortar" of culture do not give way easily. As I noted above, arguments over terms provide the energy by which culture defines and redefines itself. Cultural arguments are the primary sites of ideological struggle. Hence, the discourse surrounding the trial, by highlighting our representations of boxers and of Tyson both for boxing fans and for those with very little interest in boxing, become fragments from which future texts about boxers, about Tyson, and about African American athletes are constructed. Further, because of the relatively high profile of this case, its discourse stands to be a larger than ordinary fragment for those in the present and future who attempt to understand the nature of athletes, African American athletes, boxers, African Americans, and so forth. These discourses change our perceptions, even if only slightly. Moreover, critiques of this trial, such as this one, also work as fragments, adding to the discourse surrounding the trial, challenging the ways in which discourse oppresses, and suggesting that there are other ways in which the trial might have been framed had it taken place in a different culture.

Finally, this study also points to some of the benefits of an amended archaeological/genealogical study, even if some would balk at my use of either of these terms. This study has focused on the objects of discourse, the particular constructions of African American boxers, of Tyson, and so forth, that were created as a result of power relations of our current regime of truth. Further, this study traces out the ways in which these objects of discourse work within what could be considered to be oppressive depictions of boxers, African Americans, and Tyson. Further, as I have noted, the essay was constructed with a particular goal in mind, the goal of transforming the existing relations, to force us to reevaluate our culture's current constructions of each of these objects. It is my hope that one of the outcomes of this essay will be to force us to question the potential dangers associated with essentializing a person such as Tyson according to his race and profession, especially when we allow this essentialism to arise in the context of a trial for such a heinous crime. When the judgments we make of each other, whether in the courtroom or in one-on-one interactions, are based primarily on the grounds of cultural bricks and mortar, we do an injustice to our ability to self-reflexively rethink such assumptions.

NOTES

1. As I originally wrote a draft of this paper, television stations were keeping me attuned to the latest developments in the O.J. Simpson case and subsequent trial. I could not help but wonder at the time if the same racial schemes would be at work culturally as people began to contemplate the guilt or innocence of Simpson. It seems to me reasonable at this point to observe the repositioning of O.J. Simpson from a spokesmodel, upper-class African American athlete to, almost immediately once he was suspected of murder, a black male who had grown up in ghettos, ran in gangs, and was only temporarily saved by athletics. The narrative of Simpson's life was told and retold in such a way that it fit much more smoothly with the telos

of murder. That is, while an articulate Hertz spokesperson is not a ready-made murder suspect, a ghetto-raised black athlete fits much more easily into overall cultural narratives of crime and violence.

A recent essay that looks into the Tyson trial and reaches some similar conclusions to the ones in this essay, although making fairly different arguments about culture and utilizing a title that I find problematic in its titular use of the term "rape," is Lule, "The Rape of Mike Tyson."

2. Indeed, as will be briefly hinted at in this essay, Washington was repositioned "away from" the ordinary discourses that surround African American women (i.e., promiscuity, primitivism) and was positioned instead as, arguably, "white." In addition to direct "links" to Caucasians, she was a Sunday school teacher, upper middle class, a college student, a woman naive about the ways of the world, a woman from a city of literal picket fences, a woman easily taken advantage of by the more knowledgeable and hostile Tyson.

3. I am indebted to Thomas Lessl for his suggestion of this metaphor.

4. I construct my snapshot from a review of those newspaper and magazine articles dealing specifically with the rape accusations, trial, and verdict, as indexed by *Newsbank* and *Infotrac*.

5. One cannot help but notice when watching the film that Tyson's story is one of being trusted and aided by various elder whites (e.g., Cus D'Amato, Jim Jacobs) who act as his father and brother, and then betrayed and manipulated as soon as the black presence emerges (e.g., Robin Givens, Don King).

6. It is also interesting to note that Desiree Washington's picture and stories about her were most often featured in the main sections of newspapers and in the "news" portions of news broadcasts.

7. Indeed, the reason that Desiree Washington had to be transfigured into an "atypical" African American is that the stereotypical representation would have led to an assumption of Tyson's innocence. If she had been the sexually promiscuous and exotic black female rather than the shy Sunday school teacher, beauty queen, and college sophomore, the story would have been one of primitive passion rather than pugilistic rape.

WORKS CITED

Albert, Barb. "Appeal Rests on Witnesses, 911 Call." *Indianapolis Star,* 14 Feb. 1993.
———. "Boxer Grilled on Inconsistencies." *Indianapolis Star,* 9 Feb. 1992.
———. "Crude Tyson Talk Called a Red Flag." *Indianapolis Star,* 1 Feb. 1992.
———. "Experts Say Jurors' Doubts Won't TKO Tyson Conviction." *Indianapolis Star,* 16 Dec. 1992.
———. "Formidable Lawyers Ready for Title Match." *Indianapolis Star,* 26 Jan. 1992.
———. "Prison or Not: Tyson Gets Word on Sentence Today." *Indianapolis Star,* 26 Mar. 1992.
———. "Remorseless Tyson Draws 6-Year Term." *Indianapolis Star,* 27 Mar. 1992.
———. "State vs. Michael G. Tyson." *Indianapolis Star,* 11 Feb. 1992.
———. "Tyson to Fight Appeal Denial." *Indianapolis Star,* 7 Aug. 1993.
———. "With Tyson Jury Selected, the Sparring Can Now Begin." *Indianapolis Star,* 30 Jan. 1992.
Ali, Muhammad, and Richard Durham. *The Greatest: My Own Story.* New York: Ballantine, 1975.
Anderson, Dave. "The Humiliation of No. 922335 Mike Tyson." *New York Times,* 29 Mar. 1992.
———. "Tyson Faces Newest Challenge." *New York Times,* 26 Mar. 1995, p. S9.
Benjamin, Playthell. "Who Lost Tyson?" *Village Voice,* 25 Feb. 1993, pp. 148, 103.
Berger, Phil. "Which Tyson Will Emerge from Behind Bars?" *New York Times,* 27 Mar. 1992, p. B1.

Berkow, Ira. "After Three Years in Prison, Tyson Gains His Freedom." *New York Times,* 26 Mar. 1995, pp. S1, S9.

———. "It Seems That Tyson Has a Shot." *New York Times,* 18 Feb. 1993, p. B13.

Boyer, Peter J. "The Lost Boy." *Vanity Fair,* Mar. 1992, pp. 162–67.

Callahan, Tom. "Lawyers to Their Corners: Former Heavyweight Champion Mike Tyson Faces the Most Crucial Fight of His Young Life. *U.S. News and World Report,* 3 Feb. 1992, pp. 52–53.

Condit, Celeste Michelle. "The Rhetorical Limits of Polysemy." *Critical Studies in Mass Communication* 6 (1989): 103–22.

Corliss, Richard. "The Bad and the Beautiful." *Time,* 24 Feb. 1992, pp. 25–26.

———. "In Judgment of Iron Mike." *Time,* 10 Feb. 1992, p. 77.

———. "Tragedy of an Ex-Champ." *Time,* 26 Aug. 1991, p. 67.

"Desiree Washington: She KO'd Iron Mike but Remains More Victim Than Victor." *People,* 28 Dec. 1992, p. 90.

"Fallen Champ: The Untold Story of Mike Tyson." Dir. Barbara Koppel. Tristar Television, 1993.

Foucault, Michel. *The Archaeology of Knowledge.* New York: Pantheon, 1972.

———. "What Is an Author?" In *The Foucault Reader,* pp. 101–20. New York: Pantheon, 1984.

Gelarden, R. Joseph. "Lawyer for Tyson's Accuser Warns of Smear Campaign." *Indianapolis Star,* 10 Sept. 1991.

———. "Low-Key Garrison in Spotlight after Tyson KO." *Indianapolis Star,* 1 Feb. 1992.

Gelarden, R. Joseph, and Barb Albert. "Rape Victim Wants Tyson Imprisoned Until Rehabilitated." *Indianapolis Star,* 22 Feb. 1992.

Glauber, Bill. "Tyson Booked, Says He's Innocent." *Sun* [Baltimore, Md.], 12 Sept. 1991.

Hoffer, Richard. "Out of the Darkness." *Sports Illustrated,* 3 Apr. 1995, pp. 44–49.

———. "Up from the Canvas." *Sports Illustrated,* 27 Mar. 1995, pp. 52–58.

hooks, bell. *Outlaw Culture: Resisting Representations.* New York: Routledge, 1994.

Hull, Anne V.; Sheryl James; and Thomas French. "Why Tyson Lost and Smith Won." *St. Petersburg Times* [Fla.], 12 Feb. 1992.

Leerhsen, Charles, and Peter Blum. "A Fight for the Rest of His Life." *Newsweek,* 23 Sept. 1991, p. 63.

Lule, Jack. "The Rape of Mike Tyson: Race, the Press and Symbolic Types." *Critical Studies in Mass Communication* 12 (1995): 176–95.

McDarrah, Timothy, and Florence Anthony. "Tyson in Solitary." *New York Post,* 6 May 1992.

"Mike Tyson Convicted of Raping Teen Beauty, Faces 60 Years in Jail." *Jet,* 24 Feb. 1992, pp. 16–18.

"Mike Tyson Sentenced to Six Years, Appeal Filed Immediately." *Jet,* 13 Apr. 1992, pp. 16–17, 51–52.

Nack, William. "On Trial." *Sports Illustrated,* 20 Jan. 1992, pp. 46–49.

Oates, Joyce Carol. "Rape and the Boxing Ring." *Newsweek,* 24 Feb. 1992, pp. 60–61.

Shipp, E. R. "Baptist President's Support for Tyson Is Assailed inside and outside Church." *New York Times,* 16 Mar. 1992, p. A10.

Stepp, Laura Sessions. "Baptist World Center in Turmoil." *Washington Post,* 10 Mar. 1992.

Steptoe, Sonja. "A Damnable Defense." *Sports Illustrated,* 24 Feb. 1992, p. 92.

Treen, Joe, and Bill Shaw. "Judgment Day." *People,* 24 Feb. 1992 pp. 36–41.

Willis, Paul. "Shop Floor Culture, Masculinity and the Wage Form." In *Working Class Culture: Studies in History and Theory,* ed. John Clarke, Chas Critcher, and Richard Johnson, pp. 185–98. London: Hutchinson, 1979.

Wulf, Steve. "Two Champs Are Back." *Time,* 3 Apr. 1995, pp. 56–57.

Ziner, Karen Lee. "Tyson, Accuser Square Off over Rape." *Journal-Bulletin* [Providence, R.I.], 26 Jan. 1992.

6 ... *The Day the Niggaz Took Over: Basketball,*
Commodity Culture, and Black Masculinity

This chapter looks to explicate the historically informed image of empowered Black masculinity as it is represented in popular culture in general and the game of basketball in particular. The sign of masculinity in question is equally problematic for those who work to repress it as a potential source of power as well as those who look to champion its political possibilities. In doing the analysis I will constantly make reference to the problematic sign "nigger," arguably one of the most controversial words in the English language because of the obvious racial connotations this term has always had in American society. Yet for purposes of this chapter the word "nigger," which in contemporary society has become "nigga," is a recurrent image of both race and class significance that specifically comments on Black male culture in such a way that its historical impact cannot be denied.

At a personal level, I have never been a strong proponent of the "positive image" school of African American cultural criticism. Thus I will openly apply the highly contested term "nigga" to various sectors of popular culture. The application of this discursive pattern is fundamental to the arguments that I am compelled to make regarding race, class, masculinity, and commodity culture as expressed specifically through basketball and the image of Charles Barkley.

Clearly the actual power involved in using this term comes from the individual or group using it. In my mind there has always been quite a difference between this term and its usage by white society and the conversant usage of it by African Americans, much like those things which may have special meaning within a particular family but are very problematic when used outside of the enclosed unit. To ignore this difference would be critically negligent. I, like the problematic subjects who appear in this chapter, will explore this function as it applies to the subject at hand without reservation as to the potential reluctance it may cause on the part of those who feel my usage also encourages others to use it for their own purposes. Those whites who use the word will undoubtedly do so whether I use it or not. And those who feel it should be censored altogether are equally unaffected by my usage.[1]

"STOP ACTING LIKE A NIGGER"

> I'm a nigger in America / And I don't care what you are / Cause I'm a capital N-I-double G-E-R.
>
> —Ice T, "Straight Up Nigger"

> Q: What's the difference between a Black man and a nigger?
> A: Only a nigger would answer that question.
>
> —Dialogue from Bill Duke's *Deep Cover*

My knowledge of the politics surrounding the often contested linguistic sign known as "nigger" began at an early age. While a student in junior high school, I can remember one of the many African American female teachers who dominated my early education doing what she thought was her bit to "uplift the race" through constant reprimand of unacceptable behavior. Whenever a Black student would begin to act outside the various codes of preferred behavior, this particular teacher would pull the student aside and suggest in her sternest voice that perhaps he or she should "stop acting like a nigger." (Interestingly, white students never seemed to misbehave in the teacher's mind, or at least were never publicly reprimanded for it.)

At this time it was quite confusing to me what this very popular phrase, one I also heard throughout the neighborhood and at church, actually meant. Since the dictates of racism had already been teaching me that "nigger" was a derogatory name used for all Black people, I often wondered what she meant by "acting like a nigger" since we were all thought of as niggers anyway. We were simply acting like ourselves, right?

Yet as time passed I realized that "nigger," in addition to being a racially specific term, was an equally encoded class-specific term as well. In this sense, the Black teacher was not suggesting that we stop being Black, but that we stop imitating the lower-class behavior of those Blacks who, in her own words, would "never amount to nothing anyway." Her concerns were more specifically of a class nature, though the ominous racial imagery could not be denied.

Since she clearly did not see herself as a nigger, she was not making the assumption that all African Americans were niggers. Instead she was suggesting that in the populous context of the middle-class social ladder, the public school system, we should all learn to move away from the confines of lower-class behavior into the more acceptable realm of middle-class behavior, which, incidentally, based on her use of the racially specific term, we all thought was exclusive to whiteness.

Though the teacher's identity politics were somewhat convoluted, if not bordering on self-hatred, her point, nonetheless, was quite obvious upon reflection. In order for Black people to be successful in this world of both race and class hierarchies, they must constantly try and maintain standards of behavior that reflected those most associated with white middle-class existence. Anything less, according to the popular Right Guard deodorant commercial, "would be uncivilized."

These childhood lessons seem to have a recurrent viability in the world of African American culture. The cultural politics of race and class, and their application to masculinity, have always provided for some of the most illuminating instances of African American discourse, be it in a public or a private sense. The constant reappearance of the nigger, both linguistically and through visual imagery, is one way we can explicate the subtle nuances of African American existence, especially as it relates to cultural production. To study this looming presence in contemporary society allows for a clear understanding of the way in which the politics of the nigger has functioned historically as well as the possible realignment of these politics relative to the dictates of contemporary culture.

With this in mind, I am interested in analyzing the political history of this sign, its various forms relative to popular culture, and the recent reincarnation of the nigger as it relates to the world of professional basketball—a contemporary field where cultural politics are often at work, but seldom fully appreciated.

REAL NIGGAZ DON'T DIE!

What is a nigger? In many ways this question seems to bear an obvious answer. "Nigger" is a derogatory term rooted in the economy of slavery that has been used as a way of linguistically marginalizing the already marginalized African American subject. Though dictionaries suggest that the term refers to a lazy, shiftless person, it is impossible to deal with the history of this term without calling forth the racial imagery that it conjures up. To complicate matters, the word itself has long had a conflicting meaning and usage in various sectors of the Black community. As is my focus in this chapter, the real question becomes how has this term been redefined or "co-opted" through the powerful African American vernacular and how this functions in regard to contemporary popular culture.

According to cultural historian and political scientist Charles Henry, "the bad nigger or black bad man tradition is characterized by the absolute rejection of established authority figures" (93–94). Cultural critic Mel Watkins, in his voluminous history of Black comedic address, *On the Real Side,* applies these same sentiments to the world of comedy, in both its public and private incarnations: "bad Niggers were merely African-Americans who long before the sixties Civil Rights movement, refused to participate in the elaborate hoax that had defined American racial relationships and stood up for their rights as citizens" (462). In his further exploration of this historical figure, Watkins goes on to explain that bad niggers "insisted upon being treated as equals, rejected traditional obsequious postures when interacting with whites, and refused to adopt trickery and deception as a means to a desired end because those strategies superficially appeared to affirm inherent white superiority" (462).

Using the ideas of both Henry and Watkins, it becomes evident that "nigger" in this context was far from simply a derogatory image imposed upon African Americans by racist white society. As the quotes reveal, these figures were in a sense heroic, if not revolutionary, for their refusal to be defined by the limited racial reasoning perpetrated by the regressive elements of white society and culture. The bad nigger embodied the notion of resistance at the highest level as his presence defied all acceptable norms of behavior, decorum, and existence.

On the other hand, the bad nigger was an ambivalent figure in relationship to Black culture at large, especially women. As the code of survival dictates, the bad nigger was, of necessity, equally threatening to both the white community and his own community as well. This is clearly the case as it relates to women. In understanding the bad nigger through the oral tradition of toasts and signifying, Henry suggests that the obvious sexism of this genre typically portrays women "as prostitutes or targets for sexual aggression." He adds that "the sexual assertiveness of both men and women in this genre does not compensate for the degraded status accorded women" (58).

A contemporary example of this problematic status of the bad nigger exists throughout rap music, especially gangsta rap. In this regard, Ice Cube has stated on his inaugural solo record, *Amerikkka's Most Wanted*, that he is simultaneously a "bitch killa" and a "cop killa," an example which clearly sees no distinction between Black women and the popular imagery that has emerged between the racially oppressive police force and African American males. It is in this sense that the complex configuration of the bad nigger becomes quite substantial when we attempt to understand its function in popular culture.[2] How do we fully accommodate the revolutionary impetus so closely linked with the bad nigger's refusal to be restrained by white oppression, but at the same remain free of celebrating many of the pathological aspects of this characterization, especially in regard to women?

One possible way of further exploring this dual assertion is to explicate the class dynamics of this term that are so often ignored in favor of focusing exclusively on the racial components that are involved. It is also necessary to foreground the gender-specific nature of masculinity featured in this analysis as it is a commentary on the role of Black masculinity in popular culture. For all intents and purposes, the bad nigger is really an exercise in the politics that define lower-class Black masculinity. The meaningful explication of this phenomenon in contemporary society offers the multiple and contradictory possibilities that can be articulated when using the linguistic sign as a firm endorsement of empowerment and resistance.

THE WRONG NIGGA TO FUCK WITH

Contemporary culture has offered a redefinition of the bad nigger at multiple levels. Not only has time allowed for the gradual disappearance of the modifier "bad," as this term itself has undergone a doubling specific to oral culture, wherein it has been used interchangeably with the word "good." In addition, the spelling of the word "nigger" has also changed over time to the now-ubiquitous "nigga."

African American contemporary culture is dominated by the aura of rap music. Much of rap music has featured a respelling of common words so as to indicate a distinctively Black difference in both spelling and meaning. This respelling is also used to closely approximate the actual murmuring of Black speech patterns.

The redefining process through oral culture has a long history in African American culture. For instance, with regard to jazz, pianist and composer Bobby Timmons provides the nuance of vernacular discourse in his classic tune "Dat Dere" (that there). This practice is also quite consistent with what Henry Louis Gates, Jr., has referred to as the "signifying black difference" which is specific to African American literature. Thus, when rappers talk about a Black "thang," they are not simply misspelling "thing," they are participating in a historical tradition that lies at the essence of African American cultural practice: redefining artifacts so as to make them specific and central to Black culture and experience. With this in mind, several rappers, and other contemporary producers of culture, filmmakers, comedians, etc., have referred to themselves or each other as "nigga," clearly referencing history while at the same time commenting on the contemporary nature of their own lower-class, male-centered existence.

How has the modern-day nigga changed from his previous incarnations? It is here that the question of class becomes quite evident. As already stated, nigga is a class-specific term, especially when used in and among African Americans. The term is the exclusive domain of lower-class Black culture.

A good example of this can be found both in the figure Malcolm X and in his popular comparison between what he describes as the house nigger and the field nigger. Malcolm X has always been popular among African Americans because he embodied the tenants of the bad nigger, but eventually took this ethos to a higher level by using this marginalized position to code his political consciousness. In many ways Malcolm X is the ultimate empowered sign of Blackness as a result of his fusion of bad nigger imagery and revolutionary political ideas.

As Spike Lee's depiction of this famous figure revealed in a very telling scene, one reason Malcolm was so highly admired was his refusal to acquiesce to the demands of white authority in the form of the police. Upon entering the neighborhood Muslim restaurant after witnessing Malcolm X and the Fruit of Islam defy police authority, an overexcited eventual convert named Benjamin says to Malcolm, "I have never seen no nigger, ah excuse me, Negro, stand up to the police like that." This scene conveys two very important bits of information. First of all, it is apparent that Benjamin's interest in Malcolm X has a great deal to do with his staunch defiance of accepted protocol for Black males when being confronted by police. Malcolm is strong in the face of all sorts of possible adverse responses. Benjamin's recognition of this bad nigger quality has to do with the fact that this behavior is uncommon, yet impressive for Malcolm's sheer defiance of foregrounded authority. It is at this point that Malcolm instructs the young man that the responsibilities of being a Muslim far exceed the simple notion of defiance, though many regard this, both then and now, as the most salient quality to be derived from Malcolm's legendary presence.

Cornel West describes Malcolm's defiance in these terms: "his profound commitment to affirm Black humanity at any cost and his tremendous courage to accent the hypocrisy of American society made Malcolm X the prophet of Black rage" (48). It is apparent that Malcolm's strong impression on Benjamin functions in quite the same way that is here described by West, the notion of Black rage being the key to Benjamin's newfound understanding of assertive Black masculinity.

What also becomes apparent from this exchange in the film is Lee's subtle transformation of Malcolm's character from connoting Black rage exclusively to the problematic depiction of Malcolm as ultimately being easily assimilated into the pantheon of American heroic endeavors. This shift from the resistant power of lower-class autonomy to that of assimilated respectability, more befitting of the leaders of the civil rights movement, is clearly conferred through Benjamin's slip of the tongue, as he changes from "nigger" to "Negro" in mid-sentence. "Negro" is defiantly a term that communicated a less confrontational position of class identity in the highly charged 1960s. Lee's representation of Malcolm X can in many ways be reduced to the lessons learned from this quote: the subtle transformation of a revolutionary into an acceptable American icon of proper political significance.

We can learn similar lessons from studying the actual rhetoric of Malcolm X himself. In one of the classic excerpts from Malcolm's published and recorded speeches, we get the distillation of the class-based paradigm as it relates to cultural identity. In "Message to the Grassroots," Malcolm sets up the distinction between "house niggers" and "field niggers." What is interesting in the speech is that Malcolm initially starts out talking about the house "negro," but he stops to make this declaration: "in those days he was called a house nigger. And that's what we call them today, because we've still got some house niggers running around here" (11). Clearly the term "nigger" was considered more appropriate to make his point about the class differences that would eventually evolve out of this particular element of slave culture.

According to Malcolm, the house nigger "identified himself with his master, more than the master identified with himself," while the field nigger, who was in the majority, "hated" his master. The rest of the example hinges on the response by either side to the metaphorical master's house catching on fire. The house nigger would try harder than the master to put out the fire, while his counterpart would "pray for a wind," hoping that the house would burn to the ground.

This masterful series of metaphors reveals what has now become the domain of class politics in contemporary Black America. The house nigger, through his close association with the master, is to be thought of as assimilated within white culture, while "the masses," the field niggers, are thought of as what Los Angeles historian and cultural critic Mike Davis has called the "revolutionary lumpen proletariat," revolutionary by necessity, owing to their extremely marginal status in society. We are to assume that as time progressed from slavery, the house niggers were the ones who would adopt various monikers as a way of distancing themselves from the negative impact of the word "nigger," while on the other hand, several of the field niggers would go on to be associated with the imagery of the bad nigger, which would eventually be refigured as the nigga. The farther one gets away from the field, the less likely one is to embrace the imagery of the field, meaning the looming signifier of the nigga.

This is clearly the case in contemporary society, as a number of middle-class, image-conscious African Americans have attacked the constant use of the word "nigga" in popular culture by rappers and comedians. In response, there are those who see this otherwise negative imagery as an opportunity both to distance themselves from white society by respelling and ultimately redefining the word, and also to separate themselves from the less spectacular mundane confines of middle-class Black existence at the same time. Henry sees the bad nigger as actively establishing "visibility and identity" and as being the "epitome of selfish individualism" (94).

These characteristics have great value in the mediated world of popular culture, where performers are trying to remain viable in a financial sense, as well as in a public sense. Thus, the convenient embrace of nigga imagery has a lot to do with the financial dictates of the cultural marketplace and less to do with actual class status or real societal threat. It is then possible to read this embrace of nigga imagery as a refusal to be defined by others, but as an opportunity to redefine oneself.

This is best illustrated by popular rapper Hammer. In the summer of 1990, Hammer was the figure who took rap into the highest echelons of popular culture through his massively popular second album *Please Hammer Don't Hurt Em*. Hammer's unparalleled financial success made many question whether he was still sympathetic to the lower-class ethos that circulated throughout the rap world, a world which at that time was still popular primarily only among Black youth. He was repeatedly charged with the ultimate crime in the world of pop cultural Blackness, "selling out." In response, Hammer suggested that his music was intended for the racially transcendent category of "all people," while in turn criticizing those gangsta rappers who highlighted the music's hard masculine street edge.

Yet Hammer's video "Pumps and Bump," released in late 1993, features him in his garish $22 million house juxtaposed against the surroundings of several scantily clad female dancers. Hammer is dressed in tight bikini trunks, with his seemingly enlarged penis foregrounded for all to see. His sexual gyrations and suggested atmosphere of orgy place him in the context made popular by Miami-based rapper Luke of 2 Live Crew fame. Another video, "It's All Good," not only features him in the urban attire associated with gangsta rappers, but this record was also produced by the paragon of gangsta rap, Dr. Dre.

These images are a far cry from the religious imagery that was quite prevalent during his earlier popular phase. Hammer's change, from the assimilated mainstream entertainer to the currently more popular and financially viable gangsta, indicates Henry's assertions of visibility and selfish individuality to the fullest. Hammer has clearly gone from being a race-transcending figure of massive popular appeal to being a nigga owing to convenience and the practicality of the constantly fluctuating trends of the music industry and popular taste. It is in this sense that West cautions, "there are numerous instances of field negro with house negro mentalities and house negro with field negro mentalities" (51).

Ultimately the contemporary embrace of nigga iconography operates in a very convenient sense. The association of oneself with this imagery allows one to remain "down" with the program of hypermasculinity that is so closely linked with lower-class ghetto existence. At the same time this posture also allows the individual the opportunity to be financially successful without having to bear the burden of selling out. The convenient embrace of the nigga mentality is one that can be turned on and off at will. Thus, one can be "hard," and at the same time make as much money as possible. This newly conferred status is once again consistent with Henry's idea of "selfish individualism."

Clearly there was a time when one was more closely judged by one's rhetoric and, maybe more important, one's actions. This situation is connoted in the formerly Black phrase "walking the walk and talking the talk." Both were necessary if one was to be thought of as instrumental in the struggle toward racial equality. After the 1960s civil rights movement, though the dismantling of structural racism and group empowerment were never fully realized, African American popular culture took on entirely different dimensions. The possibilities of a sustained presence by African Americans were now quite viable in a limited but more substantial sense than previously allowed. This is especially true in regard to the music industry and professional sports. As time passed, it became a regular occurrence for Black performers in either venue to make large sums of money which offered the possibility of financial independence in capitalist America. This extreme level of newfound freedom, while on one hand creating the modern image of the irresponsible Black male spendthrift or indulgent addict who ended up penniless after his playing days were over, offered an opportunity for individual Black male empowerment at a financial level that, arguably, had never before been realized.

This situation created a series of new dilemmas for those concerned with the culturally responsible as well. First of all, for the Marxist-minded among us, it became necessary to ask whether Black people's making exceptionally large sums of money was progressive or simply another example of cultural hegemony at work. Secondly, for those who were concerned with an empowered racial agenda, the question became whether or not the successful individual had any responsibility to the Black "community" once he/she gained this status. At a larger level, it is important to ask what it means to have the financial independence normally associated with whiteness, but still have to bear the albatross of being a racial other in regard to the larger society. In a very simplified form, the question became, Is it possible to be both Black and rich, especially since we have for so long assumed Blackness to be indelibly linked with poverty?

Clearly it is possible to be financially well off and still be associated with the imagery of the nigga. While racial imagery remains constant, capitalist society does allow for fluctuation in class status in an individual sense. As I alluded to earlier, there are multiple examples of this in rap music, where the cultural politics of race and identity are always at work. But one of the most interesting examples that exist outside of rap takes place throughout professional sports. My concentration here is on basketball, the ultimate collection of niggas. This sport has the largest percentage of Black players of the three major sports, in addition to a few African Americans in high-level administrative positions, though full empowerment at the level of ownership has still eluded Blacks.

THE '90s NIGGA

> I'm a '90s nigga . . . I told you white boys you've never heard of a '90s nigga. We do what we want to.
>
> —Charles Barkley, 1992

The above-mentioned declaration was made following a nationally televised NBC basketball game in which then Philadelphia 76ers forward Charles Barkley had missed a questionable three-point shot late in a very important game. Barkley's comments were made to a group of reporters from his home-town newspapers. In response to criticism over the ill-advised shot, Barkley defended his actions by referencing his racial and economic status within the world of professional athletics and the larger domain of African American identity.

At one level the comment is indicative of the attainment by professional athletes in general and Barkley specifically of an extremely high level of economic viability as a result of their value as entertainment commodity which circulates throughout mediated popular culture. Barkley's financial status and the similar status shared by many of his sports peers definitely allows them to do "what they want to do." Financial stability at an extreme level certainly confers a strong sense of freedom in capitalist America. Thus, his statement is in many ways an obvious one in the sense of economics.

Yet this economic meaning is enhanced when one considers the racial overtones of the statement. The use of the constantly contested word "nigga" is a very clear reference to the racial politics of his statement. This prototype has had a recurring role in sports from the earliest days of Jack Johnson to Barkley's most recent reincarnation of this image. What becomes most important about this image, though, is the strong sense of defiance that codes its historical legacy. Here we have Barkley taking on a looming symbol of power, the professional sports media. The Philadelphia media, for Barkley, represents the power of the dominant discourse, clearly having the ability to define and redefine the most pertinent issues of the day, in this case an ongoing critical denigration of Barkley, both professional and personal.

Barkley's role is often enhanced when contrasted against much more mainstream imagery. It is for this reason that Joe Louis was often talked about as a "credit to his race," simply because his image of accommodation seemed less threatening in comparison to his menacing predecessor, Jack Johnson. The same is true today as the problematic image of Barkley is often seen as the underside of the much less confrontational image of Michael Jordan.

In this same statement, Barkley suggests that they, meaning the white media, want "their Black Athletes to be Uncle Toms," clearly enunciating the racial politics that define the situation. The media, a primary organ for the continued proliferation of racial hierarchies, are more comfortable having Black athletes remain in their allotted space as quiet performers and entertainers, speaking only when spoken to, and then only to affirm their circumscribed place in the extant racial hierarchy, where white males continue to "own" the services of the players and white-owned media outlets continue to reinscribe this world through their media coverage.

In Barkley's world this subservient posture, referenced here as that of the "Uncle Tom," is completely unacceptable. He responded by initially reducing his critics to "white boys," thus rhetorically emasculating them from men to boys, and then reinforcing this deconstruction of masculinity by defining himself as a "'90s nigga," an individual who does what he wants to do. In this construction, Barkley embraces African American culture—both historically, as emphasized through the folkloric reference of the bad nigga, and in a contemporary sense, where his identification of himself as a "nigga" places him in the same camp as many rap artists who use the label as a sense of identity and resistance. The "'90s nigga" with his placement within African American history and culture is superior to the powerless image of a generic "white boy." The fact that Barkley's individual financial status is far superior to that of the sports reporters with whom he is conversing underscores his elevated status even more. Not only are these "white boys" inferior in a physical sense that references the domain of masculinity, but they are seen as insufficient through their class status as well.

The point communicated through this rhetorical example concerns identity politics and the way in which African American males, through sports, can create a space of resistance and free expression that announces a relative notion of empowerment, while at the same time acknowledging the racial and class hierarchies that still dominate sports and society as a whole. Consistent with Black expression through the historical medium of music, sports in contemporary society has allowed for the recurrent voicing of African

American aesthetics and ultimately serves as an extension of the discourse that has traditionally defined culture. Basketball is an excellent example of what jazz used to be for African American males, and what rap has become: a cultural space where aesthetics, politics, and an overall sense of Blackness could be communicated to both marginal and mass audiences.

What complicates this cultural expression is the racial and financial hierarchy that defines the actual playing of the game. Though African Americans occupy a commanding position as players in both major college and professional basketball, they are still underrepresented in regard to positions of authority in control of the actual administration of the game. This situation is even worse when we consider that no professional franchise is owned by an African American.[3] Yet this situation mirrors a similar one in the music industry, where Black performers have, in essence, defined American music, both artistically and financially, but have seldom been granted the opportunity to occupy major positions of authority in the record industry, though there are some subtle exceptions in each case.

This underscores a historic relationship wherein African Americans have consistently been allowed to "perform" for the benefit and privilege of adoring white audiences. Though this relationship has often been enunciated, what might be of more interest is the relationship between Black performers and their own Black audiences. With this particular performer/audience relationship, the question becomes, What culturally specific means are being used to address this audience, or what subtle cultural codes are being presented which these audiences can extrapolate into a more sustained dialogue between performer and audience? In what way does the resulting cultural product become an intrinsic component of the definition of African American culture? The exchange of nigga imagery within the culture bridges these concerns in such a way as to highlight the difference between dialogue at an insular level and dialogue that is subsumed by the larger society. Fortunately or unfortunately, the massive proliferation of valuable Black imagery in a public sense has made the private manifestations exclusive to Black culture, like the previously segregated "chitlin circuit," almost nonexistent.

The other problem that exists in this analysis is the way in which those African American performers who play the game of basketball at a professional level are compensated quite well for their exploits, yet this compensation is relative to their existence in an institutional structure that compensates their owners in excess of what the players make and is legitimated through our understanding of corporate interest and the notion of ownership. Yet it is still quite difficult to talk about a financially oppressive relationship when we are referring to individuals who often make money in excess of one million dollars. In fact, because the average salary in the NBA is so high,

there are those who consider these multi-million dollar athletes equal participants in the same economic system as the team owners, thus nullifying any
reason to engage this elite practice critically.

The problems of African American subordination to a racial hierarchy,
and the seeming contradiction between this obvious exclusion and the high
level of compensation for the athletes involved, indicate a compromise that
uses the relative freedom afforded to individuals, yet also employs this same
freedom as another way to maintain an overall societal situation that continues to oppress African Americans at a group level.

My analysis of Barkley's replication of nigga imagery in basketball is not
without ambivalence. Ultimately the attention focused on Barkley comes
from the fact that most athletes seldom have anything at all to say, much less
anything of substance, while Barkley seems to enjoy adding to his own
spectacle by his constant recitation of sound bites. He becomes a spokesman
by default.

Although one side of Barkley's persona clearly reveals a potential threat to
the racial status quo—and this is the side that the media play up—there is
another side to his public image that is quite problematic. For instance,
Barkley once suggested after a tough loss that it was the type of event that
encouraged him to go home and "beat his wife," once again linking himself
with the duality of threat to all possible parties ("bitch killa, cop killa") that
informs this persona. He has also openly declared his intentions to run for
governor of his home state of Alabama upon retirement from the NBA, but
as a Republican, and he has publicly expressed his admiration for and friendship with the conservative media figure Rush Limbaugh.

This in an overt demonstration of political naiveté in which he assumes
that his open embrace of conservative values is somehow a liberation from
what he considers the prevailing liberal attitude and lack of real power of
most Black politicians. Barkley's embrace of Republican politics easily goes
along with his income level and the notion of selfish individualism so closely
tied to the historical nigga. This also reveals the extent to which he defines
himself as nigga when convenient, yet his personal politics allows for a
distancing from that same group concept whenever necessary.[4]

Barkley's embrace of this trendy image is a situation much like Clarence
Thomas's short-lived position as nigga during his famous confirmation hear-
ings, when he suggested that they were akin to a "high tech lynching for [an]
uppity Negro." Though the overt formality of the congressional proceedings
would have made it difficult to pull off, the word "nigga" could have easily
been substituted here in place of "Negro." In both cases the notion of the
individual is prominent until the obvious demonstration of racism forces him
to embrace the identity of the group. The convenient embrace of this imagery

makes it less than plausible as a widely accessible position of empowerment, but the ability to embrace it all does suggest some potential for broader resistance in a pop cultural world where that is seldom the case.

"IT'S GOTTA BE THE SHOES"

There is no doubt that the NBA has ascended in popularity and cultural significance over the last fifteen years. One of the most important motivating factors in this elevation has been the increased association the league and various players have with a number of corporate sponsors. The NBA over time has indeed transcended the relatively narrow parameters of sports and has truly become an entertainment venue on par with the best of Hollywood and the music industry. This is especially true when you consider that the 1979–80 championship finals were played on tape delay as opposed to being played in prime time as is now the staple.

How has this association with corporate sponsors transformed the game in such a relatively short period of time? While there are many sponsors who now use the image of the league in some form for marketing purposes, the most visible are the basketball shoe companies, especially Nike. I am concerned here, less with a corporate history of Nike as presented in Donald Katz's *Just Do It.* Instead, what is interesting is the way in which this corporate association has been used to foreground the game's cultural significance and promote the NBA as a first-rate entertainment source, as well as the obvious: sell basketball shoes.

During the 1984 college basketball season, the Georgetown Hoyas, on the way to their first national championship, wore a specially designed Nike basketball shoe, which was eventually worn by many African Americans as a strong sign of both racial and cultural exemplification. The shoe had a multicolored gray and blue design that stood out in contrast to the otherwise bland white shoes worn at the time by most other college basketball teams. The distinctive shoes went quite well with the roughhouse persona developed by the Hoyas and their two most obvious visual signposts, center Patrick Ewing and head coach John Thompson.

Black men, throughout their association with the game of basketball, have developed several distinct styles of play and, by extension, an overall persona that goes along with their mediated image. The style most recently perpetrated by Michael Jordan is quite flamboyant and highly conscious of spectacle in its presentation. This style emphasizes the physical attributes of its practitioner and concentrates on rapid moves to the basket and gravity-defying lay-ups and dunks. The most visible proponents of this style in the past have been Elgin Baylor, Connie Hawkins, Julius Erving, and most recently Jordan.

Another prominent style displayed throughout the history of the game has been the no-nonsense, straight-up, defensive-minded game that relies on brute strength and intimidation, while calling little attention to itself. The players who have practiced this style have often been referred to as "blue-collar," suggesting a strong connection between this style and the less glamorous but highly necessary labor of those who exist in a factory-type working-class environment. The most visible proponents of this style, basketball's version of the nigga, have been players such as Bill Russell, Wes Unseld, Moses Malone, and most recently Barkley.

Georgetown displayed this intimidating style in 1984 and throughout the tenure of coach Thompson, which has included players such as Patrick Ewing, Alonzo Mourning, and Dikembe Mutombo, all now NBA stars who, like their coach, embody those same qualities. This point is enhanced when we consider that Thompson's most visible menace from the 1984 team, Michael Graham, sported a bald head well before Jordan made it fashionable, and possessed an intimidating stare and an overall thuggish court demeanor that foregrounded Georgetown's penchant for embracing the nigga as their conscious role model on their run for the championship.

Thompson's imposing 6 foot 10 inch, 300-pound frame added to the intimidation factor off the court that his players liked to display on the court. Nelson George states, "Black male authority figures—as opposed to stars— were few and far between during Ronald Reagan's presidency, but Thompson filled that role with gusto, expressing thoughts fearlessly and receiving reactions that ranged from hostility to outrage to shock" (206). Along with this assertive image, the highly stylized basketball shoes brought a significant visible flair to their game and overall persona.

The colorful shoes and their easy association with the currents of popular African American fashion assisted in Georgetown's being defined as a "Black" team. For instance, George describes his own reaction to his initial encounter with John Thompson and Georgetown while he was still a student at St. Johns: "No way could I root against an overwhelmingly Black squad coached by an imposing Black man from Chocolate City, U.S.A. Just the sight of Thompson standing across the court from me sent a spasm of pride through me" (206).

Like the multicolored warm-up suits that were used as a cool replacement for the traditional coat and tie worn by coach George Raveling during his tenure as head coach at the University of Iowa, or the equally colorful sweaters worn by Bill Cosby during his highly popular NBC situation comedy, Thompson, the all-Black team, and the Nike Georgetown basketball shoe set the team apart as a strong purveyor of African American cultural identity, using sport and commodity culture in achieving this end. The fact that the team featured no visibly important white players added to this Afrocentric association.

One of the most interesting demonstrations of the cultural significance enjoyed by Georgetown of the 1980s was seen in Spike Lee's directorial debut, *She's Gotta Have It* (1986). In the film Lee plays the memorable character Mars Blackmon, a Brooklyn "b-boy" who sports the Georgetown shoes along with a Georgetown Starter jacket and a huge gold nameplate necklace. Mars's character is an obvious demonstration of the extremes of popular Black male youth culture, as his trendy attire and utter disregard for mainstream existence foreground his marginal societal status.

Mars Blackmon represents a comedic version of a popular phrase from the Hughes brothers' *Menace II Society:* "America's worst nightmare; young, Black, and don't give a fuck." This threatening posture defines a large segment of the current generation of underclass Black male youth that the mainstream media have spent so much time displaying in recent years. Their status as ultimate outsiders to the benefits of middle-class life, both Black and white, as well as their embrace of this menacing quality distinguishes them in such a way that the presence is inseparable from almost any discussion of contemporary American society and culture.

The image of Mars Blackmon, however, proved to be very popular in terms of mainstream media appeal, as he enjoyed great success in several commercials with Nike superstar Michael Jordan. Though Mars personified this image in the film, he was somehow made into a less threatening being who used his comedic edge to facilitate the selling of the Nike basketball shoes.

In one of the most memorable commercials, Mars, after a series of unfortunate mishaps while trying to play against Jordan, finally decides that Michael's prowess clearly emanates from his special brand of Nike basketball shoes, "Air Jordans." Mars therefore declares, "It's gotta be the shoes," here suggesting that the special ability provided by the Nikes makes it possible for one to emulate Jordan's exploits on the court. Here athletic ability is reduced to the ability to purchase the trendy Air Jordans, while Jordan's image becomes indistinguishable from the commodity that he markets.

As the Air Jordan commercials persisted, it became increasingly evident that what had made Mars Blackmon and his Georgetown associations so problematic had now been reversed so that the allure of Mars Blackmon/ Spike Lee could be equally profitable in a mainstream sense by extolling the virtues of the ever popular and media-friendly Jordan. Lee's presence is quite like that of Barkley, a compromised image of Blackness for mass consumption in return for the financial power to challenge the racial status quo elsewhere. This oscillation between the menacing qualities of the specifically Black Georgetown imagery and the more mainstream form of Blackness associated with Jordan and Blackmon/Lee defines the contemporary state of commodity culture as it relates to basketball and African American culture. Those things which are seemingly problematic from a racial perspective can be equally profitable to those which appear to be less confrontational.

Although Georgetown and Thompson were seen as too "Black" by some, they were also seen as authentically "Black" by enough others whose purchasing power still made their style of shoes a profitable venue for Nike. In many ways the early success of the Georgetown shoe assisted, directly or indirectly, in the eventual explosion of the subsequent series of Air Jordans that would follow throughout Jordan's career. In both cases, commodity culture prevailed, by selling either a militant form of Blackness or a less confrontational version which still utilized the prevailing sign of Blackness, but in a much different way.

As the image of Georgetown began to fade from prominence, Nike would eventually pick up on the same theme with a different twist. This is where their association with Charles Barkley, which relied on some of the same nigga thematics, comes into play. Barkley, like John Thompson, is quite an imposing physical specimen. His size is certainly something more closely linked with a football player. His highly aggressive style of play on the court and his recurrent altercations off the court have clearly enhanced his modern-day bad-boy image. Nike has picked up on this theme by, among other things, featuring Barkley in a series of advertisements in which he was pitted against fictional character Godzilla in a series of battles that Barkley, aided by his Nikes, always won.

Yet what is most interesting about Barkley's association with Nike is the very popular and controversial commercial that ran during the latter part of the 1993 NBA season. The commercial in question relied on black-and-white imagery and a personal narrative to create an intimate connection between the text in question and the spectator. In the commercial Barkley declares, "I am not a role model," and goes on to explain why he should not be seen as exemplary in any way other than as a basketball player. This statement is one that had been echoed many times before by Barkley in real life. With this commercial Nike had taken the real and made it a central part of their shoe-selling ventures.

As a matter of fact, Barkley has openly challenged the relationship between individual and group as it pertains to African Americans. The commercial was a direct response to those critics who have constantly suggested that Barkley's nigga-like actions are not proper for a man of his stature who has such influence on very impressionable children. The constant accusation that he is not a good role model clearly informs this commercial. Yet upon deeper investigation, the political dynamics of this assertion become evident.

If we look at the image of African American males throughout the media, we find a series of regressive images that receive a great deal of attention, in the public through the media as well as in private conversations. To state that the image of the Black male in popular media is a negative one is no real revelation; we see or hear this in one form or another on a regular basis. In response, the media and the underlying ideology have suggested that since the only Black males who are successful seem to be athletes or entertainers, then they, by default, become role models for Black youth. This construction reveals the monolithic mentality that mainstream American ideology has placed upon African American culture and the way in which this ideology is reified through media.

Since the imagery of African American culture is often limited to one domain—the reigning image of Cosby in the early 1980s or the prevalent image of the gangsta in the 1990s—African American youth must look up to their athletic role models, and these role models must in turn act accordingly for their adoring fans. The entirety of the race, or at least Black men, is judged by the actions of a few. What complicates this scenario is the fact that professional basketball has such a wide appeal to a mass audience that young white males are somehow indirectly implicated in this whole role-model debate. Thus, calls for Barkley to be a good role model are really calls for him to "stop acting like a nigga" because too many impressionable white youth might try and imitate the behavior.

Black male youth, according to this perverted racial logic, have no other role models, while the fear is that middle- and upper-class white male youths might look to this image as the ultimate form of rebellion against their own mundane suburban lives. In this sense, Barkley's impact is the modern-day version of what various southern white citizens' councils were concerned about when they sought to repress the influences of "nigger music" (rock and roll) upon their youth during the turbulent 1950s and 1960s. Barkley's declaration that he is not a role model can be viewed once again as the embrace of the individual over the proposed group, and at the same time it can be seen as Nike's way of selling rebellion, while never compromising their ability to sell shoes. Thus commodity culture facilitates the articulation of the recurring nigga and all the political situations that feed off its constant use.

The recurrence of nigga imagery through the game of basketball is another indication of the way in which contemporary popular culture has found profitability through the selling of the most strident forms of African American discourse. No longer off limits, all forms of Black popular culture are fair game for representation within the massive circuit of entertainment. It therefore becomes difficult to talk about those forms of African American culture which are being repressed or minimized because of a dominant ideological discourse. Instead we have seen the constant proliferation of African American male imagery in popular culture, which references the most threatening aspects of this legacy, while also making this a very profitable venue for all involved. In other words, the presentation of these images is the most effective way of disseminating Blackness for a mass audience, made possible by its simultaneous profitability as consumer culture.

NOTES

1. Much of my recent research has to do with the expression of this image in contemporary culture. There are also several public examples of this usage that inform my invocation of the word and the charged political nature that surrounds it. Most notable is the recurrent presence of the word in the O.J. Simpson trial and its attachment to former LAPD officer Mark Fuhrman. The exchange between Furhman and defense lawyer F. Lee Bailey demonstrates the potential power embodied in the word, as do the infamous Furhman tapes and the articulation of the word by Furhman as a "smoking gun" for the defense. Also, filmmaker Quentin Tarantino has aroused much controversy over his use of the word in several of his films, and he was interrogated by Black actor Denzel Washington on the set of *Crimson Tide* for his repeated usage of it. For a further discussion of Tarantino's usage, see my article "Tarantino's Mantra."

2. For an extended discussion of the politics of the term "nigger," or its contemporary embodiment, "nigga," in rap music, see my essay "Check Yo Self Before You Wreck Yo Self."

3. See Nelson George, "Joining the Club," pp. 218–22 in *Elevating the Game*, on African Americans in front office and ownership positions in the NBA. At this writing there are no African Americans in majority ownership positions in the league, though the Los Angeles Lakers made a highly publicized move when Magic Johnson was announced to have purchased a small percentage of the team from owner and former boss Jerry Buss. The same is true of Isiah Thomas's interest in the expansion Toronto Raptors.

4. There is an interesting image of Barkley on the cover of the November 1995 *GQ* magazine. Barkley is pictured in a yellow and black bumblebee-striped bathrobe with sweat dripping down his bald head and cheerfully glistening face. Also visibly apparent is his gold necklace. This picture is in contrast to the normally cool image of high fashion and masculinity that *GQ* displays on its cover. While *GQ* covers are generally reserved for white male celebrities, Barkley's exception foregrounds an image closely aligned with a Black pimp, like Max Julien's character Goldie in the 1973 cult film classic *The Mack* or as popularized in the books of writer Iceberg Slim. These images certainly reference the nigga, but obviously contradict the image of an aspiring Republican governor from a southern state.

REFERENCES

Boyd, Todd. "Check Yo Self Before You Wreck Yo Self: Variations on a Political Theme in Rap Music and Popular Culture." *Public Culture* 7, no. 1 (Autumn 1994): 289–312.
———. "Tarantino's Mantra: 'Pulp Director Has Wrongheaded Approach to the N-word.'" *Chicago Tribune*, November 6, 1994, p. 26.
Gates, Henry Louis, Jr. "Talkin' That Talk." In Gates, ed., *"Race," Writing, and Difference*, pp. 402–409. Chicago: University of Chicago Press, 1985.
George, Nelson. *Elevating the Game: Black Men and Basketball*. New York: Simon and Schuster, 1992.

Henry, Charles. *Culture and African American Politics.* Bloomington: Indiana University Press, 1991.

Malcolm X. "Message to the Grassroots." In George Brietman, ed., *Malcolm X Speaks.* New York: Grove Weidenfeld Press, 1990.

Watkins, Mel. *On the Real Side: Laughing, Lying, and Signifying— The Underground Tradition of African-American Humor That Transformed American Culture from Slavery to Richard Pryor.* New York: Simon and Schuster, 1993.

West, Cornel. "Malcolm X and Black Rage." In Joe Wood, ed., *Malcolm X: In Our Own Image,* pp. 48–58. New York: St. Martin's Press, 1992.

PART THREE . . . *Hollywood Sports Films and Contested Identities*

CHRIS HOLMLUND

7 ... *Visible Difference and Flex Appeal: The Body, Sex, Sexuality, and Race in the "Pumping Iron" Films*

Pumping Iron (Butler and Flore, 1977) and *Pumping Iron II: The Women* (Butler, 1984), two documentaries about bodybuilding contests, provide an ideal opportunity to look at the relationships operating between body, desire, and power in the United States today. Taken as a pair, these films are a veritable melting pot of sex, sexuality, race, and sales. Intentionally and unintentionally, they reveal how the visible differences of sex (to have or have not) and race (to be or not to be) mesh with ideology and economy in contemporary American society, and within film fictions. In both films sexuality is adroitly linked with sex and race at the expense of any reference to history or class. The body is marketed as a commodity in its own right, not just as the silent support for the sale of other commodities.

An analysis of the way popular film reflects and shapes the categories of body, sex, sexuality, and race remains an urgent project for film theory. Despite the incorporation of critiques made by the women's, black, and gay movements of the 1960s, 1970s, and 1980s—indeed, in some ways because of these critiques—we continue to see and speak about the body as the last bastion of nature. While the sexual and civil rights movements make it clear that inequalities predicated on sex, race, or sexual preference are socially established and maintained, the strategies they employ are nonetheless often based on an idea of the body as unified and unique.[1] Difference is either flaunted (black power and cultural feminism, black and women's separatism) or elided (the "we're just like you" policy of the National Gay Task Force since 1973), but the body remains the silent support of and rationale for political praxis. Even within theoretical discourses, the biological status of the body lingers on, masking and motivating a series of power relations. (One has to think only of the multitude of feminist critiques of Lacan's penis/phallus confusion.)

Everyone has difficulty acknowledging the extent to which the body is a social construction and an ideological support because, to invoke Freud, the body (our own and the Other's) is the object and the origin of our earliest fears and desires. The associations established between the body and power are particularly hard to acknowledge when, as is often the case, several kinds of visible difference or its correlates are intermingled: when sex is added to race, or when gender is conflated with sexuality. The original ambivalent attitudes we hold toward the body are then multiplied many times over.

The rush to ignore and deny sexual, racial, and gender differences so that there will be more money for straight white men—initiated and/or encouraged by the Reagan government and other right-wing forces—further obscures the roles assigned to the body today. More than in the sixties and seventies, we forget that the ways we look at and speak about the body are historically variable. Knowledge and power of and over the body function within what Foucault calls an "apparatus." Since we live in and create this apparatus, it is hard for us to realize that it is "a formation which has as its major function at a given historical moment that of responding to an *urgent need*."[2]

The reliance of Western society on images of the body to sell products and promote fictions compounds our confusion. Mass media and advertising see to it that we consume visible difference daily. Foucault notes that starting in the 1960s, "industrial societies could content themselves with a much looser form of power over the body."[3] The joint success of the civil rights and sexual liberation movements, in perverse combination with the post-World War II advertising and mass-media boom, has affected "the kind of body the current society needs."[4]

The question for media analysts is to define *what* kind of body this is, or what kind of bod*ies* are needed and/or tolerated by current societies, and to describe how the apparatus of body and power functions in popular culture today. The *Pumping Iron* films furnish a wealth of raw material for such an analysis. Since they deal with bodybuilding, it would seem apparent from the very start that the bodies we see are *not* natural. After all, they are clearly the products of individual obsession, created with great effort in the gym, through dieting and even drugs. Moreover, the contestants clearly try to "sell" their bodies, first to the contest judges, then to a burgeoning group of bodybuilding entrepreneurs who promote a vast array of products. Yet though the contestants' bodies are obviously and necessarily constructions, up for comparison and sale, there is an overwhelming need on the part of the judges, the audiences, and even many of the contestants to see bodies as representative of "Body" with a capital B, a natural and God-given essence, segregated and defined, as the films and contests themselves are, according to sex and gender roles.[5]

Body, capital B, participates in myth, not history. References to the mythic status of these extra-muscular bodies appear throughout both films, reinforcing our perception of bodies as "Body." Both men and women are associated with heroes and heroines, gods and goddesses. The contestants compete for the titles of Mr. and Miss Olympia, respectively. The theme song of *Pumping Iron* tells us, "Everybody [every body?] wants to be a hero / Everybody wants to live forever." *Pumping Iron II* opens with shots of mountains and power lines, then shows Bev Francis, the 180-pound Australian power lifter turned bodybuilder, seated next to and looking up at statues of muscular goddesses. Similar shots of other women recur later, though then the emphasis is on femininity via statues of Venus.

A sense of history is not absent from these films, however. On the contrary, because they are documentaries (albeit staged documentaries), the spectator knows that the contests have taken place, and that the characters are real people. Moreover, because these characters are social actors, the spectator also assumes that the issues they discuss in *Pumping Iron II* (and ignore in *Pumping Iron*) are of contemporary concern. Paradoxically, though, the historical references inherent in the form of documentary hide the fact that the *Pumping Iron* films are films, with narrative and visual strategies. Like the bodies they chronicle, they too become part of nature.[6]

In order to separate myth from history in these films, and in order to evaluate the representation of men and women bodybuilders in the broader context of the societal organization of body and power today, it is necessary to separate artificially the terms they entangle. Therefore, in what follows, I look in turn at how sex/gender, sexuality, and race are perceived and constructed as visible, physical differences, in the film narratives and images. The conclusion recombines the three categories and discusses how history is obfuscated by representation and sales: within the competitions, within the films, and within society at large.

Because women are the subjects of *Pumping Iron II,* the fact of visible difference based on sex is inescapable. It displaces the competition as the central topic of the film narrative. In order to define which woman has the best and most well-defined body, the judges feel compelled to define "body" in relation to "woman." The contestants, too, wonder about the relationship between gender (femininity or masculinity), sex (female or male bodies), and bodybuilding. The film makes their questions its own, marshaling images and sounds to ask: Is a woman still a woman if she looks like a man? Where is the vanishing point?

In contrast, *Pumping Iron* simply chronicles the 1976 Mr. Olympia contest. The reason why is obvious in retrospect: because men are the norm in patriarchal society, visible difference cannot be an issue. The association of muscularity with men poses no conflict between sex and gender: muscular men are seen as "natural."[7] As Richard Dyer says of male pinups: "Muscularity is a key term in appraising men's bodies. . . . Muscularity is the *sign* of power—natural, achieved, phallic."[8] What then could be more natural, more familiar, more right than men pumping iron?

Images of muscular women, on the other hand, are disconcerting, even threatening. They disrupt the equation of men with strength and women with weakness that underpins gender roles and power relations, and that has by now come to seem familiar and comforting (though perhaps in differing ways) to both women and men. Because of this threat to established values, *Pumping Iron II* has an edge of excitement and danger missing from *Pumping Iron*. Yet *Pumping Iron II* is not wholeheartedly in favor of muscular women; on the contrary, it is both ambiguous and ambivalent. Contradictions abound within the narrative and between the narrative and the images.

On the surface of the narrative, *Pumping Iron II* seems to promote strong women and to treat women in the same way as men. As the sequel to *Pumping Iron*, it has the same narrative structure: both films begin with interviews of the top contenders, intercut with training scenes; both climax with the bodybuilding contest.

On a deeper level, however, *Pumping Iron II* treats women very differently than *Pumping Iron* treats men. *Pumping Iron* does not need to ask "What is man?" while *Pumping Iron II* cannot do anything else. When the question "What is woman?" is asked about women bodybuilders, it seems topical, even liberal. In actuality, however, it is centuries old, and standard Hollywood practice. Steve Neale could be describing the basic plots of the *Pumping Iron* films when he writes: "While mainstream cinema, in its assumption of a male norm, perspective and look, can constantly take women and the female image as the object of investigation, it has rarely investigated men and the male image in the same kind of way: women are a problem, a source of anxiety, of obsessive inquiry; men are not. Where women are investigated, men are tested."[9]

Of course, there are individual moments within the narrative which contradict both the deep and the surface levels of the film. At these times the majority of spectators in the contest audiences and the film theater are aligned with the more muscular and articulate women. Although the conventionally prettier and sexier Rachel McLish has her ardent supporters, on the whole, Bev Francis and Carla Dunlap appear more intelligent and more likable. Throughout the film, Bev and Carla come across as outspoken and independent, good sports and good sportswomen, while time and again Rachel is characterized as a whining, cheating, Bible-belting brat.

Similarly, the film does not encourage spectators to adopt the positions articulated by the universally white male International Federation of Body-builders (IFBB) officials: on the contrary, they look ridiculous. In a key pre-contest sequence, Ben Weider, chairman of the IFBB, intones: "What we're looking for is something that's right down the middle. A woman who has a certain amount of aesthetic femininity, but yet has that muscle tone to show that she is an athlete." The retort of one of the younger male judges seems far more logical and far less patronizing: "That's like being told there is a certain point beyond which women can't go in this sport. What does that mean exactly? It's as though the US Ski Federation told women skiers that they can only ski so fast." In the final contest scenes the officials' competence as officials is thrown into question: even with the help of a calculator, they are unable to total the women's scores.

Moments such as these, where the audience is encouraged to identify with strong women and to reject "dolls" and patriarchs, are certainly victories for feminism. But they must be evaluated in the context of the entire film, and especially in the context of the film images. The images of *Pumping Iron II* are more ambiguous than the narrative because society defines how we look at women's bodies very narrowly indeed.

When bodybuilding is understood just as a sport, the analogy between bodybuilding and skiing made by the young judge and endorsed by a certain part of the film narrative is absolutely valid. The problem is that, unlike skiing, bodybuilding for women entails confronting and judging the near-naked female body. One has only to turn to Freud to appreciate why, for the male spectator especially, the female body is fraught with both danger and delight.

In Freud's analysis, men see women not just as different, but also as castrated, as not men. The male subject simultaneously recognizes and denies difference: the woman is different, *unheimlich* even,[10] yet she is also the same, just missing a part.[11] At one and the same time he desires and dreads the woman's visible difference: it evokes his fears of the loss and/or inadequacy of the penis, while simultaneously establishing male superiority based on posses-sion of the penis. In the essay entitled "Fetishism," Freud maintains that men negotiate castration anxiety caused by "the terrifying shock of . . . the sight of the female genitals" in three different ways: "Some become homosexual in consequence of this experience, others ward it off by creating a fetish, and the great majority overcome it" and choose women as their love objects.[12]

In *Pumping Iron II* in particular, the problems posed by the images of female bodies provoke responses involving all three of Freud's strategies: homosexuality, fetishism, and heterosexuality. Male ambivalence toward women's bodies is omnipresent. A fear of visible difference and a fear of the

Carla Dunlap poses in *Pumping Iron II: The Women*

abolition of visible difference paradoxically coexist, so tightly are body and power interconnected here.

The images of the more muscular women inflame male anxiety because they threaten the abolition of visible difference. In an article on a made-for-TV movie about women bodybuilders, Laurie Schulze comments: "The danger to male heterosexuality lurks in the implication that any male sexual interest in the muscular female is not heterosexual at all, but homosexual: not only is *she* 'unnatural,' but the female bodybuilder possesses the power to invert normal *male* sexuality."[13] Since Bev Francis looks and moves "like a man," homophobic patriarchal ideology whispers that men who find her attractive must be gay, and, further, that women who find her attractive must be lesbians. Bev's muscles, dress, heavy facial features, and "unfeminine" body language evoke the stereotype of what a lesbian looks like: the butch, the lesbian who is immediately recognizable as such, visibly different. Women who find Bev attractive would, as a result, be defined as fems, lesbians who, in Joan Nestle's words, are "known by . . . their choices," while butches are "known by their appearances."[14] In each case, the stereotypes of what kind of bodies gay men and lesbians find attractive are constructed around the phallus: gay men are assumed to be wimps who worship "he-men," while lesbians are assumed to be women who *are* "he-men" or women who worship "he/she-men."

The film narrative attempts to circumvent the stigma of homosexuality evoked by Bev's muscles by having her repeatedly insist that she is a woman, not a man, and by repeatedly showing her accompanied by her trainer/boyfriend, Steve Weinberger. But these narrative strategies cannot be successful in allaying male castration anxieties and/or homophobia in general, especially since they are reinforced by a fear of loss of love. Where men are concerned, Freud mentions this fear only in passing:[15] for him women, far more than men, are concerned about the loss of love attendant on the abolition of visible difference. Indeed, in Freudian terms, loss of love, not castration, constitutes the most significant *female* anxiety.[16] Adrienne Rich, in contrast, argues that "it seems more probable that men really fear . . . that women could be indifferent to them altogether" than that "the male need to control women's sexuality results from some primal male 'fear of women.'"[17]

In *Pumping Iron II,* the association of muscularity, masculinity, and lesbianism invokes these fears of a loss of love for spectators of both sexes, though in different ways. If heterosexual men see Bev as a lesbian, she is threatening: lesbians incarnate sexual indifference to men. If heterosexual women see Bev as a lesbian, they must reject her: to like her would mean admitting that they themselves might be lesbian, which would in turn entail the abnegation of traditionally feminine powers and privileges.

The overwhelming majority of the female characters in *Pumping Iron II,* from the bodybuilders themselves to the one female judge, fear that a redefinition of femininity will entail the loss of love, power, and privilege.[18] It is fear of loss of love that motivates one of the women to say, rather inanely, but nonetheless quite sincerely and even persuasively, "I hope really that they stick with the feminine look. . . . I mean, really, a woman's a woman. That's my philosophy. I think she should look like a woman. And I think that when you lose that, what's the point of being a woman?"

Most of the images in *Pumping Iron II* espouse the same philosophy. In general, they function to defuse rather than provoke male and female spectators' anxieties about muscular women by fetishizing women's bodies and by making them the objects of heterosexual desire. The differences between the two *Pumping Iron* films illuminate how these strategies work. In four areas in particular—mise-en-scène, costume and props, development of secondary characters, and framing and camera movements—sexuality is surreptitiously linked with sex and gender in such a way as to support heterosexual and patriarchal ideologies.

The settings of both films consist largely of gyms and competition stages. In addition, the "stars" of each film are interviewed at home, in their hotel rooms, and backstage before the final, climactic contest. *Pumping Iron II* adds something more, however. In two sequences involving groups of women bodybuilders, the beauty of the female body is evoked via lyrical images, even as individual women debate the essence of femininity. The first of these is set in Gold's Gym in California. It opens with a series of shots of women lifting weights. Then the camera moves with the women through the door marked "Ladies Only" into the shower room. There, through lather and steam, naked female bodies are glimpsed. The scene is a fetishist's delight: the camera pans and cuts from torsos to biceps to necks to breasts to heads. The second sequence again involves a group of women and is shot in a pool outside of Caesar's Palace. The camera movements, the editing, even the lighting, echo those of the Gold's Gym sequence, only here doubly frozen bodies—the female statues—add to the camera/spectator's titillation and admiration of muscular but distinctly feminine women's bodies, portrayed as so many water nymphs. In each sequence, the images counteract the threat posed by muscular, active women by placing them in traditionally sexy, feminine environments (showers and pools) and by showing them in stereotypical ways (frozen, fragmented, or both). Needless to say, Bev Francis and Carla Dunlap are not present in either group: they represent alternative possibilities of femininity.

The costumes and props used in both films further align sexuality, nature, and the body. The most striking example of this process occurs in the photo sessions for bodybuilding magazines included in each film. Rachel McLish flexes for the camera, holding dumbbells and wearing feathers, chains, and a tiger suit; Arnold Schwarzenegger wades knee deep in women, then plays in the ocean and poses against the sky; Lou Ferrigno, Schwarzenegger's chief competitor, crouches somewhat awkwardly next to a cheetah. While the shots of Rachel add a spice of sadism missing from the shots of the men, all testify to an imbrication of sexuality, sex, gender, and nature.

Pumping Iron II again differs from *Pumping Iron*, however, in its creation of a category of secondary characters, "boyfriends," with no equivalent in the first film. Again and again, not only Bev but also Rachel and Lori Bowen are shown with their men. Lori's fiancé (a male exotic dancer—the object par excellence of a certain class-linked, heterosexual female desire) even proposes to her in front of the camera. Throughout, the film imperceptibly but inflexibly imposes what Adrienne Rich would call a "compulsory heterosexual orientation" on the female bodybuilders.[19] Only Carla is seen in an all-female environment, accompanied by her mother and sister and without a boyfriend or male trainer. In an interview, she described how she told George Butler that she would be seen with her boyfriend, who was married, only if Butler was willing to pay for the divorce costs.[20] In *Pumping Iron*, on the other hand, only Arnold Schwarzenegger is constantly surrounded by women, glorying in his supermasculinity. But these women are nameless and interchangeable bodies, not secondary characters of note.

Finally, the way in which the two films are shot differs radically. As is obvious in the discussion above of the Gold's Gym and Caesar's Palace pool sequences, *Pumping Iron II* positions women as fetishized objects of the camera's and spectator's gaze far more than *Pumping Iron* does men. Except in the case of scenes involving Bev, the camera movements, editing strategies, framing, and lighting resemble those of soft-core pornographic films. It comes as a surprise to learn that the camera person in *Pumping Iron II* is a woman, Dyanna Taylor, best known for a documentary about the first women's team to climb Mount Annapurna. Although in interviews she has said that she wanted to capture the excitement of bodybuilding by using light-weight cameras and multiple setups, this has very little impact on how the spectator, and the film, look at near-naked women. Though muscular, breasts and buttocks still appear as tits and ass. Marcia Pally graphically describes the voyeurism of the opening shots as follows:

> Close to the woman's skin, the camera slides along her nude body. It runs down a leg, around the soft, flat stomach, and over the hip bones like a steeplechaser barely acknowledging a shrub. It sweeps across her back to the nape of her neck, and then to an arm more venous than most. It circles a shapely thigh brushing her body with a motion that is part caress but more a search. It scans her surface and takes note; like the cop in any *policier*, it knows what to remember and what to reveal. The case under investigation is the nature of femininity; the female body lies here in evidence.[21]

The men's bodies in *Pumping Iron* are not filmed in the same way: they are not panned or framed like this, nor is lighting used to the same effect. Because the male body in patriarchal societies is not *acknowledged* to be either mysterious or problematic, it is simply not displayed for the spectator's investigation and consumption to the same extent as the female body. In actuality, however, it is intensely problematic: the threat of castration is everywhere present and everywhere hidden. Repressions of and allusions to the precarious status of the male body permeate the visual strategies of *Pumping Iron*. These male bodybuilders are freaks just as Bev Francis is: they are *all* too muscular. Lou Ferrigno's subsequent casting as the Hulk and Arnold Schwarzenegger's success as Conan the Barbarian and the Terminator are not coincidental. Their excessive muscularity has made them oddities and has only increased male anxiety and awareness that, to quote Richard Dyer again, "the penis is not a patch on the phallus."[22] This is why, in contrast to the emphasis on tits and ass in *Pumping Iron II,* the camera never focuses on the bulge in Arnold's and Lou's bikinis or pans their naked bodies in the shower: to look might reveal too much or too little, threatening the tenuous equation established between masculinity, muscularity, and men.

The fear of visible difference joined with the fear of an abolition of visible difference thus makes it exceedingly difficult to separate sexuality, sex, and gender in the *Pumping Iron* films and in society as a whole.[23] Although *Pumping Iron II* relies for its dramatic tension on the possibility of a separation between sex and sexuality, the contradictions between and within narrative and image reassure us of the continuation of the status quo: sex, gender, and sexuality are one, indivisible.

A similar politics of conflation operates in the films' representation of race. Yet there are significant differences between the way sex and sexuality and race and sexuality are linked, both in these films and in the society they portray and address. Visible difference based on sex must be determined according to secondary characteristics such as muscularity because of the fact that the primary characteristic, ownership or lack of a penis, is hidden. Although, or maybe paradoxically *because,* it is there in plain sight, racial difference is not incessantly discussed and examined the way sexual difference is. In the Reagan U.S., as opposed to in past or present colonial societies, race is ignored and overlooked, hidden by discourse the way sexual difference is hidden on the body. A significant number of Americans prefer to "export" racial discrimination overseas—to South Africa, for example—rather than acknowledge it at home. When race is discussed, it is often presented via stereotypes, as it would be in colonial discourse.[24]

The *Pumping Iron* films incorporate both strategies—silencing and stereotyping—in the relationships they establish among race, body, and power. Neither is about racial difference, but again, especially in *Pumping Iron II,* race plays a significant role. In *Pumping Iron* race is not regarded as an issue, even though the Mr. Olympia competition takes place in South Africa. Here blacks are simply minor characters of no real importance to either the narrative or the images. In *Pumping Iron II,* however, race is constantly visible in the person of Carla Dunlap, one of the four major women characters and the winner of the Miss Olympia title. Yet the film narrative and images and Carla herself downplay her color, concentrating instead on the issues of sex, sexuality, and the body. Carla stands out less because she is black than because she spearheads the revolt against enforced femininity and because, as mentioned earlier, she is the only woman who is not involved with men.[25] Her articulateness, her sensitivity toward and support of the other women athletes, and her interactions with her mother and sister make her extremely appealing to both feminists and nonfeminists. What is interesting is that, despite her autonomy and despite the fact that she is more muscular than many of the other women, she never poses a threat of homosexuality the way Bev does because, by comparison with Bev, she still looks and moves like a woman. Carla plainly knows how to apply makeup and how to dress seductively. Because images override narrative, the possibility that she might actually be a lesbian or that she might be the object of lesbian desire is passed over, silenced: only the most visible lesbians are recognized as such, in the film and in society as a whole. If anything, *Pumping Iron II* underlines Carla's grace and femininity: a sequence showing her practicing synchronized swimming—that most graceful of sports, one of the few Olympic events so far open only to women—is inserted, not coincidentally, right after she challenges the judges' authority to define women's bodybuilding according to their ideas of what women should be. Accompanied by melodic, andante piano music, she swims, slowly and sensuously, in an azure pool. The setting and the sounds could not be more romantic. The dual threat posed by her muscularity and her feminism is contained and displaced by an emphasis on her femininity and sexuality.

But the most ambivalent sequence involving race, sex, and sexuality is Carla's free-form posing routine, performed to Grace Jones's song "Feel Up." The song begins with jungle noises, moves on to a sexy, upbeat message of independence and strength, and ends with jungle noises again. Carla's choreography complements the two moods of the song, passing from mystery and bewilderment to flashy self-confidence to mystery again. Although neither the song nor Carla's routine is racist, the jungle sounds and Carla's seductive posing routine might easily be reabsorbed within the framework of racist images and attitudes that permeate mass-media representations of blacks. As Gloria Joseph says, "The very presence of black women shrouded in sexual suggestiveness is loaded in particularly racist ways" because racists conceive of black women as "being intrinsically nothing but sexual."[26] The combination of exoticism, blackness, femininity, and sexuality is also, as Sander L. Gilman points out, reminiscent of Freud's equation of female sexuality and the dark continent.[27]

Given the tensions within the film and within society, the judges' choice of Carla as Miss Olympia can be seen, in Foucauldian terms, as a response by the power apparatus to an urgent need in society.[28] Threatened by the specter of the abolition of visible difference (muscular women), the male judges consciously and unconsciously affirm their need for visible difference by choosing a woman who still looks like a woman (different) and who is black (different). The judges' decision can be seen as a simultaneous recognition and disavowal of racial difference. This ambivalence, as Homi Bhabha provocatively argues in "The Other Question," links the racial stereotype with the sexual fetish:

> Fetishism is always a "play" or vacillation between the archaic affirmation of wholeness/similarity—in Freud's terms: "All men have penises"; in ours "All men have the same skin/race/culture"—and the anxiety associated with lack or difference—again, for Freud, "Some do not have penises"; for us "Some do not have the same skin/race/culture." . . . The fetish or stereotype gives access to an "identity" which is predicated as much on mastery and pleasure as it is on anxiety and defence. . . .[29]

Most important, however, the "identity" of the fetish or the stereotype masks history. It is synchronic, not diachronic. Edward Said offers another, potentially more historical, version of the ambivalence which characterizes how the racial other (in his analysis, the Oriental other) is seen: "The Orient at large vacillates between the West's contempt for what is familiar and its shivers of delight in—or fear of—novelty."[30]

Here, in the appeal to and the denial of history, is the key to how and why *Pumping Iron* and *Pumping Iron II* confront both the threat of sexual and racial difference and the threat of the abolition of sexual and racial difference. The muscular bodies we see, whether black or white, male or female, are all sold to us as new and improved versions of an old product. *Pumping Iron* downplays visible difference in its search for the ultimate meaning of generic "man." The film spectator and the audience at the Mr. Olympia competition take it for granted that Arnold Schwarzenegger should and will win the contest: after all, he is the most muscular, most articulate, most virile, and most Aryan man around. *Pumping Iron II* plays up the visible differences of sex and race in its search for the new woman who can still be admired and loved. The title song, heard at the beginning and again at the end, betrays the film's preference for a male-oriented, heterosexual eroticism, especially because the start of the film combines the suggestively seductive lyrics with slow pans of a woman's naked body on a tanning bed: "I am the future / Beyond your dreams . . . / I got the muscles / Future sex / I got the motion / Future sex / I got the body / Future sex / Touch this body / Feel this body." From the start, therefore, it is clear that women bodybuilders will be defined by their feminine sex appeal. The men who profit from the sport of bodybuilding, including director George Butler, know that the future of women's bodybuilding depends on "how well it can be marketed to the general public—on how many women can be made to want to look like . . . Rachel McLish, and, to a lesser degree, on how many men can be made to want to sleep with them."[31]

The strategy behind *Pumping Iron II* is thus a marketing strategy. As a film, it wants to make, package, and sell history, not just watch it. *Pumping Iron II* aspires to be more than the chronicle of a contest, more than a sequel subtitled *The Women*. In his eagerness to promote and sell women's bodybuilding, director George Butler staged not only the events leading up to the contest, but also the contest itself. He spent months booking Caesar's Palace and convincing Bev Francis to participate, confident that Caesar's was the last frontier and that Bev would inevitably cross it. As in television coverage of sports events, "the worlds of sport and show business meet upon the ground of stardom and competition" in both *Pumping Iron* films.[32] Unique to these films, however, is the way the spectacle of the competition and the spectacle of the film are merged with the spectacle of the near-naked, and therefore supposedly natural, body.

In the final analysis, because they emphasize and appeal to the body, the *Pumping Iron* films resemble advertising far more than sports documentaries or show-business dramas. As Marcia Pally says, watching *Pumping Iron II* is like watching one long Virginia Slims commercial: "You've come a long way, baby."[33] The skillful combination of sex, gender, and sexuality, the silencing or stereotyping of race, and the complete bracketing of class readily recall basic advertising principles. In both films, slick images and hip music repetitively say the same thing: there is no history, there is no work, there is only leisure and sex. Both films repress the history of bodybuilding and the largely working-class affiliation of its contestants and audiences, choosing instead to emphasize the body as art, sculpture, and timeless spectacle.[34] Only a few sepia stills of nineteenth-century strong men, glimpsed at the beginning and end of *Pumping Iron*, testify to the popular and fairground origins of the sport. No mention is made in *Pumping Iron II* of early strong women such as Mme Minerva, Mme Montagna, the Great Vulcana, or Katie Sandwina, the Lady Hercules. While it is obvious in *Pumping Iron II* that the Miss Olympia competition in many ways resembles striptease shows and beauty contests, no mention is made of the very recent (1970s) history of female bodybuilding contests, where models and strippers posed only to titillate the largely male audiences of the men's competitions.

Today female bodybuilding has moved closer to being a sport. Nonetheless, the nagging suspicion remains that the "long way" traveled by the women of *Pumping Iron II* dead-ends in the chance to be treated, once again, as advertising objects. Now attractive white female as well as male bodybuilders motivate spectators to buy protein and vitamin supplements, to use certain bodybuilding machines, to join health clubs, and to consume magazines, books, and, of course, movies.[35] As always, sales are more important than sports, and much more important than social commentary. Far from abolishing stereotypes based on visible difference, *Pumping Iron II* and *Pumping Iron* as well visually position the body as spectacle, then sell it as big business. In both films, the threat of visible difference and the threat of the abolition of visible difference are contained and marketed—as flex appeal.

NOTES

This chapter was originally published in *Cinema Journal* 28, no. 4 (Summer 1989): 38-51.

1. In the case of the women's movement, organizing around the issues of abortion, rape, physical abuse of women, and pornography is often based as much on the idea that the body should not be violated as on the idea that women have a right to choose for themselves. Unfortunately, organizing predicated on the inviolability of the body frequently overlaps in highly problematic ways with New Right interests.

2. Michel Foucault, "The Confession of the Flesh," in *Power/Knowledge: Selected Interviews and Other Writings, 1972-1977* (New York: Pantheon Books, 1980), p. 195.

3. Michel Foucault, "Body/Power," in *Power/Knowledge*, p. 58.

4. Ibid.

5. No doubt because the *Pumping Iron* films seek to legitimate bodybuilding as "natural" and "healthy," neither film mentions steroids, though male bodybuilders in particular often use them. At one point in *Pumping Iron* Lou Ferrigno takes handfuls of pills, but they are probably vitamins. Except for an oblique—and catty—suggestion by Rachel McLish that Bev Francis may have used steroids ("the question is not how she did it [i.e., how she got so big], but where she's at right now"), *Pumping Iron II: The Women* also shies away from the question of drugs. Alteration of the female body through costume (Rachel's bikini top is judged illegal because it is padded) and breast implants (an issue the judges say they ignore because such implants are too hard to detect) are the only artificial interventions the film acknowledges.

6. The effacement of production is typical of documentary film and classic narrative cinema. Following Edward Buscombe and Roy Peters, Garry Whannel describes how these cinematic conventions have been adapted to television sports coverage in order to "minimi[ze] audience awareness of the mediating effect of television." The visual style of television sports coverage has in turn influenced the *Pumping Iron* films as sports documentaries. See Garry Whannel, "Fields in Vision: Sport and Representation," *Screen* 25, no. 3 (May-June 1984): 101. See also Edward Buscombe, ed., *Football on Television* (London: British Film Institute Television Monograph, 1974), and Roy Peters, *Television Coverage of Sport* (Birmingham: Stencilled Paper, Centre for Contemporary Cultural Studies, 1976).

7. As Kate Millett points out, however, "the heavier musculature of the male, a secondary sexual characteristic and common among mammals, is biological in origin but is also culturally encouraged through breeding, diet and exercise." Moreover, physical strength has little to do with gender roles and power. On the contrary: "At present, as in the past, physical exertion is very generally a class factor, those at the bottom performing the most strenuous tasks, whether they be strong or not." Kate Millett, *Sexual Politics* (Garden City, N.Y.: Doubleday, 1970), p. 27.

8. Richard Dyer, "Don't Look Now," *Screen* 23, no. 3-4 (September-October 1982): 67-68.

9. Steve Neale, "Masculinity as Spectacle," *Screen* 24, no. 6 (November-December 1983): 15-16.

10. Sigmund Freud, "The 'Uncanny,'" in *On Creativity and the Unconscious* (New York: Harper and Row, 1958), pp. 122-61.

11. Freud's analyses encompass both perspectives, but the second is the more basic. Susan Lurie critiques Freud's assumption that men and boys are the norm: "In psychoanalysis the meaning of woman is fixed not as difference, but as 'mutation' in the context of a desired sameness." Susan Lurie, "The Construction of the 'Castrated Woman' in Psychoanalysis and Cinema," *Discourse* 4 (Winter 1981-82): 54. For similar critiques, see also Stephen Heath, "Difference," *Screen* 19, no. 3 (Autumn 1978): 51-112, and Karen Horney, "The Dread of Woman," in *Feminine Psychology* (New York: W. W. Norton, 1967), pp. 133-46.

12. The first of the three choices Freud discusses is homosexuality. Homosexuals, he argues, openly acknowledge the primacy of the phallus: men are taken as sexual objects because they possess the penis, which the child imagines that the mother he loved also had. Yet this solution is unacceptable to society. Fetishism is preferable because "it endow[s] women with the attribute which makes them acceptable as sexual objects." Unlike homosexuality, fetishes are not prohibited by society; on the contrary, as Freud remarks, "they are easily obtainable and sexual gratification by their means is thus very convenient." For these reasons, "the fetishist has no trouble in getting what other men have to woo and exert themselves to obtain." Sigmund Freud, "Fetishism," in *Sexuality and the Psychology of Love* (New York: Macmillan, 1963), p. 216.

13. Laurie Jane Schulze, "*Getting Physical*: Text/Context/Reading and the Made-for-TV Movie," *Cinema Journal* 25, no. 2 (Winter 1986): 43.

14. Joan Nestle, "The Fem Question," in *Pleasure and Danger: Exploring Female Sexuality*, ed. Carole S. Vance (London: Routledge and Kegan Paul, 1984), p. 233.

15. Sigmund Freud, "Anxiety and Instinctual Life," in *New Introductory Lectures on Psycho-analysis* (New York: W. W. Norton, 1965), pp. 77-78.

16. Ibid., pp. 76-77. Karen Horney would agree, though as usual her evaluation of this phenomenon is critical both of the phenomenon and of Freud's position. See, for example, Karen Horney, "The Overvaluation of Love," in *Feminine Psychology*, pp. 182-213, and "The Neurotic Need for Love," in ibid., pp. 245-58.

17. Adrienne Rich, "Compulsory Heterosexuality and Lesbian Existence," *Signs* 5, no. 4 (Summer 1980): 187.

18. No doubt Freud would argue that those women in the film (Bev, Carla) or in the audience (feminists, lesbians) who do not fear the loss of love by men do so only because they covet the phallus/penis directly. They have not made the requisite substitution of baby for penis.

19. See Rich, "Compulsory Heterosexuality and Lesbian Existence," pp. 631-60.

20. Marcia Pally, "Women of 'Iron,'" *Film Comment* 21, no. 4 (July-August 1985): 62.

21. Ibid., p. 60.

22. Dyer, "Don't Look Now," p. 71.

23. The confusion of these three categories, as Gayle Rubin convincingly argues, is all the more easily accomplished because in English "sex" refers both to gender and gender identity and to sexual activity. See Rubin, "Thinking Sex: Notes for a Radical Theory of the Politics of Sexuality," in Vance, ed., *Pleasure and Danger*, p. 307. In sharp contrast to many feminists, Rubin refuses to see women's experience of sexuality as engendering. For her "sexual oppression cuts across other modes of social inequality, sorting out individuals and groups according to its own intrinsic dynamics. It is not reducible to, or understandable in terms of, class, race, ethnicity, or gender." Ibid., p. 293.

24. See, for example, Homi K. Bhabha, "The Other Question . . . ," *Screen* 24, no. 6 (November-December 1983): 18-36.

25. According to Nik Cohn in *Women of Iron: The World of Female Bodybuilders* (n.p.: Wideview Books, 1981), p. 59, Carla's own experiences agree with the film's privileging of sexual difference over racial difference. As an adult, Carla has found sexual discrimination to pose more problems than racial discrimination. As a child, she was sheltered from racial prejudice by class privilege:

> Of all the top women bodybuilders, she was the only black. A lot of brothers and sisters had asked her if that was a dilemma. She always told them *No*, and that was the truth. She had never been taught that color was a limitation. Those were not the kind of roots she'd grown from.
>
> Her childhood had been wonderful. Her father was a chemist in Newark, and his children were provided with everything they needed. Carla had four sisters and a brother. They lived in a huge house. There were horses and boats, and lots of space to breathe in. *A typical American middle class background*, she called it. They summered on a yacht.

26. Gloria I. Joseph, "The Media and Blacks—Selling It Like It Isn't," in *Common Differences,* ed. Gloria I. Joseph and Jill Lewis (Garden City, N.Y.: Doubleday, 1981), p. 163.

27. Sander L. Gilman, "Black Bodies, White Bodies," *Critical Inquiry* 12, no. 1 (Autumn 1985): 238.

28. See Foucault, "The Confession of the Flesh," in *Power/Knowledge,* pp. 194–95.

29. Bhabha, "The Other Question," 27. Bhabha goes on to suggest that blacks themselves participate in the creation and perpetuation of the stereotype, much as women desire to be seen as different and consent to be fetishized out of a fear of loss of love.

30. Edward Said, *Orientalism* (London: Routledge and Kegan Paul, 1978), pp. 58-59.

31. Charles Gaines, *Pumping Iron: The Art and Sport of Bodybuilding* (New York: Simon and Schuster, 1981), pp. 220–22.

32. Whannel, "Fields in Vision," p. 99.

33. Pally, "Women of 'Iron,'" p. 60.

34. While in the history of Western art men have traditionally been portrayed as muscular, "the shape to which the female body tends to return . . . is one which emphasizes its biological functions . . . most often suggested by a softly curved cello shape. . . ." Charles Gaines, *Pumping Iron II: The Unprecedented Woman* (New York: Simon and Schuster, 1984), p. 20.

35. There is a clear racial as well as a sexist bias in the advertising business surrounding women's bodybuilding. Gloria Steinem writes: "Though she has great beauty and the speech skills of a first-class actress, Carla Dunlap has been offered no television commercials. Even the dozens of bodybuilding magazines have declined to put this first black woman champion on the cover." Gloria Steinem, "Coming Up: The Unprecedented Women," *Ms.* 14, no. 1 (July 1985): 109.

8 . . . A Left/Right Combination: Populism and Depression-Era Boxing Films

No one makes it out on their own.
— Maya Angelou

Baseball may be the self-appointed "national pastime," and football and basketball may get higher television ratings, but more films have been made in Hollywood about prizefighting than any other sport.[1] By pitting one fighter against another with only their hands to do battle, and by roping the combatants off from the rest of the world, boxing presents a dramatic metaphor for the rugged individualism that has traditionally been a central element of Hollywood's mythology. But while fight films celebrate the ideal of self-sufficiency, those made during the Depression era also question the sport's underlying myth of omnipotent individualism. Responding to the concerns that many in the United States felt about the country's future during the 1930s, these Depression-era boxing films endorsed a populist ideology, mythologizing the often ethnic or black fighter whose success depends upon group support and whose actions promoted traditional agrarian notions of the common good.

Professional boxing in the United States has always attracted youth from subaltern groups who have very little opportunity for self-determination. As immigrant communities settled in cities after the Civil War, their young men would often learn to fight in order to protect their neighborhoods against incursions by other ethnic groups. With the limited work opportunities available in these urban slums, boys who showed special aptitude in street fighting, and were willing to undergo intense training and physical punishment, would perfect their pugilistic skills in the hope of becoming professionals.[2] Only a select few who entered the ring were able to attain wealth and fame, and even fewer succeeded in overcoming the effects of crooked management. Given their tendency to overspend as a way of compensating for their poor background, their lack of any other marketable skills, and the often devastating effects of the punishment they took, boxers usually had a bleak future. According to Steven Riess, "many retired fighters, especially the club boxers who didn't have any substantial fame, ended up about where they had started out."[3]

During the 1930s, jobless rates of 25 percent and higher for young people prompted an especially large number of working-class young men to try their hand at prizefighting.[4] Around eight thousand boxers entered the ring as professionals in the U.S. during that decade, although only a small percentage of those achieved title contender status.[5] The popularity of boxing as one of the few avenues to the American Dream in those lean years may explain the large number of Hollywood films about prizefighting made during the 1930s. Such Depression-era films depict boxing as a means of advancement for disenfranchised urban youth, and at the same time use the sport as a metaphor for the economic hard times.

Warner Brothers dominated the Depression cycle of boxing films, presenting them in the form of the aesthetically spare, "socially conscious" melodramas which were the hallmark of the studio in the 1930s. Not that other Hollywood studios left the making of boxing pictures entirely to Warners. MGM, Warner Brothers' political and stylistic opposite, made one of the most commercially successful boxing films of the decade, *The Champ* (1931). Unlike most of the later Depression-era films about boxing, *The Champ* makes a last-ditch effort to endorse the old myth of individual self-reliance, essentially discounting any notion that social or economic forces might put limits on the rise to success.

Wallace Beery stars as Andy, a punch-drunk ex-heavyweight champion who lives a roller-coaster life in Tijuana with his young son Dink (Jackie Cooper). The ex-champ has occasional hot streaks at the crap table, but much of the time he is drunk and broke. Dink's mother, Linda (Irene Rich), and her wealthy second husband, Tony (Hale Hamilton), offer to take custody of the boy so as to give him a more stable home life and a chance to go to school, but Dink prefers to stay with his father, who loves him intensely. Anxious to better provide for Dink, Andy steers clear of the casinos and bars long enough to get a fight with the heavyweight champ of Mexico. For most of the bout the Mexican fighter punishes the out-of-shape American, but Andy somehow knocks out his opponent with a desperation punch. Despite his victory, the strain and punishment of the fight prove too much for Andy, and he dies of a heart attack in his dressing room. The film ends with Dink crying uncontrollably at the loss of his father and running into his mother's arms.

The Champ responds to concerns about the Depression through the class opposition between Andy and Tony as potential fathers for Dink. Meanwhile, the hard times which befall the Wallace Beery character are shown as resulting not from the general economy, but from his weakness and lack of discipline. The film never acknowledges that Andy's problems with gambling and alcohol could be linked to his lack of marketable job skills, and it suggests that he is simply punchy from too many blows to the head. Because *The Champ* gives no institutional or social explanation for this vocational injury, it makes Andy seem like a big child—lovable, but physically and intellectually inferior to the successful Tony.

In his discussion of Hollywood's thematic paradigm, Robert Ray describes how American films often avoid taking sides in ideological debates, preferring instead to assert that an unlimited potential for new achievement and wealth in America can overcome contradictions or conflict.[6] According to Ray, classic Hollywood's avoidance of choice between conflicting value systems usually results in a narrative structure that splits the film's "moral center" from its "interest center." *The Champ* sets up this split by endorsing Tony as representative of family, traditional morality, and the work ethic (even though by his own account his status and wealth derive more from inherited privilege than from individual achievement), while casting the film's star (Wallace Beery) as an underdog for whom the audience roots despite his weaknesses. Sneak previews of *The Champ* confirmed Andy as the center of viewer interest. An initial version of the film in which he loses to the Mexican champion before dying received such a poor response from test audiences that MGM head of production Irving Thalberg ordered the last scene reshot so that the American wins the fight. At a second preview of the revised version in which Andy wins, the audience cheered the final scene.[7]

The Champ also avoids the need for choice by displacing the class conflict between Andy and Tony into frontier imagery of conquest presented in the defeat of the Mexican champion.[8] Richard Slotkin describes how, as early as the 1870s, the newly developed mass-circulation press sought to effect a similar displacement of the class warfare that had erupted between workers and the corporate order. Even if the cause of the workers represented the "values of self-government and freedom of opportunity" on which the country was founded (and for which the Civil War had ostensibly been fought), such demands for political and economic self-determination threatened to undermine the profits of big business.[9] To avoid this obvious contradiction between corporate interests and egalitarian ideals, the press used the imagery of race war taken from the mythology of the frontier to describe the class conflict between workers and management. Working-class people were often likened to "redskin savages" as a way of undermining their ability to use democratic institutions in battles against landlords and employers. Such comparison recast class conflict in terms of "a choice . . . between 'savageism' and civilization."[10] More than fifty years later, *The Champ* still employs this strategy by shifting its focus from the class conflict between Andy and Tony to the fight between the white American boxer and the Mexican champ. In making this shift, the film also counts on audience antagonism toward Mexico left over from a recent conflict with the United States. In 1927, after the Mexican Congress passed legislation claiming a bigger share of the profits from oil that American companies were pumping in Mexico, Washington had threatened military intervention.[11] The defeat of Mexico's heavyweight champion provides a convenient means by which domestic class anger, fueled in American society by the Depression, can be projected outward onto the racial other. As the two fighters represent their respective countries, the U.S. can also symbolically reassert its claim to new frontiers and natural resources which make class warfare unnecessary at home.[12] *The Champ* not only succeeds in performing this displacement but knocks out two of the inconvenient "lower" characters with one punch—defeating the Mexican and at the same time enabling Andy to die heroically. The film's last image of Dink in his mother's arms becomes a Social Darwinist affirmation of "progress and right order" achieved through the removal of "inferior" peoples in favor of those better fit to survive the Depression.[13]

Another early 1930s film about prizefighting, Warner Brothers' *Winner Take All* (1932), depicts a similar prizefight between a Mexican and a U.S. boxer, but with somewhat different implications. *Winner Take All* tells the story of an Irish fighter from New York, Jimmy Kane (Jimmy Cagney), who has ruined his health by fighting too often and therefore goes to a dude ranch in New Mexico for a rest cure. At the desert resort, he meets a young widow named Peggy (Marian Nixon), whose little boy Dickie (Dickie Moore) is also ill. Soon after meeting Jimmy, Peggy receives a letter from her insurance company stating that it will not honor her late husband's life insurance policy because he had missed several premium payments just before his death. To cover Peggy's and Dickie's expenses at the spa, Jimmy decides to go to Tijuana and win the money in a prizefight. Jimmy's victory over a Mexican boxer functions like the climactic fight in *The Champ*, displacing any stand the film might take against the insurance company with race war imagery of European-American conquest of the West. By showing the greed and indifference of the insurance company, *Winner Take All* seems to be a relatively left-wing film; nevertheless, like most socially engaged Hollywood stories, it avoids an in-depth examination of class conflict, allowing the exploiters of the working class, in the words of Charles Eckert, "to recede like ghosts as quickly as they are glimpsed."[14]

This political waffling might be best explained by *Winner Take All*'s use of a populist ideology. Populism had a strong influence on Depression-era Hollywood—as it had during periods of economic crisis dating back to the nineteenth century—because it flattered the audience and at the same time preserved the essential values of capitalism. It had developed originally to articulate the support of middle-class rural Americans for the rights of the individual in the face of industrial revolution and growing corporate control of the economy. In all its later incarnations, populism nostalgically longed for a return to the land from big, immigrant-filled cities, and it sympathized with farmers or small-town mercantile capitalists rather than with the corporate executives, advocating local rather than federal government.[15]

The combination of progressive idealism and sentimental conservatism in populism made it appealing to both sides of the political debate. Its attacks on monopoly capital and its defense of the "common man" appealed to the left, but the solutions it offered—free enterprise, the work ethic, return to the land—also fit the conservative agenda. Hollywood liked this broad appeal, its "safe patriotic cure-all which demanded change in the form of past achievement," because it combined "Depression cynicism with the American Dream."[16]

Winner Take All embodies this hybrid ideology. On the one hand, the insurance company's refusal to pay off the policy of Peggy's late husband represents the type of corporate greed and indifference that from the left populist viewpoint was largely responsible for the economic hardship of the 1930s. On the other hand, Jimmy's solution to Peggy's financial problem also portrays a conservative response to this crisis: through the heroics of the small capitalist, the rugged individualist, who works not only for his own success but also for that of the community, the country will be saved.[17] His cure finished, Jimmy returns to New York to resume his boxing career, promising to send for Peggy and her son as soon as Dickie has finished his treatment. Jimmy, however, soon meets and becomes infatuated with an attractive young society woman, Joan Gibson (Virginia Bruce). As Joan and her friends make their rounds from ringside to nightclub table to her Park Avenue apartment, they embody another of the favorite populist villains, "the degenerate children of the wealthy class, spoiled and lazy wastrels who carelessly permit business affairs to deteriorate."[18] Joan interferes with Jimmy's business as a boxer by leading him on romantically. Although at first mildly excited by Jimmy's "primitive" energy, she never takes the boxer seriously as a lover. Jimmy, on the other hand, is obsessed with winning Joan, even going so far as to have plastic surgery to repair his broken nose and a cauliflower ear after she comments that he would be handsome without those battle scars. Despite warnings from his manager about Joan's insincerity, to protect his new face Jimmy abandons the aggressiveness in the ring that had earned him a shot at the lightweight title. When he learns, however, that she has skipped his title fight to go on a cruise to Cuba, Jimmy returns to his former style of all-out attack to finish off his opponent and win the championship just in time to board the ocean liner before it sails. Jimmy finds Joan with a blue-blood beau and exacts his revenge, knocking down the boyfriend and then Joan herself. His break with Joan not only removes her as the distraction that almost ruined his boxing career but also lets him be a hero whose title victory serves the film's populist "community"—in this case Jimmy's hardworking trainer, his honest manager, and Peggy, who agrees to marry him after all. In other words, individual assertiveness succeeds because of, and has value for, a supportive group—an idea consistent with the collectivist ideology of the New Deal, which provided Hollywood with still another way to attract a large audience by not aligning itself against capitalism.[19]

Differences between city and country life in several of these thirties boxing films also functioned as a displacement for more troubling conflicts between the working and ruling classes. Populism depicted the city as the home of shysters and sharpies, the monopolists and rich society snobs who have caused the Depression, a place where "the success ethic has given way to the jungle ethic."[20] Rural areas, on the other hand, recalled the country's agricultural past, its traditional values of self-help, its rugged individualism, yet also its good-neighborliness.

Even though prizefighters in the 1930s came largely from ethnic and racial groups who lived in large urban centers, several Depression-period films depict boxers who escape the city to find a better life in the country. Jimmy Key in *Winner Take All* finds his future family in the New Mexico desert. Ward Guisenberry (Wayne Morris), the boxer in *Kid Galahad* (Warner Brothers, 1937), is himself a farm boy who wins the heavyweight title with the help of his city-wise manager, Nick Donati (Edward G. Robinson), but finds true happiness by marrying Donati's sister Maria, who lives in the country with her mother. In *They Made Me a Criminal* (Warner Brothers, 1939), the manager of city-bred boxer Johnny Bradfield (John Garfield) kills a reporter and then frames the fighter for the crime. To avoid the police, Johnny goes on the lam, winding up on a date farm in Arizona. The farm is a kind of reform school for a group of juvenile delinquents (the Dead End Kids), and for Johnny as well, as he soon becomes a positive role model for the boys, helps to save the business from financial ruin, and falls in love with the social worker sister of one of the youths.

Whether or not the prizefighters in these films succeed in escaping to the country, their ability to survive the dangers of the city and the fight racket depends on the help of others. Although the boxers have plenty of rugged individualism, each of them also finds that he cannot make it to the top—or deal with the dangers and tragedies of the fight game—alone. For example, Ward Guisenberry in *Kid Galahad* relies on his manager Nick and Nick's girlfriend, Louise (Bette Davis), to keep gangster Turkey Morgan (Humphrey Bogart) at bay and help him win the title. In *Knockout* (Warner Brothers, 1941), the wife and trainer of Johnny Rocket (Arthur Kennedy) save him from killing himself in the ring. And after he is blinded in the ring, Danny Kenny (Jimmy Cagney) in *City for Conquest* (Warner Brothers, 1940) relies on his trainer and manager to set him up with a newsstand business. As is evident from these examples, however, the people who help the boxer tend to be family members or childhood friends. By such qualification of the individualism of the prizefighter, Hollywood carefully avoids endorsing collectivism of a more dangerous political stripe. One hundred years earlier, de Tocqueville had described this ideological compromise when he noted how "the circle of family and friends" fits well into the American mythology of individualism: "with this little society formed to his taste, [the individual] gladly leaves the greater society to look after itself."[21]

The family-like groups in these films not only reduce the political threat of the large social collective, they also offer a patriarchal structure in which female characters can contribute to the action without threatening traditional gender roles. In order to attract the female moviegoer, sports films have often included sizable roles for women in stories focused on the athletic exploits of male performers. A *Variety* reviewer commented on this strategy in writing about *Kid Galahad*, calling the major role played by Bette Davis "the thread that holds the story together" and what "will make *Galahad* acceptable to the women."[22] In Depression-era boxing films, as in American narrative sports films as a whole, the good guys are those who balance individual strength and initiative with the interests of the group; positive female characters function in that group as part of a support structure for the male protagonist. Conversely, the successful progress of the male hero through the narrative to victory (often decided by a climactic contest) depends on his avoiding or escaping a second type of female character—the conventional "bad" girl—who would distract him with her sexual allure.

In the case of Depression-era boxing films representing the family as a contained image of collectivism, female characters assume a supportive or distracting role based on whether they contribute to or undermine the formation of the boxer's "family." In *Kid Galahad*, Louise altruistically adopts a sister-like role, helping the young boxer Ward to become part of the Donati family rather than acting on her own romantic interest in him. The best example of this support occurs in *Golden Boy* (Columbia, 1939), in which Lorna Moon (Barbara Stanwyck) does double duty as reliable partner in the families of two male characters. While engaged to boxing manager Tom Moody (Adolphe Menjou), Lorna helps him persuade Joe Bonaparte (William Holden) to fulfill his potential in the ring. After she falls in love with

Bonaparte, however, she redirects her supportive efforts to convincing Joe to return to his family.

Just as the family is used to contain the collectivist impulse, so the critique of self-interest is limited to the figure of the gangster or the crooked manager who seeks to exploit the prizefighter. These films avoided the idea that the rugged individualism celebrated by populism "had actually helped create the monopoly capitalism the populists resented," and that "laissez-faire had been more a cause of the Depression than its solution."[23] Therefore, in *Kid Galahad* and *Golden Boy,* gangsters try to take control of the boxer's career for their own gain; in *They Made Me a Criminal,* a dishonest manager frames his fighter for murder; and in *City for Conquest* and *Knockout,* crooked managers use foreign substances to cause the fighter/protagonist to lose.

The infiltration of organized crime into boxing during the 1930s resulted in part from economic forces set in motion by corporate interests and the free market. The Temperance Movement, which had succeeded in installing Prohibition in 1920, drew its support not only from rural Americans threatened by the growing number of immigrants settling in urban areas but also from industrialists concerned about the effects of alcohol on worker productivity. The enormous profits that Prohibition made available for bootleggers provided the capital with which organized crime infiltrated the fight game, displacing the professional politicians who had largely controlled prizefighting up to that time.[24] Once on the inside, mobsters such as Frankie Carbo, a.k.a. Mr. Big, who was the prime mover in prizefighting from the mid-1930s until the late 1950s, made enormous profits from betting on fights that they had fixed.

After mob control of prizefighting was established, its gambling operations continued to function very much in accordance with the practices of capitalist entrepreneurship that had spawned it. As James Smith points out, "betting a known stake against the possibility of improving on it amid sometimes dangerous uncertainties" describes not only gambling but the mythology of "the whole American experience," from the opening of the West to European-American settlement to the contemporary promise of economic opportunity through investment in business which forms an integral part of the American dream.[25] Realization of this similarity demonstrates, as Smith also notes, that while "gamblers are usually assumed to be alienated from traditional values," in fact "gambling is preeminently social, and goes so far as to echo prevailing cultural values."[26] Even though, as the 1930s boxing films show, the gamblers who controlled professional prizefighting used extreme measures—including intimidation and violence—to reduce the "uncertainties" threatening their investment, one need look no further than the previously mentioned U.S. government threats to invade Mexico or the violent strikebreaking tactics of various industries in the early 1930s to see that such practices were common in American capitalism.

By adopting a populist view of the causes and solutions for the economic problems of the Depression, Hollywood boxing films could appear socially conscious while avoiding deep analysis of the real economic issues. Nonetheless, with the possible exception of *The Champ,* these films at least attempted to represent the problems of ethnic working-class youth, who saw boxing as a possible means of escape from the mean streets of America's urban slums. Moreover, while these films celebrate individuals of extraordinary physical strength, self-confidence, and tenacity, they also demonstrate that from the maze of forces at work in the business of professional boxing, as from the often brutal world of the inner city, "no one makes it out on their own."

> The world that the prizefighter comes from is one that understands the hypocrisy surrounding the commercialization of the body in a bourgeois, Calvinist-tinged culture.
>
> —Gerald Early

Like their Hollywood counterparts, the two prizefight pictures of the 1930s that featured African American boxers, *Spirit of Youth* (Grand National, 1937) and *Keep Punching* (MC, 1939), tell the stories of young fighters saved from the dangers of the big city through the guidance of friends and family who return them to rural populist values of hard work, self-discipline, and community. Following this narrative formula allowed the white producers of these "race" films to appeal to African American audiences, but without contradicting the bourgeois values endorsed by the Hollywood pictures that were shown 80 percent of the time in black theaters. Moreover, *Spirit of Youth* and *Keep Punching* starred real champions, Joe Louis and Henry Armstrong respectively, giving them a veneer of biographical realism which authenticated their populist stories as a historically valid response to the skepticism caused by the Depression.

Of course, for most African Americans, the limited economic opportunity of the 1930s was nothing new; Louis's management team was well aware that for a black man even to get a shot at the heavyweight title, he would have to reassure white Americans that he presented no threat to the racial status quo. That meant a change from the surly "jungle killer" image that white sportswriters had constructed for Louis to the "mother-loving, clean-living, humble young man" that is Joe Thomas, the lead character in *Spirit of Youth.*[27] Armstrong, because he fought in lighter weight classes, was affected less by the racial symbolism of beating white opponents. But, like Louis, he still had to overcome white resistance to black champions as well as the general "pugilistic depression" of the 1930s resulting from a "rash of 'foul fights' and criminal dealings."[28]

The country/city opposition that structures both these films displaces racial conflict rather than the class difference avoided by the Hollywood boxing movies. As Daniel Leab notes, the majority of theaters for black audiences were located in the South, where on the screen, as in the ring, overt interracial conflict was taboo because of whites' fear that it "might upset the theory of [their] social superiority or imply social equality."[29] Furthermore, Hollywood operated under the assumption that the response of southern audiences to racial themes was a bellwether for audiences in the North.[30] Even a film made a decade later, *Body and Soul* (1947), which Robert Sklar has called "as close to a work of the left as any produced to that time in Hollywood," risked direct conflict between an African American boxer and his white manager only when it was motivated by the black character's loyalty to a white friend.[31] Instead, both *Spirit of Youth* and *Keep Punching* present segregated worlds and narrative conflicts that pit black against black: the young boxer and his supporters against the gambler and the sexualized woman who hope to lead him astray and then bet on his opponent.

While they ostensibly endorse these dominant discourses of class and race, both films also reverse the race film convention of casting dark-skinned blacks as the criminal heavies.[32] The gambler villains, as well as the women who plot with them, are instead very "white" in their appearance, mannerisms, and speech patterns. This reversal of convention refers to the racial barriers that were a historical reality for both Louis and Armstrong, yet the retention by the two films of black-against-black narrative conflict allows them also to displace white racism. As a result, *Spirit of Youth* and *Keep Punching* make room for what Manthia Diawara has called the "resisting spectator" aware of "the impossibility of an uncritical acceptance" of Hollywood films and the influence they had on race films.[33]

Spirit of Youth and *Keep Punching* not only subvert their segregated worlds and black-on-black conflict by characterizing the villains in white cultural terms, they also reject the populist demonization of urban life altogether. While the young protagonists may return to the down-home values of hard work, self-discipline, and community, both films also concede that the city is a place of greater opportunity. Like the young blacks in Julie Dash's *Daughters of the Dust,* who are reminded to take their African culture north with them, these two fighters survive because they retain their racial identity, yet they also know that the economic possibility of northern cities does not exist in the South.

The Henry Armstrong character's fictional middle-class southern family functions, then, more as part of the film's attempt to relieve white anxiety about a black champion than to dismiss the need for northern migration. In fact, *Keep Punching* pokes fun at black middle-class distaste for prizefighters as representatives of the race. When the Armstrong character's father complains to his wife that their son's prizefighting in the northern city "isn't respectable," she reminds him that he has not turned his nose up at the checks Henry has sent home. After Henry wins the title, the film's last scene refers again to the material base for middle-class morals as Fanny, Henry's home-town sweetheart who also opposed his chosen career concedes, "Maybe I was a little too fussy about what you ought to do."

Both Louis and Armstrong understood the contradiction between the need for bourgeois respectability to overcome racial prejudice, and the realities of the prizefighting business in particular and life for a black male in white America in general. Before launching his career, Louis's two African American managers, Julian Black and John Roxborough, had earned their living as gamblers. Although he eventually became one of the best fighters of the decade and the only boxer ever to hold three titles simultaneously, Armstrong had started out on the club circuit in Los Angeles "winning, losing, or boxing to a 'draw' according to instructions."[34]

Spirit of Youth and *Keep Punching* acknowledge the importance of what Gerald Early means when he describes Joe Louis as a "blues hero" whose success should be measured less by the middle-class standards of respectability than by the simple fact that he "got over." Early calls such success a type of "underground victory," "used by both Black preachers and Black hustlers, the autobiographical summing up of both the sacred life and the profane life."[35] Henry Armstrong's success as a fighter, combined with his work as a minister after he left boxing, suggests that this description applies equally well to him. While Early admits that such an idea of success may result in a "complex meshing of two distinct cultural attitudes, a meshing that is not always balanced and does not always work well," its ultimate defense must be that it produces something more than the "stereotypical put-upon and distressed Black American male."[36] Along these lines, *Spirit of Youth* and *Keep Punching* portray the trainers and managers who help the young protagonists succeed as by necessity just as skilled in the urban culture of nightclubs and gambling as those who seek to exploit them. The films avoid the simplistic message that "crime doesn't pay," which, as Thomas Cripps notes, often elicited laughter from black audiences.[37] Even the femme fatale character in both stories returns the fighter to his home-town girlfriend and thereby saves him from ruin, showing the interest both movies have in demonstrating the necessary coexistence of middle-class morality and a blues aesthetic for living.

Put simply, these films balance the abstraction of middle-class values with the economic reality of selling the black body. Rather than reveal middle-class hypocrisy about money, *Spirit of Youth* stays closer to the biographical truth of Louis's working-class background and never even raises bourgeois concerns about the respectability of prizefighting. The ring scenes in both films, along with narrative digressions for jitterbug numbers and comic turns by a Mantan Moreland or Hamtree Harrington, might have been misinterpreted by some whites to reinforce stereotypes of blacks as "rhythmic," "fun-loving," and an essentially physical rather than intellectual people. They are instead both a way of expressing individual and racial identity, and a means of moving up.[38]

NOTES

1. Ronald Bergan, *Sports in the Movies* (New York: Proteus, 1982), p. 14. A program entitled *Knockout! Hollywood's Love Affair with Boxing* shown on American Movie Classics in 1992 stated that more than 400 films have been made about boxing since 1910.

2. Steven Riess, *City Games: The Evolution of American Urban Society and the Rise of Sports* (Urbana: University of Illinois Press, 1989), pp. 109-10.

3. Ibid., p. 113. From 1870 to 1920, the Irish dominated professional prizefighting just as they did baseball, producing nine world champions during the 1890s, and more champions and contenders than any other group up until World War I. As their opportunities in other areas of the national economy improved, however, Irish dominance over the sport declined, and different ethnic groups gradually moved into professional prizefighting. After the turn of the century, Jewish fighters began to win titles; they were second only to the Irish in the number of champions they produced during the 1910s. Boxing also provided men of Italian and Eastern European extraction with their first major successes in professional sports during the same decade; it would be another generation before a player of Polish or Italian extraction would win a Major League batting crown. Italian Americans retained their major role in prizefighting through the end of the Second World War; by that time the Jews had followed the Irish out of the inner-city neighborhoods, replaced as boxers by African Americans and Chicanos. While boxers of Jewish, Italian, and Eastern European backgrounds who fought before World War II were generally smaller, and therefore in lower weight classes, promoters could still generate a high degree of interest and draw large crowds by setting up fights between opponents from these ethnic groups, and by billing the contests as struggles for national or religious pride. Riess, *City Games*, pp. 110-16.

4. Otis L. Graham, Jr., provides the statistic that 50 percent of Americans between the ages of 15 and 19 were unemployed in 1933. He also notes that "young people waited an average of two years after schooling before finding a job in the 1930s, and about 25 percent never found employment until the war." "Years of Crisis: America in Depression and War, 1933-1945," in *The Unfinished Century*, ed. William Leuchtenburg (Boston: Little, Brown, 1973), p. 381.

5. Riess, *City Games*, p. 112.

6. Robert Ray, *A Certain Tendency in the Hollywood Cinema, 1930-1980* (Princeton: Princeton University Press, 1985), pp. 55-69.

7. A description of these test screenings and the change in the end of *The Champ* appears in Samuel Marx, *Mayer and Thalberg: The Make-Believe Saints* (New York: Random House, 1975), p. 170.

8. I am using here Charles Eckert's idea of displacement as he describes it occurring in "proletarian" or "socially conscious" films of the 1930s and 1940s. Using both Freudian psychoanalysis and Lévi-Strauss's study of myth, Eckert sums up this process as a combination

of displacement "as Freud defines this term (the substitution of an acceptable object of love, hate, etc., for a forbidden one)," and the transformation of unsolvable dilemmas like that in myths in order to "resolve the dilemma at another level, or to somehow attenuate its force." See "The Anatomy of a Proletarian Film: Warner's *Marked Woman*," in *Movies and Methods*, vol. II, ed. Bill Nichols (Berkeley: University of California Press, 1985), p. 420.

9. Richard Slotkin, *Gunfighter Nation: The Myth of the Frontier in Twentieth-Century America* (New York: Atheneum, 1992), p. 19.

10. Ibid., p. 20.

11. Josefina Zoraida Vazquez and Lorenzo Meyer, *The United States and Mexico* (Chicago: University of Chicago Press, 1987), pp. 134-38.

12. Slotkin, *Gunfighter Nation*, p. 13.

13. Ibid., p. 21.

14. Eckert, "Anatomy," p. 415.

15. Peter Roffman and Jim Purdy, *The Hollywood Social Problem Film* (Bloomington: Indiana University Press, 1981), pp. 46-47.

16. Ibid., p. 64.

17. Ibid., pp. 47-48.

18. Ibid.

19. As Mark Roth has shown, Warners celebrated this same social model in backstage musicals such as *42nd Street*, in which the director plays an FDR-like figure "both inducing and supported by a strong sense of community." "Some Warners Musicals and the Spirit of the New Deal," in *Genre: The Musical*, ed. Rick Altman (London, Boston: Routledge and Kegan Paul and the British Film Institute, 1981), p. 41.

20. Roffman and Purdy, *Hollywood Social Problem*, p. 60.

21. Alexis de Tocqueville, *Democracy in America*, ed. J. P. Mayer, trans. George Lawrence (Garden City, N.Y.: Anchor/Doubleday, 1969), p. 506. This quote by Tocqueville appears in Ray, *Tendency*, p. 61.

22. *Variety*, June 2, 1937. Reprinted in *Variety Film Reviews* (New York: Garland, 1983).

23. Roffman and Purdy, *Hollywood Social Problem*, p. 63. My point that these films condense the trait of extreme self-interest into criminal characters so as to mark it as an aberration and therefore avoid examination of the role of individualism in larger social problems is again indebted to Charles Eckert's description of a similar process in his article on *Marked Woman*. See "Anatomy," pp. 420-24.

24. Riess, *City Games*, pp. 171-72, 177-81.

25. James F. Smith, "Where the Action Is: Images of the Gambler in Recent Popular Films," in *Beyond the Stars: Stock Characters in American Popular Film*, ed. Paul Loukaides and Linda Fuller (Bowling Green: Bowling Green State University Popular Press, 1990), p. 178.

26. Ibid., p. 181.

27. Jeffrey Sammons, *Beyond the Ring: The Role of Boxing in American Society* (Urbana: University of Illinois Press, 1988), p. 97.

28. Ibid., 96, 80.

29. Daniel J. Leab, *From Sambo to Superspade: The Black Experience in Motion Pictures* (Boston: Houghton Mifflin, 1976), p. 181. This quote describing southern white attitudes toward blacks is from James H. Stevenson's unpublished master's thesis, Howard University, 1948, reprinted in Sammons, *Beyond the Ring*, p. 100.

30. Thomas Cripps, *Slow Fade to Black: The Negro in American Film, 1900-1942* (New York: Oxford University Press, 1977), p. 110.

31. Robert Sklar, *City Boys: Cagney, Bogart, Garfield* (Princeton: Princeton University Press, 1992), p. 185.

32. Cripps, *Slow Fade*, p. 329

33. Manthia Diawara, "Black Spectatorship: Problems of Identification and Resistance," in *Black American Cinema*, ed. Diawara (New York: Routledge, 1993), pp. 212, 219.

34. Gilbert Odd, *Encyclopedia of Boxing* (New York: Crescent Books, 1983), p. 12.

35. Gerald Early, *Tuxedo Junction: Essays on American Culture* (New York: Ecco Press, 1989), p. 178.

36. Ibid.

37. Cripps, *Slow Fade*, p. 342.

38. Michael Eric Dyson describes a similar dual meaning for black sports heroes in his essay "Be Like Mike?: Michael Jordan and the Pedagogy of Desire," in *Reflecting Black: African-American Cultural Criticism* (Minneapolis: University of Minnesota Press, 1993), p. 67.

9 . . . Baseball in the Post-American Cinema, or Life in the Minor Leagues

> The icons of our world are in trouble.
> —Lee Iacocca

At the beginning of *Nation into State: The Shifting Symbolic Foundations of American Nationalism,* a historical and literally concrete exploration of the symbolic landscape of the United States, political geographer Wilbur Zelinsky explores a variety of meanings attached to the concept of "nation." Distinguishing between nationhood and statehood (closely related but not synonymous concepts), he tells us:

> If we distill the notion of nationhood, or peoplehood, to its essence, it is the shared belief among a sizable group of individuals (too large a number for personal contact to be feasible among all) that they are united in the possession of a unique and cherished social and cultural personality.[1]

Zelinsky goes on to point out "how impossible it is to define the nation without simultaneously defining nationalism," for, as he puts it, "belief in the existence of the former automatically breeds some level of allegiance, or even passion, for that rather mystical, romantic concept." Both nation and nationalism, he suggests, are "forms of social consciousness," but both are also social *constructions* and *artifacts*—even if, on the one hand, the nation is born and sustained "only when enough people . . . believe in its existence," and, on the other, the sense of nationhood, the consciousness of national identity, "must *appear* to be the *natural* upwelling of sentiments based upon a mutual discovery of commonalities rather than something imposed from above."[2]

One would be hard pressed to deny this description of national identity as it is lived indigenously from within (rather than seen objectively from without). Nonetheless, contemporary experience in the postmodern America of late capitalism would seem to belie it. While most Americans currently believe in the existence of the nationalist state (living as they are under its increasing compulsions), they do so in an increasingly alienated and negative mode. On the one hand, the supposed "superiority" of our democratic mode of government has been paradoxically leveled by what might be seen as our *ideological triumph.* Citing such events as "*perestroika,* the destruction of the Berlin Wall, the capitalization of the Eastern Bloc," to which I might add the collapse of communism and the state power of the Soviet Union (against which the United States heretofore defined itself), cultural critic Bill Brown points out that "the daily headlines of 1990 . . . depict a decade wherein the ideological frontier, the global line of resistance to capitalist democracy, is fading." The "very success of American ideological monopoly," he suggests, "precipitates cultural loss, the loss of 'America' itself, the dispersal of 'America,' 'America' appearing, all at once, everywhere and therefore nowhere."[3] Thus, the foundational myth of "American exceptionalism" that has been, as John Agnew says, so much "an integral part of American history" seems increasingly baseless.[4]

On the other hand, this recent (and to some degree "sudden") national "baselessness" caused by America's ideological success (its consequence: a peculiar and paradoxical sense of alienation) is matched by the blatant failure of capitalist democracy as it has been experienced "at home." The most spectacular examples are the nation's trillion-dollar deficit and the savings and loan scandal, but more concretely visible are crises in health care and pension funds, factory layoffs and closures, and the alarming realization and growth of an American underclass who stand—actually and symbolically—as "homeless." Governmental response has only widened the gap between real experience and state "representation." A most telling example is President Bush and his top White House aides' response to the failing economy as "a public relations problem, not a policy issue," as one newspaper report put it.[5]

Daily events in the United States narrate a foundering of belief in the nation as well as a nearly complete loss of faith in the state. In the street and across the media, one is exposed to an "upwelling of sentiments" based less upon, as Zelinsky puts it, the mutual discovery or maintenance of "commonalities" than upon the mutual (and generally hostile) discovery and promotion of differences. On the one hand, the current economic situation has pervaded the national consciousness in the form of a general "depression" that might be seen as the new "commonality" binding Americans together. But this commonality is purely negative. Listening to a local CBS radio news station on November 2, 1991, within a single hour one could hear reports about the stock market dropping sixty-three points, a training conference being held in San Jose, California, on developing "self-esteem" in the workplace as an aid to bettering the quality of production, and the results of a poll on global "competitiveness" that indicated that most Americans feel "we" are slipping in the international lineup of major economic powers. On the other hand, the economic situation in the United States not only has made American class differences appallingly obvious, but it has also fueled hostile articulations of racial and ethnic difference in the midst of a period also marked by massive and contentious immigration of Hispanics and Asians into the United States and visible demographic challenges to the coherence of America as a "white majority." Again, several myths informing a sense of national "exceptionalism" are exposed by their perversion in the current socioeconomic context. Historian Michael McGerr tells us:

> The myth of America as a uniquely middle-class society tends to mute people's awareness of class differences. The "American dream," the less than fully justified faith in social mobility, tends to reconcile both the more and less fortunate to the inequalities of capitalism.[6]

Today, the exceptionalist myth of America as "uniquely" middle-class is challenged daily on the streets and by a perversion of the exceptionalist myth of "social mobility"—namely, its current dynamic as "downward." And while the liberal rhetoric of "community" (as in "the homeless community") attempts to efface class differences, the latter's actuality is no longer "muted." The new downward social mobility foregrounds "the inequities of capitalism" and serves to further fragment a phenomenological sense of national commonality.

   This economic fragmentation informs and further amplifies social fragmentation along other lines of visible difference: race, ethnicity, and geography. On the one hand, the recent assertion and politics of racial, ethnic, and regional identities have been a *positive response* to participation in a global culture constituted primarily through new communication and media technologies and wide-ranging diasporic and transnational movement. Americans live in an age when electronic interfaces and instant communication have nearly erased the boundaries and distances of national geography. A pervasive and dispersed global network of commercial franchise has sent American Kentucky Fried Chicken to Beijing, McDonald's to Moscow, and Holiday Inns, American movies, and music videos everywhere. In the other direction, if more quietly, foreign interests have purchased American companies and real estate and are increasingly making their presence felt in the context of everyday "American" life. On the other hand, the recent assertion and politics of racial, ethnic, and regional identities have been an *embattled response* to a rising and fearsome parochialism, provincialism, and fundamentalism on the part of the white "uniquely" American middle class, whose mythic "majority" (already diminished economically) is terrified of being culturally hybridized and debased—that is, of losing its numerical and political clout and being "sent down" from its white franchise to live and play in what heretofore were the politically disenfranchised "minor leagues" of minority culture. Containing an advertisement for a series of upcoming television news "bites" on "Race and Tolerance," the same CBS news program cited earlier is explicit in this regard. "How do you view people of other colors than you are?" it asks. "And how will you feel when the white majority becomes a minority?" In sum, we are in a period significantly and simultaneously marked by a heightened sense of multiculturalism and transnationalism and by the increasing presence of racism, anti-Semitism, homophobia, and xenophobia.

It is clear that Zelinsky's description of the phenomenological experience of nationhood, the consciousness of national identity, as "the *natural* upwelling of sentiments based upon a mutual discovery of commonalities rather than something imposed from above" still holds—but it does so ironically, perversely, paradoxically, as befits what has been called our "postmodern" historical moment. That is, the only "mutual discovery of commonalities" that Americans have experienced in the last decade or so has been the discovery of the commonality of their incommensurable differences. Not imposed from above, but lived from below, this mutual discovery has indeed led to what appears to be "the *natural* upwelling of sentiments"—but these sentiments express the rejection of national identity and the embrace of globalism, on the one hand, and forms of tribalism, on the other. American nationalism, therefore, seems almost completely debased—despite its short-lived and artificial regeneration via the construction of the recent Gulf War. As Brown puts it: "If the post-Cold War, new-world order served as the condition of possibility for the 'united front' against Saddam, then this new order should also be recognized as the condition of anxiety that produced Saddam as a phantasmatic threat to the American way of life." It is, indeed, the "American way of life" that has been revealed as phantasmatic. "No longer the sign of capitalist success, no longer the defender of the free world against communist expansion, America," Brown tells us, "enters the *post-American.*"[7]

The "post-American," then, acknowledges a collapse of phenomenological belief in the existence of the "nation" as anything more than phantasmagoric, and an increasing sense that any confidence in the concept of a unified national character or belief in an enduring liberal consensus resides primarily (and sometimes only) in the familiar and communal *commercial space* of the national television set, the movie screen, and the shopping mall, where Americans are constructed and commercially (rather than politically) reenfranchised by McDonald's, Reebok, and Coca-Cola. Therefore, it is not surprising that post-Americanism shares with postmodernism a pervasive sense of loss, an "inverted millenarianism"—to use Fredric Jameson's characterization—in which "premonitions of the future" are replaced with the sense of "the end of this or that."[8] This experience of the "end" provokes intense and hyperbolic nostalgia and, among the soon-to-be-less-enfranchised, invokes images of "the good old days" satisfied by television commercials, series, and mainstream movies that are archaic, pastoral, and idyllic in tone and location. This nostalgia for a "pure" American identity is also satisfied by sports—and, most particularly, by *baseball.*

As Bill Brown suggests in an extraordinary article titled "The Meaning of Baseball in 1992 (with Notes on the Post-American)," not only has America claimed and mythified baseball against historical fact as its own "national pastime," but baseball itself has contributed to the production and containment of that mythic space we claim as "America." Brown writes that

> baseball has played a prominent role in the American Imaginary—the process by which "America" strives to see itself coherently. Of course, without its own tongue or its own *Volk,* the nation has always relied on icons, and on the designation of a national character, for instance, to assert cohesion, to imagine a community, as Benedict Anderson would put it. And baseball's ability to *archaize* America—famously exhibiting its pastoral spatiality and temporality—enables the game to establish *national fixity.* . . . In other words, baseball renders America visible to itself.[9]

Zelinsky would agree. Exploring a range of symbols, phenomena, and performances that are overtly nationalistic, he turns to the more latent statism powerfully generated by organized sports, particularly in their modern mediated form whereby national participation is primarily through spectatorship. As he points out:

> Vicarious engagement in local sport may indeed be the only social activity that binds together nearly the entire populace not only in small towns but in large metropolises as well. And, by means of radio, television, and the print media, the major sports create coast-to-coast congregations of communicants whose memberships transcend the usual barriers of class, age, religious denomination, ideology, and, recently at least, sex, ethnic, and racial group—and ultimately even region. Sport fanaticism, which in varying degree involves the vast majority of Americans, engenders an intensity of feeling on a daily basis far greater than any roused by conventional religious or political issues.[10]

In the mediated world of the twentieth century, the secular religion generated by sport is generally transnational. Americans, however, are particularized ("exceptionalized") by their expressed claim upon baseball as the National

Game. David Halberstam contends that "baseball is . . . our most mythological of sports; it has the longest history, it is by its own proclamation our
national pastime, and it harbors . . . our greatest mythological figures."[11]
Among American sports, baseball is also the one most evocative of another
mythological tenet of national exceptionalism: America as an innocent nation
in a wicked world.[12] Wearing clean white uniforms, young men engage in a
supremely rational, civilized, gentle, and moral battle played out within the
context of a simple, grassy mise-en-scène as an emotional drama that dis-
avows the implications of advertising and Astroturf. As Zelinsky points out,
the sport is "most intimately linked with the American ethos, like the flag
and apple pie, and thus nationalism."[13]

The "imagined community" generated by baseball is a *national* community. It is, however, as Brown reminds us, a national community figured as
archaic and *pastoral*. Zelinsky, too, suggests that the game's national popularity "arises from a mythic association with the pastoral theme, the fabled
Middle Landscape so central to the American Dream, and thus with the
mystique of the small town and agrarianism." He goes on to quote a powerful
statement on baseball by Michael Novak, author of *The Joy of Sports*, published in 1976, but first positions it as written "before the professional ranks
were as thronged with Afro-Americans and Latin Americans as they are
today."[14] Novak says:

> Baseball is as close a liturgical enactment of the white Anglo-Saxon Protes-
> tant myth as the nation has. It is a cerebral game, designed as geometrically
> as the city of Washington itself, born out of the Enlightenment and the
> philosophies so beloved of Jefferson, Madison, and Hamilton. It is to games
> what the Federalist Papers are to books.[15]

Thus, whatever the actual historical and multinational claims upon baseball
(and there are many), the game has long been mythologized as an American
"field of dreams"—the utopian and irreal (but therapeutically effective) site
upon which to situate an equally mythological and utopian national character.

It is hardly surprising, then, that baseball not only has appeared in innu-
merable American movies as a frequent and iconic part of the American
mise-en-scène (indeed marking it *as* American), but also has figured prominently and almost always as an allegory of American (male) experience in
quite a sizable number of narrative films, from Thomas Edison's 1899 *Casey
at the Bat* to 1942's *The Pride of the Yankees* to 1989's aptly named *Field of
Dreams*. Despite their affinity for biography and period recreation, with few
exceptions most of these films (whether comedy or melodrama) have idealized the game, introducing and yet negating its historicity, its institutional

and commercial status, and locating it instead in a hermetic, timeless, oneiric vision of America that always has a white Middle American male Casey at bat (whatever his race or origin), that always contains and synthesizes the contradictory qualities of childhood and adulthood, pastoral and urban space, individual effort and teamwork, that always defuses and privatizes cultural difference as personal idiosyncrasy and homogenizes it as "all-American." Given the game's perceived mythic function and, as Brown suggests, its status of establishing "national fixity," it is no wonder that a survey of the thirty-five American feature films made from the 1940s through the 1980s that foreground baseball reveals no fewer than nine of them as outright fantasies.[16] This close affinity between the "mythic" and the "fantastic" in relation to baseball movies constitutes the genre as generally "timeless." Brown, however, is particularly interested in the fact that recent years have seen a "rather extraordinary proliferation" of both books and movies about baseball—and he goes on to argue that, precisely at a historical moment when the daily life of Americans seems to force a continual denial of anything once remotely experienced as "national fixity," the appearance of these texts expresses dominant culture's attempts "to keep a 'national game' centered as an American object of American knowledge."[17] This desire to "center" baseball as a national game and an American object in the current political, cultural, and economic landscape, however, is tremulous at best. The most recent films about the game explicitly introduce not "fantastic elements" but "hybridizing elements" into this innocent, pure, all-American (male), and "national" pastime: namely, markers of racial, ethnic, and gender differences, of big business and commercialism, and even of international challenges to the country's iconographic claim on baseball as one of its primary national symbols.

For the most part, up until the last decade, issues of race and nationality, gender, and big business have been suppressed or deflected in American baseball features. However, there have been exceptions. Indeed, in 1909, a film called *His Last Game* not only was presumably the first baseball feature ever made, but also was a "cowboy and Indians sports film" about a Choctaw Indian, "an ace pitcher for an Indian baseball team, who refuses a bribe from two cowboy gamblers to throw the game," goes on to win with a grand-slam homer, but is finally executed for the murder of one of the gamblers (which may have been in self-defense)—first, because the stay of execution doesn't come in time, and second, because dead he poses no threat to the dominant order of things.[18] (To wit, sympathetic or not, the film affirms quite literally the Hollywood canard that "the only good Indian is a dead Indian.") And in 1937, a women's softball team provided the context for *Girls Can Play*—a murder mystery notable for being "the first sound feature film dealing primarily with women in sports" and for *not* being a comedy, "as virtually all films about women athletes would be up until the 1970s."[19] From the 1940s to the 1980s, the few other films dealing with race or gender include *The Jackie Robinson Story*, released in 1950, starring the ball player as himself in a relatively pointed look at the racial issues surrounding his career as the first African American admitted into the major leagues in 1947. The film's ultimate message, however, was that both the game and America were expansive enough to incorporate him into the dominant—and white—order of things. The tone and issue are quite different in *The Bad News Bears* (1976). The hopeless and foul-mouthed male Little Leaguers in this immensely popular comedy accept and depend upon an equally foul-mouthed but more adept girl as their star pitcher. While responding in some small degree to cultural debates in post-1960s America around gender access and competitiveness in children's sports, the film avoids comparable issues in the adult sports world. *The Bad News Bears Go to Japan* (1978) is only a somewhat prescient spin-off—taking the now-sanitized pint-sized team abroad under the aegis of a small-time promoter out to make a buck from the international encounter. The film, however, patently represses the long history of baseball as a Japanese national game and also ignores the larger international economic battle contemporaneously being waged behind its own mise-en-scène.[20]

Most interesting, perhaps, of the few films before the 1980s that introduced elements that might perturb the mythology of the game as not only all-American but also all-inclusive was *The Bingo Long Traveling All-Stars and Motor Kings*. Released in 1976 (the Bicentennial year), it focused on a barnstorming group of black ball players "on the road" in the America of 1939, but contained them in a plot that kept racial and business conflict internal, comic, and out of the white major leagues. Concerned with an economic battle between an independent club and the all-powerful, all-business Negro National League, the film started out, as Danny Peary put it, as "an interesting look at exploitation of blacks by blacks and a sharp leftist political satire ('Seize the means of production' is Bingo's motto)," but devolved into a "familiar farce."[21] Nonetheless, the film's humor is often pointed. A running gag, for example, has one of the players pretending to be first a Cuban and then a Native American in hopes of breaking into the white major leagues.[22]

Another look at the thirty-five baseball films made between 1942 and 1989 reveals that they were released in cycles. The first cycle (consisting of twenty feature films) ran from 1942 through 1958, and spanned both the Second World War and the Cold War periods, when American attitudes were fiercely nationalistic and statist. Interestingly and appropriately, given baseball as the phantasmagoria of America rendered "visible to itself," there was more than a decade's gap between this first cycle and the second, which began in 1973. Indeed, according to Zucker and Babich's *Sports Films: A Complete Reference,* only a *single* American baseball film was released between 1958 and 1973. Hardly a popular "hit," 1962's *Safe at Home* featured American heroes Roger Maris and Mickey Mantle and capitalized on "the two Yankee sluggers' assault on Babe Ruth's home run record in 1961."[23]

This remarkable fifteen-year gap certainly provokes speculation as to its causes. One possibility is that the "imagined community" and utopian national space previously figured by baseball on the screen were so completely at odds with the cultural upheavals in the America of the 1960s that this previous "imagined community" indeed could *not* then be imagined, for to do so would force the recognition that such an "imagined community" and its figuration of utopian national space was now lost—but was not yet ready to be *nostalgically redeemed.* As Zelinsky notes: "By the 1960s and 1970s, the statist faith seemed to be approaching its nadir in the United States, especially among the youthful," who were, we might add, the nation's major motion picture audience.[24] Paul Goodman, writing in 1969, is apposite—if, in hindsight, somewhat hyperbolic:

> For the first time in recorded history, the mention of country, community, place has lost its power to animate. Nobody but a scoundrel even tries it. Our rejection of false patriotism, is, of course, itself a badge of honor. But the positive loss is tragic and I cannot resign myself to it.[25]

During this period marked by the Vietnam War, urban rioting around civil rights, the generation gap, and the emergence of militant feminism, the allegorizing of baseball and its Anglo, male, and Middle American ethos was insupportable. As well, in the real world of baseball, the period from the late 1950s through the 1970s marks the sport's increasing incorporation (both figuratively and literally) of non-Anglo players, its commercially motivated and increasing diasporic team movements, and its shift from radio space to televisual space. Now fans could watch as well as listen to the game in the privacy of their own homes, but what radio hid, television displayed: an increasing racial and ethnic hybridization of the Anglo ideal. Then, too, fans watched the Oakland A's for three years running grow long hair and mustaches and identify themselves as the "Anti-War team." And, perhaps most threatening of all to the idea of national "fixity" that baseball had theretofore represented, the national public during this period watched the Brooklyn Dodgers, New York Giants, and other teams suddenly and coldly leave their "naturalized"—and arcadianly figured—birthplaces, publicly revealing themselves not as "home" teams but as "franchises" ready to sell their regional birthright for a mess of corporate pottage.

After this fifteen-year hiatus, the second cycle of baseball films began in 1973, ended in 1978, and consisted of only six features—of which, it should be noted, two were sequels to the highly successful and irreverent *Bad News Bears*—suggesting that "cycle" may be too strong a term to use here. Indeed, Zelinsky notes in relation to his own project of charting the historical and geographic dynamics of overtly nationalistic cultural phenomena that after the Bicentennial year there was a "post-1976 slump in pilgrimages to nationalistic shrines." And, generally conservative as he is in the matter, he goes on to bemoan the period's nearly complete loss of vitality in relation to "the old tried and true nationalistic symbols"—pointing to such things as the "trivialization of national holidays, the near extinction of monument building, outright desecration of the flag, and, possibly, a dismaying decline in voter turnout during presidential elections." He goes on to suggest that America in the late 1970s had the "dubious" distinction of being in the lead of the general decline of "nationalist sentiments" and "civil religions" in the industrialized West.[26]

The most recent cycle of baseball features dates from 1988. During the decade between 1978 and 1988, only three films were produced, two of them virtually unseen, the third generally acknowledged a popular success. *Zapped* (1982) was a totally forgotten fantasy along the lines of *It Happened One Spring*, and *Blue Skies Again* (1983) was a totally forgotten comedy, notable perhaps for featuring a woman as second-baseman. *The Natural* (1984) stands, then, as the only baseball film to capture the national imagination during the decade between 1978 and 1988. Again, one is prompted to speculate about the general significance of this gap—occurring, as it did, primarily during the Reagan years, from 1980 to 1988. During this period, the Republican party fully reclaimed and rearticulated America with an ex-movie star who urged the nation on, in the less pastoral and more militaristic terms of football (and *Star Wars*), to "win just one for the Gipper." We had Reagan, so perhaps we didn't need baseball to render the country phantasmagorically visible to itself. Or perhaps Reagan's persona wasn't authentic or innocent enough to be successfully linked to baseball. In this regard, it is fascinating to discover that Reagan actually made a baseball film in 1952, but *The Winning Team*, in which he portrayed presidentially named Philadelphia pitcher Grover Cleveland Alexander, did not capture the public imagination as much as did his portrayal a decade earlier of football player George Gipp in *Knute Rockne, All-American*.[27]

As the single exception to the period's general lack of symbolic "need" for baseball onscreen, it is especially interesting to contemplate the appeal of *The Natural*—a film in which gambling and corrupt ownership of the game figure darkly, although the film's combo heroic/idyllic ending totally overturns the cynical finish of the Bernard Malamud novel from which it was adapted.[28] Indeed, the film's mythic backlighting and cagey omissions cleverly function to cover up its sellout of the novel's dark conclusion. Both Roger Ebert and Mark Crispin Miller are illuminating if one juxtaposes their reactions to *The Natural*. Ebert asks, in the era of Reagan: "Why didn't they make a baseball picture? . . . Why did a perfectly good story . . . have to be made into one man's ascension to the godlike, especially when no effort is made to give that ascension meaning?"[29] And Miller suggests the appropriate response:

> [The film] climaxes with Roy Hobbs—although morally compromised, and with an open wound—belting one last meteoric homerun (slow motion, fireworks, music, cheering crowds), thereby winning—that is, *not* throwing—the big game: a finale of bogus jubilation that we might expect in a TV commercial, which figures, since the movie's script was written by BBDO's [an advertising agency] Phil Dusenberry, maker of many ads for, among other products, Diet Pepsi and Ronald Reagan.[30]

The recent cycle of baseball films really began in 1988 and has not yet ended. Nineteen eighty-eight is also the year George Bush was elected president. Not much positive has been—or could be—made of the image of Bush as once captain of the Yale baseball team. Indeed, Bush's best-known connection to baseball was derived from the remarks of Governor Anne Richards of Texas at the 1988 Democratic National Convention: "George Bush is a man who was born on third base and thought he hit a triple." Thus, it is fitting that the America this newest cycle of baseball films again renders visible after a decade seems morally tarnished, completely institutionalized and commodified, and with one exception—in its contemporary rather than period stagings—also seems generally complacent about, rather than critical of, its own symbolic debasement. Certainly, the films of the late 1980s and early 1990s still mine the rich symbolic history of baseball, but do so with few illusions about what the national pastime of America has now become. The one exception, of course, is 1989's *Field of Dreams*, a film promiscuously nostalgic and illusionary, but one that still cannot escape the project of commodifying the game. As well, in all the contemporary films, the hermetic symbolic province of the white, Anglo, Protestant, Middle American male is permeated and hybridized by the cultural differences and global shifts that mark the current moment.

There have been five baseball films in this present cycle. *Eight Men Out* (1988), a period piece, recounts the story of the infamous Chicago Black Sox scandal of 1919, in which members of the team agreed to throw the World Series for cash. In its own way a demythification of *The Natural, Eight Men*

Out focuses on relations between a corrupt management and exploited ball players who are no better than laborers and hardly heroic. As Brown points out, the film "exposes the underbelly of baseball as big business." Made in the same year, the more contemporaneously located and comic *Bull Durham* emphasizes both "the drudgery of life in the minor leagues" and "the male athlete as the object of woman's gaze."[31] *Bull Durham* also foregrounds the fact that a bright array of commercial products and logos have entered the generally pastoral and timeless space of baseball—connecting the game and players not only to the commodified social space around them, but also to the commercial logos that increasingly substitute for the symbolically impoverished, traditional icons of nationalism. Rather than flags, eagles, monuments, and even yellow ribbons, it is Pepsi Cola, Budweiser and Miller beer, Jim Beam whiskey, Oscar Meyer processed meat, and Alberto-Culver cosmetics that really let us know we're in America.[32] Thus, advertising in baseball films such as *Bull Durham* paradoxically demythifies the "innocence" of baseball, but also reenergizes its evocation of nationalism—that is, a sense of American identity enabled by the construction of a commercial space to which we can all relate and in which we can all commune. The same could be said generally of *Stealing Home,* also released in 1988.

In 1989, responding to these corruptions, bent on redeeming the essential innocence of the game as well as of the entire Black Sox team, *Field of Dreams* came from Hollywood's left field (initially no major studio wanted to assist with financing its production). Overtly linking the current American nostalgia for simpler and more innocent times with the mythology of the innocence of baseball and playing out this desire for a gentler, simpler America as a rejection and redemption of the male Oedipal scenario, the film scored a runaway hit. First contextualizing itself within a liberal discursive field, it proceeds to relocate the sport into a literally oneiric field on an Iowa farm and, by its end, to literally consume a black radical in its corn. It is important to note, as well, that for a movie set in 1988 and released in 1989, *Field of Dreams* is deliberately and peculiarly bereft of the familiar products and brand names that have come to dominate the mise-en-scène of most American movies since the mid-1970s. There are only four such familiar commercial markers, and their location in the film is instructive. A Kodak film strip and a Century 21 real estate sign are used early on in the film's opening photographic sequence—on the one hand helping to literally ground the autobiographical narration in a contemporary and familiar America, on the other not allowed to taint the mythic Iowa in which most of the film takes place. The other two logos appear only in what the film suggests (through a variety of means) as a benignly corrupt urban space: a giant Citgo sign verifies the mise-en-scène as Boston, while an unlit Pepsi logo figures vaguely on the wall of Fenway Park.

And yet the film is, as Brown notes, "a capitalist dream."[33] By the end of the movie, the words supernaturally whispered to Ray Kinsella, "If you build it, he will come" (the "it" referring to a baseball field and the "he" to long-dead Joe Jackson, expelled in the Black Sox scandal), have been transformed in meaning into something more pragmatic, something along the lines of "Since you built it, they will come" (the "it" still the baseball field, but the "they" referring to an endless stream of dissatisfied and nostalgic Americans willing to pay $20 per person for a spectacle that will fill the void left by their loss of youth, their loss of faith, their loss of national identity). Thus, despite the film's yearning to revivify dead ball players and dead fathers and give them a second chance, despite its attempts to remythify the game and a vision of America and to reenergize the "imagined community" of nationalism, *Field of Dreams* ends up selling, as Bill Brown concludes, "its own dream as a box office hit." (In this, Ray Kinsella is a visionary along the lines of a Charles Keating.) More than just linking the "dream of a meaningful sport and a meaningful America," *Field of Dreams* sells the dream of selling that dream and stages a drama of American self-consumption.[34] Indeed, the fulfillment of the film's infinite regress of nostalgic self-consumption can be found in the fact that real people make a pilgrimage to the Iowa field where *Field of Dreams* was shot, and an issue of *USA Weekend,* in a travel article titled "Make a Movie and They Will Come," suggested six "sites" and "sets" to visit in 1992, two of which provided the backdrop for upcoming baseball movies and both of which are located in the American "heartland": Huntingburg and Evansville, Indiana, where *A League of Their Own* was filmed, and Danville, Illinois, where *The Babe* was filmed.[35]

Nineteen eighty-nine, however, also saw the release of *Major League,* a film that, in the guise of a mild comedy, figures the return of the corruption so repressed in *Field of Dreams* and finds it funny. The major plot line involves a woman baseball team owner who "seeks to get out of her Cleveland franchise by organizing a team that's guaranteed to lose games—and fans."[36] Foregrounding the irreconcilable aspects of cultural difference, one of the film's running gags involves the ongoing conflict between a blonde Anglo player, identified as a fundamentalist Christian, who insists the team pray before every game, and a player from the Dominican Republic who maintains a voodoo shrine in his locker and insists on sacrificing live animals in hopes of winning. Suffice it to say that the film ends with the team winners and the Dominican culturally triumphant.

Two more baseball films were subsequently released theatrically, and another as a cable television movie. *The Babe* (1992) was a nostalgically shot and heroically oriented period biography of Babe Ruth, just barely complicated by the ball player's womanizing. *A League of Their Own* (1992) was also a period piece about women's professional baseball in the 1940s and 1950s. Despite its historical revisionism and generally feminist approach, it too is steeped in a nostalgia supported by the film's flashback structure. And, although *A League of Their Own* casts the utterly contemporary Madonna as one of the ball players, her presence on-screen does relatively little to add bite to a thoroughly enjoyable homage to a pastoral myth of community only vaguely troubled by the real vicissitudes of gender discrimination.

Madonna off-screen, however, was another matter. Befitting the paradoxes constituting the post-American moment, during the film's production, Madonna publicly trashed the nostalgic and pastoral myth of Middle American baseball reaffirmed by the film. Speaking to *TV Guide* (and thus to nearly every middle-class household in America), Madonna said of Evansville, Indiana, where she spent three months filming, "I may as well have been in Prague." It was not meant as a compliment, nor was it taken as such by the townsfolk of Evansville or one of Indiana's senators. The star went on to reveal that she has "zero interest in organized sports" and had to learn to play for the film. Blunt as usual, she told *TV Guide:* "I was enthusiastic in the beginning, but when you have to do it over and over again, you lose interest. Unless you're getting paid 12 million *dollars* to play baseball—*then* I could grow very interested."[37]

However, the made-for-cable *The Comrades of Summer* (1992) and the theatrically released *Mr. Baseball* (1992) suggest an even more overt and radical on-screen challenge to the mythological "American-ness" of baseball. Both not only acknowledge its globalization in the post-American moment, but also dramatize fumbling, comedic, and contentious attempts to reassert American sovereignty over "foreign" co-optation of the game. Shot on location in Russia before the collapse of the Soviet Union and released shortly after, *The Comrades of Summer* is a comedy about an injured ex-big league player who, short of money and product endorsements, reluctantly signs on to coach a bumbling team of Russian "bad news bears" for their first Olympic competition. So much for the Cold War. It is worth noting, however, that the film displaces the thematic of the "washed-up" ball player's dread of "being sent down to the minors" (a thematic that appears even in *A League of Their Own*) to a dread of being sent to a foreign country, and attempts through comedy both to reassert American supremacy over the game and to recognize the increasing need to adapt to foreign cultures which refuse that supremacy.

This contestation over America's symbolic ownership of baseball is made even more explicit in *Mr. Baseball,* a film informed by the current economic contestation between the United States and Japan that is paradigmatic of the post-American moment. Both the film's narrative and the discursive field that

surrounded the production of *Mr. Baseball* foreground not only the fear of
America's loss of supremacy in the international trade wars, but also the fear
of national transformation and hybridization. On November 20, 1991, the
New York Times (Late Edition) ran a news story with the headline "Japanese
Buy Studio, and Coaching Starts."[38] Primarily descriptive, seemingly flat in
tone but with a cautionary subtext, the piece is rich in irony as it reports
how, after Matsushita Electric Industrial Company's recent purchase of
MCA, Inc. (the owner of Universal Pictures), the script of a film in production titled *Mr. Baseball* was substantially rewritten. The romantic comedy
starring Tom Selleck is about Jack Elliot, a ball player let go by the New York
Yankees who signs on with a Japanese team and has to deal not only with
his own adaptation to the Japanese style of training and play, but also with
the "anti-foreign bias of Japanese baseball" and an obligatory cross-cultural
romance.[39] What is of moment, the *Times* notes, is that this is "the first movie
about Japan produced by a Japanese-owned Hollywood studio and the first
test of the Japanese promise to leave creative control in Hollywood."

Aside from the issue of whether the American filmmakers or the Japanese
corporation had "creative control" over the film, what is of most interest in
the *Times* article are the script changes related specifically to the game and
its ethos. Where the original script had Jack *clashing* "head-on with Japan's
devotion to martial spirit, group harmony, saving face, grueling workouts and
love-hate feelings for foreigners," the rewritten script "turns more completely
on the idea of . . . Jack . . . *accepting* Japanese ways before he can succeed."
The *Times* reports, as well, that "the new script sees learning to hit a baseball
in Japan as an almost mystical combination of concentration, will power and
learning to 'accept.' The earlier script emphasized plainer elements of technique." Mr. Selleck's comments on this change are as illuminating as they are
transparent. "When I originally signed on, this was just a baseball movie.
Then the studio got taken over, and it took on new overtones. . . . I got a
lot of assurances that the movie would not be compromised. . . . Yes, Jack
changes. *But he keeps himself whole as an American baseball player.* It's a
tightrope I have to walk. I'm not about to sell out for a resolution that's not
acceptable."

The article also contains comments by Robert Whiting, briefly a consul-
tant on the film and author of *You Gotta Have Wa,* a book on Americans
playing Japanese baseball. He assures the *Times* that "the Americans who do
best in Japan are not forced to accept Japanese ways," that "the adjustment
that batters make is a technical one, not anything to do with fighting spirit,"
and that the Japanese "like to think they improved baseball." "They love
stories about guys who come over and see the light and do things the Japanese
way," he adds, but "the facts don't support their contention." The *Times*

concludes with an overly coy question: "Will anyone find a deeper message from a Japanese-owned studio about the superiority of Japan?" And director Fred Schepesi replies: "I hope not. Maybe someone's going to find that sort of stuff. But you'll see that this will be a very funny, very entertaining movie with real substance underneath."[40]

This news story is utterly revealing of its cultural implication in the post-American moment. Both of its narratives (one within and the other surrounding the film) implicate cross-cultural relations and a contested claim over the same hallowed and previously all-American "national pastimes": baseball and movies. The themes and anxieties of the article and the themes and anxieties of the film duplicate each other and bespeak a fear of hybridization and loss of national identity and power—and both disavow (the news story almost hysterically and the film comically) the changed nature, situation, and symbolic integrity of both movies and baseball. We can no longer rest secure that either represents our American "national heritage." And they, in turn, can no longer secure us as particularly and "exceptionally" American. Matsushita bought Universal Pictures. And, in the face of initial national outrage followed by resigned silence, the Japanese founders of Nintendo bought the Seattle Mariners. When they made their offer of $100 million, the *New York Times* reported it as "the first time that an owner outside of North America has tried to buy a controlling interest in a major league baseball team." With appropriate postmodern and post-American logic, the deal, they reported, "was presented . . . as the best chance to keep the club in town."[41]

In "The Meaning of Baseball in 1992," Bill Brown pointed ahead to the fact that later in the year, for the first time, baseball would become an official Olympic sport. (He did not, however, anticipate *Comrades of Summer,* nor the fact that the United States would not win the gold medal.) Brown writes: "Whereas the *World* Series has always been contested within North America, in 1992 a different sort of world series will be, for the Americans, all away games. The meaning of baseball then, may lose much of its meaning; rather, the cipher may become less available as an inscriptive space in which 'American' is repeatedly rewritten."[42] And yet, if in "real life" baseball is less available as an inscriptive space in which "America" can be rewritten, it nonetheless remains a screen space in which feeble attempts to recuperate "America" and national identity can find their dramatization.

In sum, American baseball movies have always seemed symbolically connected to questions of nationalism, and as Ken Burns says, the game has served as "a kind of Rosetta stone of American history and American myth, wherein the lie is as important and certainly revealing as the truth."[43] The most recent cycle of films bear out this statement. On the one hand, the turn toward baseball movies such as *Comrades of Summer* and *Mr. Baseball* pro-vides a field of dreams that is uneasily responsive to the post-American and increasingly global moment. On the other, it could be argued that recent films—particularly the most popular of them, including *Field of Dreams* and even *A League of Their Own*—speak more nostalgically to the profound loss and failure of American nationalism than they speak to progressive hopes for a shared and equitable global future. The passage with which a rather con-servative Wilbur Zelinsky closes his book on "the withering away of the nation-state" is apposite, mourning as it does the decline of America and the passing of "American exceptionalism." Indeed, it could stand as the narration with which Ray Kinsella might more blatantly have begun *Field of Dreams:*

> No longer are all the days and hours of our lives completely immersed in the faith; no longer do all thoughts and actions fall spontaneously into the hallowed patterns. Instead we can detect elements of hysteria in a reversion to an unattainable past. Beset by other concerns, even the most ardently pious and nationalistic among us must pump ourselves up at certain mo-ments before we can simulate the proper emotions. But we dare not look within, into the dark empty center. What more can I say?[44]

* * * * *

POSTGAME MORTEM

Yet there is more to say about the "dark empty center" within—which now, in June of 1995, has been exteriorized in the empty center-field bleachers of our national stadiums, bitter fans abandoning the national pastime following the ambiguous resolution of an eight-month baseball strike that began in August 1994. There is also more to say about "elements of hysteria" in our representational "reversion to an unattainable past." The continued produc-tion of patently nostalgic or fantastic baseball movies into the mid-1990s seems tellingly at odds with the times, self-conscious and primarily ironic attempts to "pump up" and "stimulate" the emotions "proper" to some previous and lost phenomenological sense of what it felt like and meant (for some) to be an "American."

By the time the above essay was first published in the *East-West Film Journal* at the beginning of 1993, *Mr. Baseball* had been released to lukewarm public reception.[45] By April of 1995, Matsushita had become disenchanted with the American movie business and, less than happy with its investment in MCA/Universal, sold the studio to Seagram's Edgar Bronfman, Jr. Yet, in the two years intervening, several more baseball films made the summer and fall lineups—all but one comedies pitched to family audiences, and most "pumped up" by elements of fantasy. Nineteen ninety-three saw the release of *Rookie of the Year, Little Big League,* and a remake of 1951's *Angels in the Outfield.* With cameo appearances by real sluggers Pedro Guerrero and Barry Bonds, Disney's comic fantasy *Rookie* features a twelve-year-old pitcher so talented that he leads the Chicago Cubs to the World Series. In Castle Rock's comic fantasy *Little Big League,* another twelve-year-old inherits the Minnesota Twins and shapes them into a winning team. And in Disney's *Angels in the Outfield,* another little boy-child's unwavering faith leads a losing baseball club to the pennant when he evokes the help of "flying shiny people" in white robes, wings, and halos, led by a head angel named Al. In these films, we see an unabashed reversion to an "unattainable past"—the purity and faith of American male prepubescent childhood standing in for the loss of (simulating, if you will) "the days and hours of our lives" when, as Zelinsky eulogizes, Americans were "completely immersed in the faith." Zelinsky's mournful description of this loss of belief in American exceptionalism is particularly telling in relation to the function of the angels in the climactic championship game in *Angels in the Outfield.* "Beset by other concerns," he writes, marginalizing all those elements that have come to (destabilize) the center of all that was "American," "even the most ardently pious and nationalistic among us must pump ourselves up at certain moments before we can simulate the proper emotion." Playing fair (a mythological American characteristic), head angel Al explains to the young protagonist that the angels aren't going to make any assists in the big championship game, the game that really "counts." In essence, they're there "to give hope, not to interfere with our free will"—nor, one supposes, to deny our "real" ability to win the pennant. As one critic notes in a poignant response to Zelinsky's recognition of the need for even the most pious and nationalistic to "pump up" for the crucial moments, "the angels are absent during the big game, but they've given the players enough confidence to win it on their own."[46]

Two other baseball movies were theatrically released in 1994: *The Scout,* a comedy (supposedly based on the "true" story of Fernando Valenzuela) in which a Yankee scout is sent to Mexico to recruit a mentally unbalanced pitcher with a 100-mile-per-hour fastball; and *Cobb,* a Warner Brothers dramatic bio-pic that focused on the sadomasochistic love-hate relationship between sportswriter Al Stump and bigoted baseball great Ty Cobb. Nothing on the big screen, however, could compare to the small-screen representations of baseball in 1994: first, epic television coverage of the bitter baseball strike which began in August, wiped out the World Series for the first time in ninety years, lasted for 234 days, reportedly lost more than $700 million in revenue, disgusted fans, and even engaged the fruitless mediation of the president of the United States; and second, the airing on PBS of Ken Burns's epic documentary series *Baseball*—which, as it turned out, instead of complementing the 1994 World Series with a nostalgic look at the game's historical past ended up presently substituting for it.

Indeed, watching this "replacement" game was truly uncanny. Airing on the Public Broadcasting System, the nonprofit documentary series' "nine innings" filled in for the "real thing" that would have been broadcast on corporate, for-profit, network television. While owners and players argued about vast sums of money on the evening news to fans who were not amused, Burns's nationalistic history eulogized the game—as if it were dead. In general, despite its attention to scandals and labor disputes and its liberal recuperation of the Negro leagues in the "Shadow Ball" of the "fifth inning," *Baseball* was highly nostalgic and elegiac in tone, using period music played on a distant piano, sepulchral narration, and intimate reminiscence to evoke loss and remembrance. As with *The Civil War* (1990), Burns's aim was an act less of historical analysis than of constituting a collective memory.

In an article in the September 1994 *Premiere* (issued just before both the documentary and World Series were to be broadcast), Burns reflects on historian Arthur Schlesinger's comment that "the problem in our country is too much *pluribus* and not enough *unum*."[47] He goes on to say:

> If you wanted to describe my work in a nutshell, it's about *unum*. What is it that makes us cohere? The last 30 years have seen the disintegration of that which brings us together. . . . And baseball, like the Civil War, is one of these really clean shots right to the heart of who we are.[48]

Certainly, in *Baseball* the liberal Burns speaks to the discontinuities and contradictions embedded in the national pastime and sees these as emblematic of "America" as both theory and praxis: "It's about race, it's about class, it's about wealth, it's about labor and its tensions. This is a metaphor for the entire country."[49] Yet the game stands for him, finally, as a unifying nationalistic force—albeit set presently in a nostalgically re-membered past.

Thus, watching *Baseball* in lieu of the 1994 World Series and in the context of an ugly and venal baseball strike was an uncanny experience. This was particularly true whenever the series focused on labor disputes. Although it was clear that such sequences were meant to have presence and illuminate the transformation of baseball from a pastime to a business, in the context of the strike these disputes became foregrounded, emphatic, pervasive—undercutting the idealization and nostalgia with a sharper edge than Burns might have intended or anticipated. In this regard, the words of Bob Costas—one of the series' recurrent commentators—take on particular irony, uttered, one presumes, before the 1994 strike (about which the *Premiere* article says nothing):

> Through it all, there's something about the appeal of baseball that is different—and, I would say, better—than any other team sports. And there are too many people in baseball, at every level, who don't understand and appreciate that. I think every baseball owner, every player, and every representative of the players association oughta [*sic*] sit down and watch this thing, and realize what a great national treasure the institution of baseball is, and think twice about their stewardship of that institution.[50]

It will be interesting to see what happens to baseball movies in the aftermath of the 1994 strike, which ended on March 31, 1995, without real resolution of its disputes. (It is worth noting that the game's umpires also went on strike for a brief period in the spring of 1995.) There are real questions about what may happen as the 1996 World Series approaches. In the meantime, fans are disaffected. Despite major discounting of game tickets and an extraordinary amount of autograph signing by previously distant players, attendance is drastically down. Gauging public feeling, Roger Angell, writing for the *New Yorker*, recounts a telling incident at the Mets' home opener against the Cardinals:

> the moment when three young men jumped out of the stands and began scattering handfuls of paper money around the infield. Then they lined up in a row out by second base with their fists in the air, and from the press box we could see that each of them had "Greed" inked across the front of his T-shirt.[51]

At the time of this writing, as *TV Guide* appositely put it, "major league baseball has been back for more than three weeks, and while the game remains the same, images have been changed to protect the innocence."[52] Whether this innocence can ever be recuperated—through flights of film fancy in which angels shore up the confidence of post-Americans, through nostalgic hindsight in which baseball stands as the idealized image of an America that is forever lost, or through the embrace of a transnational future figured by Japanese-born All Star Hideo Nomo—remains to be seen.

NOTES

The quotation that serves as the epigraph for this essay was part of a report by CBS Radio News (7 January 1992) on American business guru Lee Iacocca's trip to Japan with President George Bush to lobby for more favorable trade relations with that country. Iacocca's comment was made prior, and thus is not in reference, to Bush's public illness during that visit.

1. Wilbur Zelinsky, *Nation into State: The Shifting Foundations of American Nationalism* (Chapel Hill: University of North Carolina Press, 1988), p. 5.

2. Zelinsky, pp. 5–6 (emphasis added).

3. Bill Brown, "The Meaning of Baseball in 1992 (with Notes on the Post-American)," *Public Culture* 4, no. 1 (1991): 60–61.

4. John A. Agnew, *The United States in the World-Economy: A Regional Geography* (New York: Cambridge University Press, 1987), p. 15.

5. Andrew Rosenthal, "President Faces Tough Choices about the Future," *Santa Cruz Sentinel,* 24 November 1991, sec. A, p. 2.

6. Michael McGerr, "AHR Forum: The Price of the 'New Transnational History,'" *American Historical Review* 96, no. 4 (1991): 1063.

7. Brown, p. 61 (emphasis added).

8. Fredric Jameson, "Postmodernism, or the Cultural Logic of Late Capitalism," *New Left Review* 146 (July-August 1984): 53.

9. Brown, 52 (emphasis added). The internal reference is to Benedict Anderson, *Imagined Communities: Reflections on the Origin and Spread of Nationalism* (London: Verso, 1983).

10. Zelinsky, p. 108.

11. David Halberstam, "Baseball and the National Mythology," *Harper's* 241 (September 1970): 22.

12. McGerr, p. 1063.

13. Zelinsky, p. 110.

14. Zelinsky, p. 110.

15. Michael Novak, *The Joy of Sports: End Zones, Baskets, Balls, and the Consecration of the American Spirit* (New York: Basic Books, 1976), p. 58, quoted in Zelinsky, pp. 110–11.

16. The fantasy films are *It Happens Every Spring* (1949), *Take Me Out to the Ballgame* (1949), *Angels in the Outfield* (1951), *Rhubarb* (1951), *Roogie's Bump* (1954), *Damn Yankees* (1958), *Zapped* (1982), *The Natural* (1984), and *Field of Dreams* (1989). Of these, it is worth noting that only *Take Me Out to the Ballgame* and *Rhubarb* do not contain supernatural elements, the former constructed as fantastic by virtue of its musical status and the latter by its plot, which posits a cat as owner of the Brooklyn Dodgers. *It Happens Every Spring* focuses on a chemistry professor's discovery of a magic compound which repels wood and his subsequent rise to fame as a star pitcher. *Angels in the Outfield* involves angels helping the Pittsburgh Pirates win the pennant. *Roogie's Bump* has the ghost of a baseball star giving a would-be major leaguer the power to pitch at lightning speed. *Damn Yankees,* also a musical, involves the selling of a soul and the transformation of an old man into a young body so that he can play for the Washington Senators. *Zapped* focuses on a high school player who develops telekinetic powers that can alter the path of a baseball. *The Natural* has a supernatural bat. And *Field of Dreams* is motivated by supernatural voices and ball players of all generations come back from the dead.

The remaining, more "realist" films (melodramas and comedies) are *The Pride of the Yankees* (1942), *It Happened in Flatbush* (1942), *Ladies Day* (1943), *The Babe Ruth Story* (1948), *The Kid from Cleveland* (1949), *The Stratton Story* (1949), *The Jackie Robinson Story* (1950), *Kill the Umpire* (1950), *The Pride of St. Louis* (1952), *The Winning Team* (1952), *The Kid from Left Field* (1953), *Big Leaguer* (1953), *The Great American Pastime* (1956), *Fear Strikes Out* (1957), *Safe at Home* (1962), *Bang the Drum Slowly* (1973), *The Bingo Long Traveling All-Stars and Motor Kings* (1976), *The Bad News Bears* (1976), *The Bad News Bears in Breaking Training* (1977), *The Bad News Bears Go to Japan* (1978), *Here Come the Tigers* (1978), *Blue Skies Again* (1983), *Eight Men Out* (1988), *Bull Durham* (1988), *Stealing Home* (1988), and *Major League* (1989).

For production information and plot synopses of baseball films prior to 1988, see Harvey Marc Zucker and Lawrence J. Babich, *Sports Films: A Complete Reference* (Jefferson, N.C.: McFarland and Co., 1987).

17. Brown, p. 62.

18. Zucker and Babich, p. 22.

19. Zucker and Babich, p. 20.

20. Brown points out that "American educators first introduced the sport to the Japanese in the 1870s," and by the 1890s "baseball had been embraced as part of Japan's own new nationalism, which solidified during the Sino-Japanese War" (64). In this context, it is interesting to note that Zucker and Babich mention three Japanese films made about baseball, all made by major filmmakers, and the two fiction films figuring baseball as the site of the corruption of Japanese culture and codes of honor by both modernity and the West. In 1956, Maseki Kobayashi made *I'll Buy You,* "an exposé of corruption in the world of Japanese baseball" (23); in 1968, Kon Ichikawa made *Youth,* a feature documentary about high school baseball (42); and in 1971, Nagisa Oshima made *The Ceremony,* in which "baseball becomes symbolic of the disintegration of traditional Japanese culture" (16).

21. Danny Peary, *Guide for the Film Fanatic* (New York: Simon and Schuster, 1986), p. 54.

22. Cuba can also claim baseball as its national sport, and Native Americans were playing to press notice (albeit under special circumstances) as early as 1905. See the extraordinary account of the game between Japanese players from Waseda University and American Indians from the Sherman Government Institute as reported in A. G. Spalding, *America's National Game: Historic Facts concerning the Beginning, Evolution, Development and Popularity of Base Ball, with Personal Reminiscences of Its Vicissitudes, Its Victories and Its Votaries* (New York: American Sports Publishing Company, 1911), cited in Brown, p. 49.

23. Zucker and Babich, p. 37.

24. Zelinsky, p. 248.

25. Paul Goodman, *Growing Up Absurd* (New York: Random House, 1969), p. 97.

26. Zelinsky, pp. 248–49.

27. The synopsis of *The Winning Team* (which co-starred Doris Day) is worth quoting from Zucker and Babich, pp. 41–42. "Major leaguers Jerry Priddy and Arnold Statz, technical advisers for this somewhat whitewashed account of Alexander's life, worked with our future president on his pitching form. Whitewashed, we say, because while the film deals with Alexander's rapid rise, fall and comeback, his disease is never identified as epilepsy.

"*The Winning Team* traces the Hall of Famer's career from his days as a telephone lineman to stardom with Philadelphia until he is struck in the head. The resultant spells of dizziness are worsened during his military hitch, and he begins to drink heavily.

"He's eventually cut by Philadelphia after his epileptic fits are mistaken for drunkenness and he becomes a circus attraction until bouncing back with the St. Louis Cardinals."

28. For two recent articles on the adaptation from novel to film (with apologia and criticism for the changes), see Peter Turchi, "Roy Hobbs's Corrected Stance: An Adaptation of *The Natural,*" *Literature/Film Quarterly* 19, no. 3 (1991): 150–56; and James Griffith, "Say It Ain't So: *The Natural,*" *Literature/Film Quarterly* 19, no. 3 (1991): 157–63.

29. Roger Ebert, *Roger Ebert's Movie Home Companion* (Kansas City: Andrews and McMeel, 1991), p. 378.

30. Mark Crispin Miller, "Advertising: End of Story," in *Seeing Through Movies,* ed. Mark Crispin Miller (New York: Pantheon Books), p. 221.

31. Brown, p. 67.

32. The relationship between advertising and the cinema (including product placement) is discussed not only in Mark Crispin Miller's "Advertising: End of Story," cited above, but also in his "Hollywood: The Ad," *The Atlantic* 265, no. 4: (1990) 41–68.

33. Brown, p. 69.

34. Brown, p. 69.

35. Monika Guttman, "Make a Movie and They Will Come," *USA Weekend,* 17–19 December 1991, p. 8. It is worth noting that Huntingburg, Indiana, was selected for its ninety-five-year-old wooden stadium, renovated for the film, and Evansville for its "venerable, brick-walled Bosse Field," and that Danville, Illinois, was selected for its wood-frame stadium—meant to stand in for Pittsburgh's Forbes Field and New York City's Polo Grounds.

36. Leonard Maltin, *Movie and Video Guide* (New York: Penguin Books, 1991), p. 746.

37. Kurt Loder, "Madonna on TV," *TV Guide,* 23 November 1991, p. 5.

38. "Japanese Buy Studio, and Coaching Starts," *New York Times,* 20 November 1991, Late Edition, sec. A, pp. 1ff.

39. "Japanese Buy Studio" points to anti-foreign bias inherent in "the fact that [Japanese] umpires have a bigger strike zone for Americans and that Japanese pitchers have walked American hitters to keep them from breaking Japanese home-run records" (sec. C, p. 21).

40. "Japanese Buy Studio," sec. C, p. 21.

41. *New York Times,* 24 January 1992, p. 1.

42. Brown, p. 49.

43. Ken Burns, quoted in "Watching Baseball on Green Fields of Memories," *New York Times,* 17 April 1992, sec. B, p. 1. Burns, who produced and directed the documentary series *The Civil War,* was then in the process of making a major series on baseball, slated for airing on public television in 1994.

44. Zelinsky, p. 253.

45. Vivian Sobchack, "Baseball in the Post-American Cinema, or Life in the Minor Leagues," *East-West Film Journal* 7, no. 1 (January 1993): 1–23.

46. Joan Ester Anderson, "Look Homeward, Angel," *Entertainment Weekly* 275 (19 May 1995): 71.

47. Ken Burns quoted in Christopher Connelly, "At the Top of His Game," *Premiere* 8, no. 1 (September 1994): 79–80.

48. Burns quoted in Connelly, p. 81.

49. Burns quoted in Connelly, p. 82.

50. Costas quoted in Connelly, p. 83.

51. Roger Angell, "Called Strike," *The New Yorker,* 22 May 1995, pp. 52–53.

52. Jim Baker, "Sportsview: TV and Baseball Still Playing Patch-up," *TV Guide,* 20 May 1995, p. 44.

CONTRIBUTORS

AARON BAKER teaches in the Interdisciplinary Humanities Program at Arizona State University. He is currently working on a book about sports in American film and television.

TODD BOYD is Assistant Professor of Critical Studies at the USC School of Cinema-Television. His academic work has appeared in *Wide Angle, Cineaste, Filmforum,* and *Public Culture.* He has also written extensively on popular culture for the *Chicago Tribune* and the *Los Angeles Times.* His book *Am I Black Enough for You? Popular Culture from the 'Hood and Beyond* is forthcoming from Indiana University Press.

JAMES FRIEDMAN is the manager of the UCLA Film and Television Archive Research and Study Center, and a doctoral candidate in the Department of Film and Television at UCLA.

CHRIS HOLMLUND, Associate Professor at the University of Tennessee, teaches Film Studies, Women's Studies, and French. She writes on queer and feminist theory and Hollywood, independent, and experimental film. With Cynthia Fuchs, she is editing an anthology on queer/lesbian/gay documentary, *Between the Sheets, in the Streets.*

HENRY JENKINS is the Director of Film and Media Studies at MIT. He has written or edited four books, including *Textual Poachers: Television Fans and Participatory Culture* and *Science Fiction Audiences: Watching Star Trek and Doctor Who.* He goes to WWF Wrestling with his son Henry Jenkins IV.

KENT A. ONO is Assistant Professor of American Studies and Asian American Studies at the University of California, Davis. He has contributed essays to *Amerasia Journal, Communication Monographs, Philosophy and Rhetoric,* and *Women's Studies in Communication.* He recently co-edited a book on *Star Trek,* called *Enterprise Zones.* His interests include cultural studies and contemporary critical theory about race, gender, class, and sexuality.

AVA ROSE was a doctoral candidate in Cinema Studies at New York University. She works as a clinical counselor and writes essays bringing contemporary psychoanalytic theories to the field of cultural studies.

JOHN M. SLOOP is Assistant Professor of Communication Studies at Vanderbilt University, and is the author of *The Cultural Prison: Discourse, Prisoners, and Punishment.* His published essays have focused on the nature of rhetorical criticism, the discourse of Public Enemy, and the public discourse concerning alternatives to incarceration. He would like to thank Todd Boyd, Jennifer Gunn, Kent Ono, Sarah

Projansky, and Shari Stenberg for their comments on his essay. In addition, he thanks Thelonius Monk daily for "Ruby, My Dear."

VIVIAN SOBCHACK is a Professor in the Department of Film and Television at UCLA. She is the author of *Screening Space: The American Science Fiction Film* and *The Address of the Eye: A Phenomenology of Film Experience,* co-author of *An Introduction to Film,* and editor of *The Persistence of History: Cinema, Television and the Modern Event.*

DAN STREIBLE is Assistant Professor of Radio-Television-Film at the University of Wisconsin, Oshkosh. He previously taught at Austin Community College and the University of Texas. He has published essays in *Film History, Screen, Velvet Light Trap, Encyclopedia of Film, Motion Picture Guide, Libraries & Culture,* and anthologies. He is the author of a forthcoming book on the history of fight films and is co-editing an Emile de Antonio reader.

INDEX